S0-ATR-480

Ancient Jewish Epitaphs

An introductory survey of a millennium
of Jewish funerary epigraphy
(300 BCE - 700 CE)

CONTRIBUTIONS TO BIBLICAL EXEGESIS AND THEOLOGY
2
edited by Tj. Baarda and A.S. van der Woude

1. J.A. Loader, *A Tale of Two Cities. Sodom and Gomorrah in the Old Testament, early Jewish and early Christian Traditions*, Kampen, 1990.
2. P.W. van der Horst, *Ancient Jewish Epitaphs. An introductory survey of a millennium of Jewish funerary epigraphy (300 BCE - 700 CE)*, Kampen, 1991.

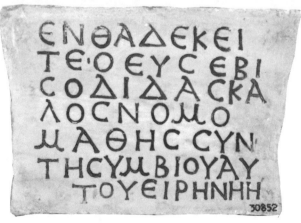

Pieter W. van der Horst

Ancient Jewish Epitaphs

An introductory survey of a millennium
of Jewish funerary epigraphy
(300 BCE - 700 CE)

Kok Pharos Publishing House – Kampen – The Netherlands

CIP-GEGEVENS KONINKLIJKE BIBLIOTHEEK, DEN HAAG

Horst, Pieter W. van der

Ancient Jewish epitaphs : an introductory survey of a millennium of Jewish funerary epigraphy (300 BCE - 700 CE) / Pieter W. van der Horst. — Kampen : Kok. –
(Contributions to biblical exegesis and theology. ISSN 0926-6097 ; 2)
Met lit. opg., reg.
ISBN 90-242-3307-0
Trefw.: Joodse grafschriften ; geschiedenis / joodse grafschriften ; filologie.

© 1991, Kok Pharos Publishing House, Kampen, The Netherlands
Cover by Karel van Laar
ISBN: 90 242 3307 0
Nugi 632 – W boek

All rights reserved. No part of this publication may be reproduced, stored in a retrieval system, or transmitted, in any form or by any means, electronic, mechanical, photocopying, recording or otherwise, without the prior permission of the publisher.

CONTENTS

Preface

This book has not been written for the specialized epigraphist. It is of an introductory nature, and as such it is aimed at students of classical philology, ancient Judaism, and theology who want to have a first orientation in the world of early Jewish funerary epigraphy. Although much work has been done in this field, a more or less comprehensive introductory survey is still a desideratum. This book is intended to fill that gap to a great extent, but not completely. Some aspects of a technical nature have been left out of account here. For the details of palaeography the student has to be referred to the standard introductions and handbooks on that matter. And onomastics has not been dealt with, partly because it falls outside my competence, partly because this aspect has been adequately covered in a number of recent publications (references will be given below). Also left out of account are the non-verbal funerary symbols that often accompany the engraved text, such as pictures of *menoroth, ethrogim, lulavim,* Torah shrines, and the like. Apart from the fact that they indicate Jewishness, not the slightest unanimity has been reached in the interpretation of the meaning of these symbols. But the controversy over it rarely affects the interpretation of the inscriptions, and this has led me to the decision to omit this material and to focus solely on the epitaphs.

The author is very grateful to the Faculty of Theology of the University of Utrecht for having granted him a sabbatical leave in the autumn of 1990, which enabled him to write this book, and also to the Faculty of Humanities of the Hebrew University in Jerusalem and the board of the Lady Davis Trust for offering him the opportunity to spend some months as a visiting professor in Jerusalem where the bulk of this book was written. Thanks are also due to my colleagues Dr. G. H. R. Horsley (La Trobe University, Bundoora, Australia) and Dr. J. H. M. Strubbe (Leiden University, Netherlands) who have been so kind to read the whole manuscript and from whose corrections and suggestions I have had great benefit. Dr. J. N. Pankhurst again improved my English, for which I am very grateful. Of course, all errors in form and contents remain mine.

Utrecht, January 1991
P.W.v.d.H.

List of Abbreviations

AE	*L'Année Epigraphique*
ANRW	*Aufstieg und Niedergang der römischen Welt*
ARW	*Archiv für Religionswissenschaft*
AS	*Anatolian Studies*
BASOR	*Bulletin of the American School of Oriental Research*
BCH	*Bulletin de correspondence hellénique*
BE	*Bulletin Epigraphique* (see under Robert in the Bibliography)
BIFAO	*Bulletin de l'Institut Français d'Archéologie Orientale*
BS	*Beth She'arim* (see under Avigad, Mazar, Schwabe in the Bibliography)
CIG	*Corpus Inscriptionum Graecarum*
CIJ	*Corpus Inscriptionum Judaicarum*
CIL	*Corpus Inscriptionum Latinarum*
CPJ	*Corpus Papyrorum Judaicarum*
CRAI	*Comptes Rendus de l'Académie des Inscriptions et Belles Lettres*
CRINT	*Compendia Rerum Iudaicarum ad Novum Testamentum*
GLAJJ	*Greek and Latin Authors on Jews and Judaism* (see under Stern in the Bibliography)
GV	*Griechische Versinschriften* (see under Peek in the Bibliography)
HTR	*Harvard Theological Review*
HUCA	*Hebrew Union College Annual*
IEJ	*Israel Exploration Journal*
IGSK	*Inschriften griechischer Städten aus Kleinasien*
IGUR	*Inscriptiones Graecae Urbis Romae*
JBL	*Journal of Biblical Literature*
JJS	*Journal of Jewish Studies*
JQR	*Jewish Quarterly Review*
JRS	*Journal of Roman Studies*
JSJ	*Journal for the Study of Judaism*
JSNT	*Journal for the Study of the New Testament*
JSS	*Journal of Semitic Studies*
MAMA	*Monumenta Asiae Minoris Antiqua*
MGWJ	*Monatsschrift für Geschichte und Wissenschaft des Judentums*
NT	*Novum Testamentum*

NTS	*New Testament Studies*
RAC	*Reallexikon für Antike und Christentum*
RB	*Revue Biblique*
REG	*Revue des Etudes Grecques*
REJ	*Revue des Etudes Juives*
Riv. Arch.	
Crist.	*Rivista di Archeologia Cristiana*
SEG	*Supplementum Epigraphicum Graecum*
TAM	*Tituli Asiae Minoris*
TAPA	*Transactions of the American Philological Association*
TLZ	*Theologische Literaturzeitung*
TPAPA	*Transactions and Proceedings of the American Philological Association*
ZAW	*Zeitschrift für die alttestamentliche Wissenschaft*
ZDPV	*Zeitschrift des Deutschen Palästina-Vereins*
ZNW	*Zeitschrift für die neutestamentliche Wissenschaft*
ZPE	*Zeitschrift für Papyrologie und Epigraphik*

b.   Bavli (= Babylonian Talmud)
m.   Mishna

I. Introduction

The use of studying ancient Jewish epitaphs is, as one author states it, that they provide us with "testimonies to Jewish living", and he goes on to remark that, whereas Jewish writings "taught how a Jew *should* live, epitaphs demonstrate how a true Jew *had* lived".[1] This certainly is a somewhat naive exaggeration, for the author does not take into account the tendency to idealize in epitaphs, but there is certainly a kernel of truth in his statement. Through Jewish literature from antiquity we come into contact with the literate and learned circles of Jewish society and so we come to know the ideas and ideals of the upper class. The voice of the common man, the 'little people', is not heard in those pages. It is precisely in introducing us to the common Jewish man and woman, their thoughts and speech and action, their fears and hopes, their griefs and joys, that inscriptions make one of their most valuable contributions to our knowledge of the world of ancient Judaism. In this sense epitaphs are certainly "testimonies to Jewish living".

Before we start to study these tomb inscriptions in order to learn more about ordinary Jewish people in antiquity, we have to discuss a number of preliminary questions. These questions are: *a*) Where can we find the publications of these inscriptions? *b*) How can we tell a Jewish inscription from a non-Jewish one? *c*) How can we determine the age or period to which an inscription belongs? *d*) What is the geographical spread of the inscriptions? These are the matters that will be dealt with in this introductory chapter.

Sources

After many scholars in the nineteenth and twentieth century had

---

[1] F. Aber, Epitaphs – Testimonies to Jewish Living, *Judaism* 6 (1957) 311.

published partial collections of Jewish inscriptions which covered only one country or city or site,[2] it was in 1936 that Father Jean-Baptiste Frey published the first volume of a comprehensive collection of Jewish epigraphical material; the second volume was published posthumously in 1952.[3] The manuscript of both volumes had been completed by 1935. So the work reflects the state of knowledge of 55 years ago, or rather, Frey's state of knowledge, for Frey was severely criticized by some leading epigraphists not only for being sloppy in the presentation of the evidence but also for having overlooked quite a number of inscriptions and for having included some that do not belong there.[4] Many of these defects were remedied for the first volume (which covers Europe) by Baruch Lifshitz, who wrote a very extensive Prolegomenon to the 1975 reprint of vol. I,[5] in which he proposed a considerable number of corrections and additions. But, unfortunately, Lifshitz died before he could start to work on vol. II (covering Asia and Egypt), which is still more deficient than vol. I. Hence it is often necessary to consult improved re-editions of this material by other scholars, whenever available. (Apart from incidental re-editions by L. Robert [see below] we refer especially to such corpora as *Monumenta Asiae Minoris Antiqua, Tituli Asiae Minoris*, and *Inschriften griechischer Städten aus Kleinasien*.) In both volumes, supplemented by Lifshitz' addenda, we find altogether some 1600 inscriptions, the vast majority of which are funerary inscriptions. In spite of all the justified criticisms, this work still remains the basic tool for research on Jewish epigraphy. It will, however, be supplanted in the near future

---

[2] The only scholar aiming at a more or less comprehensive collection was J. Oehler, Epigraphische Beiträge zur Geschichte des Judentums, *MGWJ* 53 (1909), 292-302; 443-452; 525-538.

[3] J.-B. Frey, *Corpus Inscriptionum Judaicarum. Recueil des inscriptions juives qui vont du IIIe siècle avant Jésus-Christ au VIIe siècle de notre ère,* Rome: Pontificio Istituto di Archeologia Cristiana, 2 vols., 1936-1952. This work will be referred to as CIJ; the often used abbreviation CII should be avoided since it also stands for *Corpus Inscriptionum Iranicarum.*

[4] L. Robert, Un corpus des inscription juives, *REJ* 101 (1937) 73-86, reprinted in his *Hellenica* III, Paris: Maisonneuve, 1946, 90-108, and *Bulletin Epigraphique III (1952-1958)*, Paris: Les Belles Lettres, 1974, no. 24 (pp. 101-104). A. Ferrua, Addenda et corrigenda al CIJ, *Epigraphica* 3 (1941) 30-46.

[5] New York: Ktav, 1975, 21-104.

because at the universities of Tübingen and Cambridge (UK) work on new editions of all available evidence is in progress.[6]

As long as these new editions are not yet available, we have to use the following means to supplement Frey's CIJ. First, there are some re-editions of parts of Frey's work. H. J. Leon, in an appendix to his book *The Jews of Ancient Rome,*[7] reprinted all Jewish inscriptions from Rome with many corrections and additions (most of which were accepted by Lifshitz in the reprint of CIJ vol. I). Important new inscriptions from Rome were published in 1976 by Fasola.[8] The Egyptian inscriptions were re-edited with corrections by D. M. Lewis in an appendix to the *Corpus Papyrorum Judaicarum (CPJ).*[9] For the rest of North Africa (not covered by Frey), Y. le Bohec published a comprehensive survey of all Jewish inscriptions in that area in 1981.[10] And two years later G. Lüderitz published his *Corpus jüdischer Zeugnisse aus der Cyrenaica.*[11] As for ancient Palestine, we have the 3 volumes on the Beth She'arim catacombs by Mazar, Schwabe, Lifshitz, and Avigad.[12] And for other places in Hellenistic and Roman Palestine, especially Jerusalem, there is a whole series of articles with publications of new epitaphs in various

---

[6] I owe thanks to Dr. G. Hüttenmeister and Dr. W. Horbury for information on these projects. The Cambridge project has just finished work on Egypt and the Cyrenaica; in Tübingen the project focuses on Greece and Asia Minor.

[7] Philadelphia: Jewish Publication Society, 1960, 263-346.

[8] U. M. Fasola, Le due catacombe ebraiche di Villa Torlonia, *Riv. Arch. Crist.* 52 (1976) 7-62. See also the new Roman inscription published by A. Ferrua, Iscrizione paleocristiane in una raccolta privata, *Riv. Arch. Crist.* 59 (1983) 321-333, the Jewish inscription at p. 329.

[9] V. A. Tcherikover – A. Fuks – M. Stern, *Corpus Papyrorum Judaicarum,* 3 vols., Cambridge (Mass.): Harvard University Press, 1957-1964, vol. III, 138-166.

[10] Y. le Bohec, Inscriptions juives et judaïsantes de l'Afrique Romaine, *Antiquités Africaines* 17 (1981) 165-207.

[11] Wiesbaden: Reichert, 1983. For a minor supplement see my 'Lord, help the Rabbi'. The Interpretation of SEG XXXI, 1578b, in my *Essays on the Jewish World of Early Christianity* (Novum Testamentum et Orbis Antiquus 14), Fribourg – Göttingen: Universitätsverlag – Vandenhoeck, 1990, 182-186.

[12] B. Mazar, *Beth She'arim I,* Jerusalem: Massada, 1973; M. Schwabe – B. Lifshitz, *Beth She'arim II,* 1974; N. Avigad, *Beth She'arim III,* 1976.

journals (but especially in the *Israel Exploration Journal* and *Revue Biblique*).

This brings us to another and difficult matter. The publications of most of the new finds in the field of ancient epigraphy are scattered over a very wide variety of journals in many languages and over Festschriften. The specialist must consult all of these in order to find his material. The beginner is fortunately aided in this respect by some convenient publication series. First and foremost, as far as new Greek inscriptions are concerned, there is the invaluable *Supplementum Epigraphicum Graecum* (SEG), which has appeared annually since 1923 (with an interruption from 1971 to 1976), in each volume of which the epigraphical harvest of one whole year is collected from all relevant journals and books, especially since 1976 (from 1923 till 1971 the coverage was less systematic and complete). Further, we are in the fortunate position that (by coincidence) almost immediately after the publication of CIJ vol. I, Louis Robert, who is generally regarded as the most outstanding epigrapher of our century, and his wife, Jeanne Robert, took over the annual 'Bulletin épigraphique' in the *Revue des études grecques* (from 1938 onwards). In every instalment they discuss all relevant epigraphical publications of the previous year(s), often with very substantial improvements on (and sometimes very vehement criticisms of) the publications discussed. They did this for almost half a century, until Louis Robert's death in 1985. Now all these contributions have been re-issued separately.[13] Robert always gives the references to the Jewish inscriptions in one of the opening sections of the *BE* s.v. 'inscriptions gréco-juives'. These tomes with their index volumes (and also Robert's other collected essays, *Opera Minora Selecta*[14]) are extremely helpful in tracking down Jewish inscriptions discovered after the publication of Frey's CIJ (especially in Asia Minor). It is very unfortunate that the international team of scholars who now continue Robert's *BE* (under the direction of Ph.

---

[13] *Bulletin épigraphique*, 10 vols., Paris: Les Belles Lettres, 1972-1987; *Index du Bulletin épigraphique*, 5 vols., Paris: Les Belles Lettres, 1972-1983 (not covering the final volume of *BE*). The *Bulletin épigraphique* will henceforth be referred to as *BE* followed by year and by number of the item discussed, as is the international custom.

[14] Amsterdam: Hakkert, 6 vols., 1969-1989.

Gauthier and G. Rougemont) in the *REG,* have decided to drop the entry 'Greco-Jewish inscriptions', thereby rendering a great disservice to students of ancient Jewish epigraphy.

Second, for the Latin inscriptions we have a similar useful service in *L'Année Épigraphique* (= *AE*), published as part of the *Revue Archéologique,* but since 1966 also separately, in which the yearly harvest of new publications in the field of Latin epigraphy is annually presented. The student of Jewish inscriptions will find here less to interest him since, as we will see, the vast majority of ancient Jewish inscriptions is in Greek, but the Latin inscriptions should not be neglected for that reason.

Third, for inscriptions in Hebrew and Aramaic, a tool comparable to *SEG, BE* and *AE*, is provided by Jean Teixidor in his *Bulletin d'épigraphie sémitique (BES),* published in the periodical *Syria* since 1967. Some aid can be gained also from the surveys in periodicals like *Journal for the Study of Judaism* (in its extensive and very useful 'Review of books and articles', covering the Hellenistic-Roman period), the annual *Elenchus Bibliographicus* of the journal *Biblica,* and the *Internationale Zeitschriftenschau für Bibelwissenschaft und Grenzgebiete.* The student who has consulted all these bibliographical aids,[15] can be reasonably sure that in this way he or she will have found 99% of the published inscriptions.

A rough count shows that the total number of Jewish inscriptions available is about 2000, of which some 1600 are epitaphs. Of these

---

15 It is also useful to consult the bibliographies in L. H. Kant, Jewish Inscriptions in Greek and Latin, in *ANRW* II 20, 2, Berlin – New York: W. de Gruyter, 1987, 671-713, and esp. H. Solin, Juden und Syrer im westlichen teil der römischen Welt, *ANRW* II 29, 2 (1983) 587-789 (cf. Solin's Juden und Syrer im römischen Reich, in G. Neumann – J. Untermann (edd.), *Die Sprachen im römischen Reich der Kaiserzeit,* Bonn: Habelt, 1980, 301-330); H. Bloedhorn's Appendix to M. Hengel, Der alte und der neue "Schürer", *JSS* 35 (1990), 64-72. For new Jewish inscriptions from the Arab area see F. Altheim – R. Stiehl, *Die Araber in der alten Welt* V 1, Berlin – New York: W. de Gruyter, 1968, 305-309. R. W. Suder, *Hebrew Inscriptions: A Classified Bibliography,* Selinsgrove: Susquehanna University Press, 1984, is only of very limited use. The most valuable general bibliographical guides in the field of ancient epigraphy are F. Bérard – D. Feissel et al., *Guide de l'épigraphiste,* Paris 1989 (2nd ed.), and the section 'Epigraphik' in the annual *Archäologische Bibliographie,* published by the Deutsches Archäologisches Institut.

1600 funerary inscriptions, some 1000 form the basis of the present investigation. That not all epitaphs have been used for this study is due to the fact that circa 600 of these inscriptions either contain nothing more than some barely legible letters because they are badly damaged, or contain just a name without any additional information. We have used only such inscriptions as yield more data than just names.

Identifying Jewish inscriptions

The second preliminary problem we have to address is the extremely tricky question of how to tell a Jewish inscription from a non-Jewish one. What are are the minimal requirements for an epitaph to be regarded as certainly (or almost certainly) Jewish? In order not to blur the picture we want to draw, it is of paramount importance to make clear which criteria are valid and which are not in making this distinction. It is clear, of course, that an epitaph found in a Jewish catacomb or cemetery, containing biblical names with *Ioudaios* added, referring to biblical passages, mentioning the function of *archisynagogus*, and adorned with symbols like the *menorah*, *ethrog* or *shofar* – that such an epitaph should be regarded without the slightest doubt as a Jewish inscription. It is also clear that an epitaph found in a pagan necropolis, invoking pagan deities, and without any Jewish symbols or biblical names, is not Jewish. The problem is, however, that there are so many instances which are far less clearcut than those just mentioned. What to think of an epitaph found in a Jewish catacomb, beginning with *D(is) M(anibus)* (= to the gods of the netherworld), mentioning pagan theophoric proper names, showing no Jewish symbols, and having no references to the Bible or the synagogue? Or what of an epitaph, found *not* in a Jewish burial place and showing no Jewish symbols, but mentioning names like Isaac and Sabbatis and quoting the Septuagint?

In the Introduction to the *Corpus Papyrorum Judaicarum*, Victor Tcherikover formulated the following criteria for regarding a papyrus as Jewish.[16] A papyrus is considered as Jewish (*a*) if the word

---

[16] *CPJ* I (1957) xvii-xx.

Ioudaios or *Hebraios* occurs in it; (*b*) if technical terms like 'synagogue' or 'sabbath' appear in it; (*c*) if it originates from what are known to have been places of exclusively Jewish settlement; (*d*) if it contains Jewish names. In my opinion, when taken together, these four criteria establish a solid case for regarding a papyrus or an inscription as Jewish. Tcherikover, however, considers them to be valid indicators of Jewishness also when taken in isolation. One should object to that for the following reasons. (*a*) The words *Ioudaios* or *Hebraios* (or their Latin equivalents) make an epitaph Jewish *only* if said of the deceased person(s) or the dedicator(s), but *not*, for example, when it is said that the dead man was killed by a Jew or that the man or woman who set up the stone forbids pagans, Jews, and Christians to efface the inscription on it (see, for example, no. 680a).[17] (*b*) Technical terms are indicative of Jewishness *only* if they are exclusively Jewish, which is not the case, for example, with the term *synagōgē* (it can mean any pagan meeting or assembly) and with several other 'Jewish' *termini technici*. This criterion applies with greater force only when taken in combination with other criteria. (*c*) Exclusively Jewish places are very rare, especially in the diaspora, except for the Jewish catacombs in Rome. But even there it is not improbable that, after these burial places ceased to be used by Jews, some pagans or Christians deposited the bodies of some of their deceased there. (*d*) Finally the criterion of Jewish names. Are there exclusively Jewish names? Actually, there are very few names (if any) "which can be demonstrated to have been used only by Jews, and never by Christians or pagans, whether in the same or other geographic areas".[18] Highly instructive in this respect is the name Sambathion (and its variants) of which Menachem Stern has proved beyond any reasonable doubt that, whereas in the Hellenistic period it was by and large a typically Jewish name (as a hellenized form of the Hebrew Shabbetai), in the Roman and Byzantine periods a great

---

17 When an epitaph is referred to with a number without any other indication, the number always refers to Frey's CIJ.

18 R. S. Kraemer, Hellenistic Jewish Women: The Epigraphical Evidence, *SBL 1986 Seminar Papers*, Atlanta: Scholars Press, 1986, 191. J. Oehler's collection of Jewish inscriptions in his Epigraphische Beiträge zur Geschichte des Judentums, *MGWJ* 53 (1909), is marred by his including many inscriptions on the basis of names supposed to be exclusively Jewish.

many non-Jews adopted it without being aware of its original connotations.[19] And, it should be added here, Jewish symbols are not an
absolute guarantee for Jewishness either since these could be used
also by Jewish Christians or even by gentile Christians.[20]

It may be clear by now that the matter is far from being simple. A
rigorous application of criteria would require us to regard an epitaph only as Jewish when a number of criteria reinforce one another, e.g., Jewish burial place plus Jewish symbols and epithets (for
instance, *philentolos*, 'lover of the commandments'), or biblical
names plus Jewish technical terms and functions (for instance, *archi-
synagōgos*, 'head of the synagogue'). Such a methodological strict-
ness runs the risk of excluding valuable material the Jewishness of
which is not manifest enough. On the other hand, methodological
slackness runs the risk of including non-Jewish material that may
blur the picture. It is better, for the sake of clarity, to keep on the
strict side, without being extremely rigorous. That is to say, application of two or three criteria together is to be much preferred above
applying only one, the more so since in late antiquity Judaism,
Christianity, and paganism were not always mutually exclusive categories.[21]

Dating inscriptions

The third problem we have to deal with briefly is that of dating the
inscriptions.[22] This is a problem because actually the only really

---

[19] Stern in *CPJ* III (1964) 43-56.

[20] See e.g. E. R. Goodenough, *Jewish Symbols in the Greco-Roman Period*
II, New York: Pantheon, 1953, 13; idem, An Early Christian Bread Stamp,
HTR 57 (1964) 133-137 (137: "at least some Christians, probably many, carried
over strictly Jewish symbols into their new faith"). For the use of 'Christian'
symbols by Jews see P. Figueras, *Decorated Jewish Ossuaries*, Leiden: Brill,
1983, 17 and 22-23.

[21] So rightly Kraemer, *SBL 1986 Sem. Pap.* 191.

[22] See for concise but good expositions A. G. Woodhead, *The Study of Greek
Inscriptions*, Cambridge: Cambridge University Press, 2nd ed. 1982, 52-66. G.
Klaffenbach, *Griechische Epigraphik,* Göttingen: Vandenhoeck & Ruprecht,
1966, Ch. 8. J. E. Sandys – S. G. Campbell, *Latin Epigraphy,* Groningen:

certain evidence for dating an inscription is a date in the text itself, or mention of a known person or an event of known date. But there are regrettably few Jewish epitaphs which provide such data.[23] Some inscriptions can be dated more or less precisely on the basis of names, e.g. Aurelii are always later than 212 CE. And sometimes the form of the monument on which the inscription has been engraved is of some help in fixing the date more precisely.[24] But almost the only other clue remaining then is the style of the lettering or the form of the letters. However, the criterion of the character of the writing and the shapes of the individual letters is far less precise than is often supposed. It is a valuable method especially for the early period of Greek writing (seventh through fifth centuries BCE) because the various alphabets then underwent a rapid development[25] But by the end of the fifth century BCE the letters and the technique of writing them had completed this development. The classical style of the fourth century was never eclipsed and was preserved almost throughout antiquity (in spite of the introduction of a few new letter-forms in the imperial period, which do not often occur in our evidence). That is why outstanding epigraphic authorities are sometimes widely at variance on the date of an inscription as assessed by the forms of its letters. A discrepancy of two or three centuries in dating inscriptions has more than once proved possible. Only a very thorough and constantly maintained acquaintance with all possible variations in letter shapes from region to region and from period to period may sometimes enable an expert to be more precise than, say, indicating just the century in which the inscription was probably written.

Bouma's Boekhuis, repr. 1969, 200-203. A. E. Gordon, *Illustrated Introduction to Latin Epigraphy*, Berkeley – Los Angeles: University of California Press, 1983, 40-42.

[23] Only a number from Leontopolis (Tell el-Yehudieh) provide exact dates.

[24] This is well illustrated by the study of the tombstones in the shape of a door by M. Waelkens, *Die kleinasiatischen Türsteine*, Mainz: Philip von Zabern, 1986.

[25] See e.g. Klaffenbach, *Griechische Epigraphik,* Ch. 4; B. A. van Groningen, *Greek Palaeography,* Leiden: Sijthoff, 1967, 13-20; B. F. Cook, *Greek Inscriptions*, London: British Museum, 1987, 6-20.

There is virtual agreement that all inscriptions discussed in this book date from the period between Alexander the Great and Muhammad. (The word 'millennium' in the subtitle of the book is thus a slight exaggeration, although a couple of inscriptions taken into account here do indeed date almost certainly from the late seventh century.) The vast majority of our epitaphs, however, date from the first five centuries CE, according to the epigraphical experts. We will simply take over the datings by Frey, Robert, and other specialists, being well aware of the uncertainties. As a matter of fact, for our purposes it is not of great importance to differentiate between earlier and later inscriptions, because hardly any clear lines of development in whatever respect are discernible.

Our focus is on the Greek, and to a lesser extent on the Latin inscriptions, the Semitic ones (in Hebrew and Aramaic) being only a small minority in this period.[26] From the seventh/eighth century onwards, Greek and Latin epitaphs recede into the background and Hebrew becomes the predominant language in Jewish funerary epigraphy. That has been Frey's (and our) criterion for taking the seventh century as the closing period of ancient Jewish epigraphy.

Geographical spread

Finally we will have to say a few words about the geographical distribution of the epitaphs. A glance at Frey's CIJ reveals immediately how uneven this distribution is. Of his 1540 inscriptions, some 530 are from Rome; this number should by now be corrected to ca. 600. There is no other city of the ancient world that has yielded so many Jewish inscriptions. (By way of contrast, Alexandria, which had a much larger Jewish population than Rome, has only 18 inscriptions in CIJ.[27]) The rest of Italy, including the islands, yields 128 items in CIJ. The whole of Europe outside of Italy yields only 70 items in

---

[26] From the pre-Hellenistic Israelite period only very few tomb-inscriptions have been preserved; see K. A. D. Smelik, *Historische Dokumente aus dem alten Israel*, Göttingen: Vandenhoeck, 1987, 68-71, 138-141, 148-150.
[27] In a later chapter we will come back to the difficult problem of the representativeness of the inscriptions.

CIJ. Asia Minor has 68 items (a number that should by now be more than doubled); Syria and Phoenicia have 78 items. Palestine has 533 items (205 of which are from Jerusalem, a number that is much higher now). Mesopotamia and Arabia yield only 9 inscriptions. And Egypt has 115 items, 80 of which are from Tell el-Yehudieh (ancient Leontopolis, the site of Onias' Jewish temple). Roman Africa was not covered by Frey. Most of these numbers have now to be corrected, but the overall picture remains more or less the same. Rome remains the leading city as far as Jewish inscriptions are concerned; even Jerusalem lags far behind. It is very odd to see that Mesopotamia, which had a very sizeable Jewish population, has preserved hardly any Jewish inscriptions. On the other hand, as we will see later, the city of Onias' temple, Leontopolis (today still called Tell el-*Yehudieh*), has yielded quite a number of very interesting poetic epitaphs.[28]

Much of this situation is due to the vicissitudes of history and to the arbitrariness of archeological discoveries. A couple of new finds may completely change the whole picture. (Imagine the discovery of a hugh Jewish necropolis of ancient Alexandria with thousands of epitaphs! The recent discovery of the great Jewish inscription in Aphrodisias was one of such chance finds which may change the picture of ancient Judaism considerably.[29]) But for the time being we have to resign ourselves to the fact that what history has handed down to us in terms of epitaphs is for a great part a matter of chance. Nevertheless, a thousand tomb-inscriptions which give us more information than only the name of the deceased, are a valuable source for the study of some aspects of ancient Jewish life and culture which should not be ignored.[30]

---

[28] On this rival temple and the Jewish settlement in Leontopolis see most recently R. Hayward, The Jewish Temple of Leontopolis: A Reconsideration, *JJS* 33 (1982) 429-443, and A. Kasher, *The Jews in Hellenistic and Roman Egypt*, Tübingen: Mohr, 1985, 119-135.

[29] See J. Reynolds – R. Tannenbaum, *Jews and Godfearers at Aphrodisias*, Cambridge: Cambridge Philological Society, 1987; and my comments in: Jews and Christians in Aphrodisias in the Light of their Relations in Other Cities of Asia Minor, in my *Essays on the Jewish World* 166-181.

[30] H. J. Leon's *The Jews of Ancient Rome* (1960) is a good example of how these inscriptions can be exploited as a quarry of information on many aspects of Jewish life in the capital of the Empire.

II. The Languages

The distribution of languages over the extant Jewish inscriptions from the ancient Mediterranean world is very revealing. A global count of all the published inscriptions as far as their languages are concerned reveals the following: 68% of the inscriptions are in Greek, 18% are in a Semitic language (either Hebrew or one of the Aramaic dialects), 12 % are in Latin, and 2% are bilingual (most bilinguals have Greek as one of the languages, so that in fact 70% of the inscriptions contain Greek).[1] The first impression one gains from these data is that Greek was the language of the great majority among the Jews in the Imperial period, probably of more than two-thirds of them. This global impression is corroborated when one looks at local or regional variations. That Jews in mainland Greece and Asia Minor would use Greek as their daily language was only to be expected. But it comes as a bit of a surprise that of the many Jewish inscriptions from Rome 78% are in Greek, whereas only 21% are in Latin and 1% are in Hebrew or Aramaic.[2] This is surprising, the more so in view of the fact that in the vast majority of Roman tomb-inscriptions Latin is the predominant language even in those of other orientals, especially the numerous Syrians in Rome.[3]

---

[1] The numbers are slightly rounded off, but there is no substantial difference between 68 and 68.1%. There are some trilingual inscriptions (Greek, Latin, Hebrew) but too few to be taken into account in these global statistics.

[2] See Leon, *Jews of Ancient Rome* 76, as corrected by Solin, Juden und Syrer 701-702.

[3] Solin, Juden und Syrer 703-704. Leon, *Jews* 77, draws attention to the fact that there is considerable variation in the use of the 3 languages in the 3 greatest catacombs (out of 7) in Rome: the Via Appia catacomb (the most Romanized of all) has ca. 63,5% Greek inscriptions and 36,5% in Latin; the Via Nomentana catacomb has 92,5% in Greek, 6% in Latin and 1,5% in Hebrew; and the Monteverde catacomb has ca. 78% in Greek, 20% in Latin, 1,5% in Hebrew/

This apparently implies that, at least from a socio-linguistic point of view, the Roman Jews lived in relative isolation, *i.e.*, they maintained their own language which was (*not* Hebrew but) Greek. One should not assume that they used Greek only on their tombstones as a kind of sacred language (comparable to the use of Latin in later Christian funerary epigraphy in the West), for their sacred language remained Hebrew, as is witnessed by the many Greek and Latin inscriptions ending in the single Hebrew word *shalom*, or the expressions *shalom 'al mishkavo* or *shalom 'al Yisra'el*. (In contrast, practically nothing is known of the use of languages in Jewish inscriptions east of the Roman Empire.)

That Greek was indeed the predominant language of the Jews becomes even more apparent when one looks at the situation in Roman Palestine. There, too, the majority of the inscriptions are in Greek, not a vast majority to be sure, but at least more than half of them (between 55 and 60%). Even the epitaphs in the famous rabbinic catacombs in Beth She'arim are for the most part (more than 75%) in Greek.[4] It is only in Jerusalem that the number of Semitic epitaphs seems to equal approximately the number of those in Greek.[5] Of course these data shed significant light on the much discussed problem of the hellenization of Judaism in the Hellenistic and Roman periods.[6] This is not the place to enter the debate about the

---

Aramaic, and 0,5% bilinguals.

[4] See Schwabe – Lifshitz, *Beth She'arim II: The Greek Inscriptions* (1974), and Lifshitz' essay L'hellénisation des Juifs de Palestine, *RB* 72 (1965) 520-538; J. N. Sevenster, *Do You Know Greek? How much Greek could the first Jewish Christians have known?*, Leiden: Brill, 1968, with Lifshitz' reaction in Du nouveau sur l'hellénisation des Juifs de Palestine, *Euphrosyne* 3 (1970) 113-133.

[5] Lifshitz, Jérusalem sous la domination romaine, *ANRW* II 8, New York – Berlin: W. de Gruyter, 1977, 457-459 (p. 459: "La proportion des textes épigraphiques grecs par rapport à la quantité des inscriptions découvertes à Jérusalem témoigne de l'emploi de la langue grecque par une partie assez considérable de la population de la ville").

[6] Of the many publications on this theme I refer here only to some epoch-making works: S. Lieberman, *Greek in Jewish Palestine*, New York: Jewish Theological Seminary, 1942; idem, *Hellenism in Jewish Palestine*, New York: Jewish Theological Seminary, 1950; M. Hengel, *Judentum und Hellenismus*, Tübingen: Mohr, 1973 (2nd ed.); idem, *The Hellenization of Judaea in the First*

measure and depth of Hellenistic influence on post-biblical Judaism, but it should be noted that at least on a linguistic level this influence was heavy and thorough. If even rabbis and their families phrased their epitaphs in Greek, there is only one natural explanation for that phenomenon: Greek was the language of their daily life.[7]

Greek

The epitaphs (and other inscriptions) amply testify to the fact that there was no such thing as a typically Jewish Greek. Apart from the vocabulary, which of course does contain such typically Jewish words as *nomomathēs, philentolos, philosynagōgos* etc., the Greek language of these inscriptions is not different from what we encounter in pagan non-literary sources from the same period.[8] For those who are used to reading only literary texts, the first meeting with these epitaphs may come as some sort of a shock. Most of them are written in a very poor and vulgar Greek, which can be read only by one who has the necessary minimum knowledge of the developments in post-classical spoken Greek. The following short sketch intends to provide that minimum of knowledge in the field of phonology, morphology, and syntax, in so far as it is required to enable the beginner to read the Jewish epitaphs.[9]

Century After Christ, London: SCM Press, 1990. In the last-mentioned book references to all earlier relevant literature can be found.

[7] See, besides the publications by Lieberman, Lifshitz and Hengel mentioned in the previous notes, also G. Mussies, Greek in Palestine and the Diaspora, in S. Safrai – M. Stern (edd.), *The Jewish People in the First Century* (CRINT I 2), Assen:Van Gorcum, 1976, 1040-1064.

[8] For an up-to-date survey of the discussion see esp. G. H. R. Horsley, The Fiction of 'Jewish Greek', in his *New Documents Illustrating Early Christianity* 5, North Ryde, N.S.W.: Macquarie Ancient History Documentary Research Centre, 1989, 5-40.

[9] Although almost a century old, K. Dieterich, *Untersuchungen zur Geschichte der griechischen Sprache von der hellenistischen Zeit bis zum 10. Jhdt. n. Chr.,* Leipzig: Teubner, 1898 (repr. Hildesheim: Olms, 1970) is still a good guide. The same applies to A. N. Jannaris, *An Historical Greek Grammar Chiefly of the Attic Dialect,* Hildesheim: Olms, 1968 (repr. of the London 1897 ed.). Most useful and up to date is F. T. Gignac, *A Grammar of the Greek Papyri of the Roman and Byzantine Periods,* 2 vols., Milano: Cisalpino-Goliardica, 1976-

Phonology

The most frequently occurring orthographical interchanges in Koine Greek are:

Interchange of αι and ε,[10] of which one finds innumerable instances in our epitaphs, e.g. κέ, κεῖτε, Αἰβρέος, αἰν, ἐνθάδαι, φιλό-ταικνος, παρθαίνος.[11]

Interchange of ει and ι:[12] e.g. δεικέα (= δικαία), βείωσας, οὐδίς, ἰς, κῖτε (= κεῖται), θάρι (= θάρρει).

Interchange of η and ι/ει:[13] e.g. ἀνίρ, ἴτις, νίπιος, δής, ῥάββη, ἰρίνι, ἠρήνη, εἰρείνη.[14]

Interchange of η and ε/αι:[15] νέπιος, συναγωγές, ἐπλέρωσε, ἤτη (= ἔτη), ἔδε (= ἤδη), ἤν (= ἐν), ἤνδηκα, μεμόριον. In the earlier period (till the second century CE) the η evidently still retained its value of

---

1981 (vol. 3 on syntax is to follow soon). For what follows I have made grateful use of the philological notes in N. Müller – N. A. Bees, *Die Inschriften der jüdischen Katakombe am Monteverde zu Rom,* Leipzig: Harassowitz, 1919; H. J. Leon, The Language of the Greek Inscriptions from the Jewish Catacombs of Rome, *TAPA* 58 (1927) 210-233; idem, The Jews of Venusia, *JQR* 44 (1953/54) 267-284, esp. 274-278; idem, *Jews of Ancient Rome* Ch. 5 ('The Language of the Jews of Rome'); C. Brixhe, *Essai sur le grec anatolien au début de notre ère,* Nancy: Presses universitaires de Nancy, 1984.

For abbreviations used in the inscriptions the reader is best referred to A. Calderini, *Epigrafia,* Torino: Società Editrice Internazionale, 1974, 68-78 (general introduction) and 247-340 (comprehensive list of abbreviations compiled by S. Daris).

[10] Gignac, *Grammar* I 192-193.

[11] Only for very specific instances will I give references to CIJ (or, if not in CIJ, to the place of publication). It did not seem wise and useful to burden the text with numerous numbers when instances of the phenomena described can be found on almost every page of CIJ. Accents and spiritus have been added by me.

[12] Gignac, *Grammar* I 189-191.

[13] Gignac, *Grammar* I 235-242.

[14] For εἰρήνη I found the following variant spellings: ἠρήνη, ἰρίνι, ἐρήνη, ἐρείνη, εἰρείνη, ἰρήνη, ἐρένη, ἠρίνη, εἰρίνη, εἰρίνι, *hirene, iren.* The spellings ἰρη (41), εἰρηη (137), ἐρη (328) and εἰρνε (349) are probably just scribal errors. With knowledge of these interchanges a form like αἰπηστάτις becomes intelligible as a variant of ἐπιστάτης.

[15] Gignac, *Grammar* I 242-249.

a long *ē*; thereafter it gradually merged with *i*, as in modern Greek.[16]

Interchange of οι and υ:[17] e.g. ὑ (= οἱ), τῦς (= τοῖς), κύμισις (= κοίμησις).[18]

Interchange of υ and ει/ι/η:[19] e.g. ὑ (= ἡ), εἰωνώς (= υἱωνός), ἱπέρ, γλικυτάτη.

Interchange of ει/ι and ε/αι:[20] e.g. ἐρήνη, ἱπήνευσε (= ἐπίνευσε), τέλεον, χέρα, χέθη (= κεῖται).[21]

Interchange of ω and ο:[22] e.g. σινβίο (= συμβίῳ), ὸς (= ὡς), ὼ (= ὁ), γραμματέος, υἱώς, ἱαιρέος (= ἱερέως).

Interchange of α and ε:[23] e.g. ἀνθάδε, ἐτάρις (= ἐτέροις), τέσσε- ρες, μυραψός.

Interchange of α and ο:[24] e.g. σαρός, ὁθάνατος.

Change from ευ to εου:[25] e.g. ἱερεούς, γραμματεούς (also the spel-ling γραμματεός is occasionally found). This change indicates that ευ was still a diphthong with the value *ew* (as is also apparent from

---

[16] Leon, Jews of Venusia 274-275, remarks that this form of itacism had clearly developed further in the (later) Venusian inscriptions than in the (earlier) Roman.

[17] Gignac, *Grammar* I 197-199.

[18] For κοίμησις I found the following spellings: κύμισις, κύμησις, κόμησις, κώμισι, κύμηση, κοίμησι, κοίμησης, κίμησις, κύμησης, κίμυσες, κύμις, *cymisis*, *quimesis* (see also N. A. Bees in *Rheinisches Museum* 71 [1916] 287-288). Even κόνωσις is found (no 359).

[19] Gignac, *Grammar* I 267-273.

[20] Gignac, *Grammar* I 249-262. That ε was sometimes pronounced as *i* seems evident also from forms like ἐνθάδι, ἐνστρίψατο, and also οἰυμύρι (= εὐμοίρει) where οι=ι=ε, on which see B. Lifshitz, La vie de l'au-dela dans les concep-tions juives, *RB* 68 (1961) 404 n. 22.

[21] For κεῖται/κεῖνται I found the following spelling variants: κεῖτε, κῖτε/ κῖντε, κῖτεν, κεῖθαιν, ἐκεῖθεν, ἐκῖθεν, κῖτη, χέθη, χεῖθε, χῖθε, χῖτε, κῖθε, χεῖθαι, κῖται, κεῖτι, κεῖτη, κέτι, κῖτει, κιτοῦται (as if from *κειτέομαι). The spellings κιετε and κικε are probably mistakes of the engraver. On the incorrect aspi-ration and the addition (or omission) of the augment see below.

[22] Gignac, *Grammar* I 275-278.

[23] Gignac, *Grammar* I 278-286.

[24] Gignac, *Grammar* I 286-288.

[25] Gignac, *Grammar* I 230-231; also Robert, *BE* 1966 no. 81 and 1972 no. 578.

ἀνασκέβασε = ἀνασκεύασαι); the same applies to αυ as is evidenced by αὐουτῆς (= *awtēs*).

Interchange of α and αυ:[26] e.g. ἀτῆς (= αὐτῆς), Ἀγουστέσιοι (= Αὐγουστήσιοι).

Interchange of γ and ι:[27] e.g. ὑγός (= υἱός; elsewhere one finds the spellings υελός, υἱώς, and ὑός, all were pronounced like *(i)yos)*, ἱερουσιάρχης, Παρηιόριος (=Paregorios).

The aspirate was no longer pronounced as is apparent from the spellings *e* and *ae* (instead of *he/hae*) for ἡ in Latin transcriptions of Greek epitaphs (on which see below) and from the confusion in spellings like *hirene* and μεθ' ἐμοῦ. Also the aspirates θ and χ were often changed into τ and κ due to loss of aspiration:[28] e.g. ἐντάδε, παρτένος, τιγάτερ, οὐκ ἡμῖν. And note the false aspiration in forms like ἀθάναθος, χῖτε and κῖθε (for κεῖται).[29] The φ ceased to be a diphthong *(ph)* and had become an *f*, as is apparent from the consequent Latin transcription with *f* and from its use in Greek transliterations of Latin words, e.g. φιλιωρουν = *filiorum,* φηκιτ = *fecit.*[30]

The ζ seems to have developed the phonetic value *dj* or even *j*: we find ζὰ βίου for διὰ βίου (once in Latin *iabiu,* no. 480), κοζουγι as a transcription of *coiugi* (= *coniugi,* cf. *cogiugi* in no. 236), and Προζεκτω for *Proiecto* (no. 286); cf. the later Greek ζάβολος for διάβολος.[31]

Some minor peculiarities are forms like μίκκη for μικρά, not uncommon in Koine Greek and preserved in modern Greek μικιός and μικκούτικος;[32] further συνγωγή and ἀρχισύνγωγος with syncope of the vowel in an unstressed syllable;[33] frequent gemination of a

---

26 Gignac, *Grammar* I 226-228.

27 Gignac, *Grammar* I 71-72.

28 Gignac, *Grammar* I 134-138.

29 Phrases like ἐντάδε χεῖθε and τετάπθο are perhaps cases of metathesis of aspiration caused by lack of knowledge of the correct forms.

30 Gignac, *Grammar* I 99-100.

31 Gignac, *Grammar* I 75. But see Horsley, *New Documents* V 15.

32 Gignac, *Grammar* II 113-114; also Müller – Bees, *Inschriften* 51, and B. Lifshitz, Inscriptions grecques de Césarée en Palestine, *RB* 68 (1961) 118.

33 Cf. *snoge* for synagogue in some Dutch-speaking Jewish circles. Gignac, *Grammar* I 302-310, gives many examples and pays special attention to the frequency of this phenomenon in Latin loanwords (309-310); in our epitaphs

consonant, e.g. in προσσήλυτος, ἀνορρύξει, Ἰούσστος, γοννεῦ-
σιν, ἄμμωμος, ἔζζησεν; and the reverse in γραματεύς, θρέμασιν,
γεναίη, ἱέρισα.[34] But here we are moving already into the field of
morphology.

Morphology

Of morphological changes brought about by phonological developments, we may note the following:
Final -ς is frequently omitted,[35] most often in κοίμησι and its variant spellings (κύμηση, etc.).
Final -ν is also omitted:[36] τή, τῶ, etc.; but sometimes it is added
where it should not be: κῖτεν, κεῖθαιν, ἐκῖθεν (all of them = κεῖται),
et al.[37]
Dropping of ν in medial position is also attested: e.g. Ἀλεξαδρέου
(= Ἀλεξανδρέως), διαφέροτα (= διαφέροντα), μησκόμενος (= μνη-
σκόμενος).[38]
Once we find a prothetic ι, in Ἰστασία for Στασία (361);[39] sometimes prothetic ε, in ἐκῖθεν for κεῖται, but see below on false aug-
ments.

Further we may notice influence of Latin upon the endings of
nouns of the first and second declensions: e.g. the nominatives
νίπιους (= νήπιος), Σελεύκους; the genitives συνγωγῆ (= synagogae), Βερνακλώρω (= Vernaculorum), both occurring only in no.
318: Δωνᾶτος γραμματεύς συνγωγῆ Βερνακλώρω. This pheno-

---

e.g. Βερνακλήσιοι = Vernaculenses.

[34] Gignac, *Grammar* I 154-165. Unique is the spelling of the name Βαρϣεοδα
(no. 108), with a *shin* in the middle of a Greek word, perhaps because Greek
knew no such sound as a *shin*.

[35] Gignac, *Grammar* I 124-129.

[36] Gignac, *Grammar* I 111-112; also Dieterich, *Untersuchungen* 88-91.

[37] Gignac, *Grammar* I 112-114. At p. 113 Gignac remarks that the very
frequent omission and converse erroneous addition of final *nun* indicates that
final nasal was dropped in the speech of many.

[38] Gignac, *Grammar* I 116-118. Gignac gives no parallels to the genitive form
-έου in a word ending on -εύς; see vol. II 85.

[39] See P. Kretschmer's review of Müller-Bees in *Glotta* 12 (1923) 193.

menon has been observed mainly in the inscriptions from Rome.[40]
Names in -ιος are often spelled with -ις: e.g. Ἀλύπις, Εὐσέβις, but
the genitives of these names are in -ιου.[41] Cf. also πεδίν for
παιδίον.[42]

Extension of the plural nominative ending -ες to the accusative is
evidenced by μῆνας τέσσαρες, ἔζησεν ... μῆνες ἕξ, etc.[43] It is also
found in an inscription of which every single word is spelled
incorrectly (by a *grammateus*!), no. 102: Γημηλλίνη νηπεία ἵτις
ἤζησεν ἤτη μεία μῆνης ἤνδηκα (= Γεμελλίνη νηπία ἥτις ἔζησεν
ἔτη μία [= ἔτος ἕν] μῆνες ἕνδεκα).

Once we find the forms γερουσιάρχων (600), instead of the usual
γερουσιάρχης, and φιλαδελφῶν (363, perhaps also 321), instead of
the usual φιλάδελφος. As to the first, nouns deriving from ἄρχω
always end in -άρχης or -αρχος, never in -άρχων. But here the writer of the epitaph was no doubt influenced by the ending of the term
ἄρχων, which is the most frequently occurring title of an official in
Jewish inscriptions.[44] As for the second, φιλαδελφῶν is also a mixed
form, based for the first half on φιλάδελφος and for the second on
φιλὸς ἀδελφῶν; it is perhaps comparable to φιλοπάτορος and
φιλομήτορος (152, both nominatives!), possibly formed after both
φιλοπάτωρ/-μήτωρ and φιλὸς πατρός/μητρός, although in this case
another factor may have been at work, namely the tendency in post-
classical Greek to transfer third-declension nouns and adjectives to
the second declension.[45]

In verbs in past tenses the (syllabic) augment is sometimes omitted, a
first step towards the more restricted use of the augment in modern
Greek (certainly not an archaism):[46] θῆκεν, ποίησεν. Forms like

---

40 See Müller – Bees, *Inschriften* 101, and Leon, *Jews of Ancient Rome* 84.
41 Gignac, *Grammar* II 25-29; at p. 28 Gignac notes that in the course of time
a new declensional type developed: κύρις, κυροῦ, κυρῷ, κῦριν.
42 Fasola, Due catacombe 49.
43 Gignac, *Grammar* II 46-47, 191-192. At p. 47 Gignac remarks that this
extension resulted eventually in the adoption of -ες as the nom.-acc. plur.
ending of the first declension in Modern Greek.
44 The variant spellings ειεροσάρχης, ιερουσιάρχης, ιερουσιάρκων are no
doubt based on folk-etymology (ιερός), facilitated by the pronunciation of γ as
ι.
45 Gignac, *Grammar* II 62-64.
46 Gignac, *Grammar* II 223-225.

ἐκῖθεν (for κεῖται), mentioned above under 'prothetic e', may in fact be cases of augment-transfer.[47]

The widespread phenomenon of replacement of second aorist endings by those of the first aorist is visible in forms like ἀπέθαναν and ἔλαβας.[48]

Syntax

Most of the inscriptions are brief and have been written in a simple Greek from a syntactical point of view. Only some features deserve attention.

There are some striking indications of the dative's obsolescence:[49] ἐν εἰρήνης, σὺν τῆς συμβίου αὐτοῦ. Hand in hand with this development goes the taking over of the functions of ἐν + dat. by εἰς + acc.: e.g. εἰς μίαν ἀπέθαναν ἡμέραν, εἰς τὸ μέσον κεῖται.[50] Sometimes adjectives and participles do not agree with the nouns they qualify: ἔτη τρεῖς,[51] ἔτη μία (for ἔτος ἕν), Ῥεβεκκα ... ζήσας, μνῆμα διαφέροντα ...[52] Once the verb does not agree with the subject, ἐνθάδε κεῖται θυγατέρες δύο (535), but here the engraver apparently started thoughtlessly with the stereotyped incipit, which almost always had the verb in the singular.[53]

---

[47] Gignac, *Grammar* II 225.

[48] Gignac, *Grammar* II 335-345.

[49] J. Humbert, *La disparution du datif en Grec,* Paris: Klincksieck, 1930. W. Dressler, Der Untergang des Dativs in der anatolischen Gräzität, *Wiener Studien* 78 (1965) 83-107.
Brixhe, *Essai sur le grec anatolien* 95-100.

[50] F. Blass – A. Debrunner – F. Rehkopf, *Grammatik des neutestamentlichen Griechisch*, Göttingen: Vandenhoeck, 17th ed. 1990, par. 205.

[51] Gignac, *Grammar* II 190, quotes instances like ἀρτάβας τρία.

[52] Curiously enough, the only 3 instances of this incorrect use of διαφέ-ροντα/διαφέρων occur in inscriptions from Jaffa. The necropolis of Jaffa yields 5 instances of διαφέρειν in the meaning of 'belonging to', but with no less than 4 different constructions: with genitive, with ἀπό + gen., with dative, and with accusative. See CIJ 937, 938, 947, 955, and an additional instance published by B. Lifshitz, Varia epigraphica, *Euphrosyne* n.s. 6 (1973/74) 29-31; see also his Varia epigraphica, *Epigraphica* 26 (1974) 84.

[53] So correctly Leon, *Jews* 86.

Sometimes appositions fail to agree in case with the substantives to which they refer: θυγάτηρ Μηνοφίλου πατὴρ συναγωγῆς or Εἰρήνα ... σύμβιος Κλωδίου ἀδελφὸς Κουίντου. The tendency to fall back into the nominative case in appositions is a well-known phenomenon in vulgar Greek, but it occurs especially frequently in Semiticizing Greek.[54]

There are several instances of the use of ὅστις for the relative pronoun ὅς, but also of τίς for ὅς or ἥ: ἐνθάδε κεῖται Οὖρσος γραμματεὺς τὶς ἔζησεν κτλ. (148). We also find ὁ for ὅς and τό for ὅ: ... ὁ ἔθρεψεν ἡμᾶς and τὸ ἐμὸν μνῆμα τὸ μετὰ πολλῶν μοχθῶν ἐποίησα (719).[55]

Sometimes the engravers had problems with indicating the age of the deceased: ἔζησεν ἐτῶν ..., with genitive for accusative, apparently due to confusion with the descriptive genitive which would be used without ἔζησεν. But we also find the following: ἐνθάδε κεῖται ... Ἰουλία ἐτῶν ἐννέα καὶ μῆνας ἐννέα. This is a confusion of 2 formulas: (a) here lies Julia of 9 years and 9 months (genit.); and (b) here lies Julia who lived 9 years and 9 months (accus.).[56]

Finally, we find some oddities like dative for nominative: ἐνθάδε κεῖται Εὐτυχιάνῳ ἄρχοντι συμβίῳ ἀξίῳ, probably again a mixing up of 2 well-known formulas: (a) here lies E. (nomin.); and (b) for E. (dat.; many short epitaphs contain only a name in the dative).[57] Also accusative for nominative: ἐν εἰρήνῃ τὴν κοίμησιν αὐτῆς; but here we may consider the possibility that, whereas in the standard formula ἐν εἰρήνῃ ἡ κοίμησις αὐτοῦ the verb to be suppleted is εἴη, in the case where κοίμησις is in the accusative the verb to be suppleted is δῷη, with God as grammatical subject. This is speculative, but the fact that in CIJ no. 358 the father of a young boy

---

54 G. Mussies, *The Morphology of Koine Greek,* Leiden: Brill, 1971, 92-94.
55 Leon, *Jews* 85, refers to many inscriptions in Rome with (ὅσ)τις as relative pronoun. Mussies, Greek in Palestine and the Diaspora 1044 n.1, suggests that τίς pro ὅς may be a Latinism (*qui*); but see Brixhe, *Essai sur le grec anatolien* 84.
56 Müller – Bees, *Inschriften* 111, and Leon, *Jews* 86.
57 As a matter of fact, in the pagan Greek tomb-inscriptions from Rome the name of the deceased is more often in the dative than in the nominatie or genitive; see I. Kajanto, *A Study of the Greek Epitaphs of Rome,* Helsinki: Societas Scientiarum Fennica, 1963, 7-8, 16-25.

prays, νῦν, δέσποτα, ἐν εἰρήνῃ κοίμησιν αὐτοῦ, lends some support to this hypothesis, since the father seems to ask the Lord to grant the boy his sleep in peace.[58]

H. J. Leon concludes from his study of the Roman inscriptions that "there must have been a distressingly large percentage of [Jewish] individuals with little or no education".[59] This is a doubtful statement since orthographical confusion is not necessarily a proof of lack of education. Moreover, we do not know to whom the wrong spellings should be attributed: to the family of the deceased or to the mason who actually engraved the text on the stone? But Leon rightly concludes that the Jews formed no linguistic island, for neither in their pronunciation of the Greek nor in their grammatical usage did they differ in any demonstrable way from the other Greek-speaking groups of the Mediterranean world of the Imperial period. "There is no evidence whatever of a Judeo-Greek or Judeo-Latin in any respect comparable with the Yiddish or Ladino of later times".[60]

Interlude

By way of transition to the Latin of the inscriptions, I will discuss very briefly the Greek inscriptions in Latin characters and the Latin inscriptions in Greek characters, all of them from Rome. There are only a handful of Greek inscriptions written with Latin letters, but there are a couple of dozen Latin inscriptions in Greek letters; and, by way of curiosity, there is one Greek inscription in Hebrew letters. I leave aside the several inscriptions in Greek and Latin which end in *shalom* (written in Hebrew) or *shalom 'al Yisra'el* (e.g. 283, 319, 349, 397, 497, etc.), and several Latin inscriptions in which the standard closing formula ἐν εἰρήνῃ ἡ κοίμησις αὐτοῦ/αὐτῆς/σου

---

[58] See also U. Fischer, *Eschatologie und Jenseitserwartung im hellenistischen Diasporajudentum*, Berlin: W. de Gruyter, 1978, 218.

[59] Leon, *Jews* 78. Jonathan Smith's remark that the Jewish inscriptions are 'relentlessly elite' is odd; see his Fences and Neighbors, in W. S. Green (ed.), *Approaches to Ancient Judaism* II, Chico: Scholars Press, 1980, 24 n. 34.

[60] Leon, *Jews* 92.

is written in Greek letters (but occasionally transliterated into Latin characters, e.g. 224 *en irene ae cymesis su*).

Of Greek in Latin transliteration two examples may suffice: 229 *Esidorus eterus en irene quimesis su* = Ἰσίδωρος ἑταῖρος, ἐν εἰρήνη <ἡ> κοίμησίς σου (Isidorus, friend, in peace be your sleep); 284 *Marcus Cvyntus Alexus grammateus ego ton Augustesion mellarcon eccion Augustesion* = M. K. Ἀ. γραμματεὺς ἐγὼ τῶν [or: ἐκ τῶν] Αὐγουστησίων, μελλάρχων ἐκ τῶν Αὐγουστησίων (M. Q. A., secretary of the Augustesians, archon-to-be of the Augustesians). We find here in the transcription several phonological elements that we have dealt with in the previous section.

Latin inscriptions in Greek letters are more frequent: e.g. 215 Σεμπρωνιους Βασειλευς Αυρηλιαι Καιλερειναι κοζουγι βοναι ετ διςκιπουλεινα ι βοναι κουν κουα βιξει αννεις XZ φηκιτ κοζουγι βμ = *Sempronius Basileus Aureliae Caelerinae coiugi bonae et discipulinae bonae cum qua vixi annis xvii fecit coiugi b(ene) m(erenti)* (Sempronis Basileus to Aurelia Caelerina, a good wife and good pupil, with whom I lived for 17 years; he set up [this stone] for his wife who well deserved it). Note the shift from the first to the third person singular. No. 239 Ειουλια Αλεξανδρα φηκι κοικι σουω Ειμερω βενεμερενδι = *Iulia Alexandra feci coiugi suo Himero benemerenti* (Julia Alexandra set up [this stone] to her well-deserving husband Himerus). Note again the hesitation between first and third person (*feci ... suo*). No. 248 Μαρκελλους ετ Σουκκα παρεντης Μαρκελλε φειλιε καρισσιμε φηκηρουντ, ἐν εἰρήνη ἡ κοίμησίς σου = *Marcellus et Succa parentes Marcellae filiae carissimae fecerunt*, ἐν κτλ. (Marcellus and Succa, parents of Marcella, set up [this stone] for their dearest daughter). No. 264 Σεβηρε ματρι δουλκισειμε Σεβηρους φιλιους = *Severae matri dulcissimae Severus filius* (For Severa, his very sweet mother, Severus, her son [set up this stone]). As a final example no. 460 λοκου Βεσουλες ανουρο ρεκεσητ κε´ = *locus Besules annorum recessit xxv* (burial place of Besula; she passed away [at the age] of 25 years). This Latin in Greek garment shows up some peculiarities to which we will presently return.

Finally, there is the curious Greek inscription in Hebrew characters. In no. 595 (from Venusia) we read, after a first line with *shalom 'al* etc.:

טפוס סהקונדינו פרסוביטרו קי מטאירינא אטונ אוגדואנטא

(τάφος Σεκουνδίνου πρεσβυτέρου καὶ Ματηρίνα<ς> ἐτῶν ὀγδοήντα, 'tomb of Secundinus the elder and of Materina, aged 80 years').

Note that the form of the numeral, ὀγδοήντα, comes very close to the modern Greek form (as does also πεντήντα, fifty, in no. 596, also from Venusia).[61]

We can only guess at the reasons why these inscriptions were engraved in characters not belonging to the language in which they were inscribed. But they are not isolated cases in that we also know, for instance, Jewish Greek writings in Hebrew characters, the most famous example of which is the late medieval Greek translation of the Pentateuch in Hebrew letters.[62] But this whole problem deserves an investigation of its own which cannot be carried out in the framework of this study.[63]

Latin

The more Romanized Jews, who were users of Latin, were on the whole probably more prosperous and therefore better educated than the Jews who spoke Greek. For this reason, and also because the Latin inscriptions are at least six times less numerous than the Greek, we find far fewer examples of aberration from correct Latin pronunciation and grammar.[64] We have already seen some instances in the previous paragraph when we discussed Latin inscriptions with Greek characters. We will now briefly present the most important of these elements in a systematic way.[65]

---

[61] See H. J. Leon, The Jews of Venusia, *JQR* 44 (1953/54) 276.

[62] See the edition by D. C. Hesseling, *Les cinq livres de la Loi,* Leiden: Brill, 1897.

[63] Some preliminary remarks are to be found in Müller – Bees, *Inschriften* 165-167.

[64] Leon, *Jews* 87. At pp. 87-92 Leon presents a good survey of the peculiarities in the Latin inscriptions of the Roman Jews.

[65] For a more detailed treatment of the matters discussed the reader can be referred to C. H. Grandgent, *An Introduction to Vulgar Latin*, New York: Hafner, 1962; V. Väänänen, *Introduction au Latin vulgaire*, Paris: Klincksieck, 1963.

Change of *ae* to *e*:[66] *Iudea, filie dulcissime, que* (= *quae*, rel. pron. nom. sing. fem.), *coiugi sue*. Sometimes the reverse may be seen: *baenemerenti* and *nominae* (abl.) are 'hypercorrect' forms (cf. *aeheeu* =*eheu*). The distinction between short and long *e* seems to have been generally observed, as is apparent from Greek transcriptions like βενεμερεντι φηκιτ. Similarly, short and long *o* are still distinguished as in ʿΟνωράτος. But short and long *i* are often confused: δουλκισειμε; and short and long *u* are never distinguished in Greek transcriptions: κουν (= *cum*), φιλιους, κονιουγι.[67]

Often *u* and *o* were mixed up: *dolurem, mensurum (= mensorum = mensium), apostuli*, ανουρο (= *annorum*). Very curious is one inscription (611, Venusia) in which twice the Greek η is used in the middle of a Latin word or a word in Latin characters: *mηnsurum* and *trηnus*, the latter word, however, being Greek: θρήνους.

The *c* is always *k*: φηκιτ, Λουκιος. Latin *v* ceased to be pronounced like *w* (e.g. Ούεσπασιάνος), but sounded like something halfway between *b* and *v* (the so-called bilabial fricative β), hence spellings like *bixit* and *venemerenti*.[68]

There is loss of nasal *n* before spirants and fricatives, especially *s*: *mesis*, (also μησις), *quostituta* (= *constituta*), *Cresces*, Κωστάντις (= Constantius), *coiugi*, etc. (contrast *bennid* = *venit*). This loss of *n* was probably compensated through nasalisation of the preceding vowel.[69] There is also loss of final *m*: e.g. *mense unu* (= *mensem unum*, note the incongruence in gender), *quattuordeci, memoria* (acc.), ανουρο (= *annorum*).[70]

In a late inscription (629, Tarente) we find *hic requiescit benememorio Anatoli filio Iusti* as evidence both of loss of final *s* in the nominative and of the pronunciation *o* for *u*; this nominative ending in *-o* has won the field in Italian and Spanish.

We find formations of the genitive plural of third declension

---

[66] Grandgent, *Introd.* 88-89; Väänänen, *Introd.* 38-39.
[67] On vowel lengths see Grandgent, *Introd.* 82-87.
[68] On the history of the *v* in late Latin see Grandgent, *Introd.* 135-137, very instructive; also Väänänen, *Introd.* 51-52. For the word *vixit*, which of course occurs very often in inscriptions, I found the following spellings: *vixit, vixsit, bixit, bissit, vexit, vixet, vicxit*, βιξιτ, βιξειτ, βειξιτ.
[69] Grandgent, *Introd.* 74, 131-132. Already Plautus repeatedly uses *mostrare*.
[70] Grandgent, *Introd.* 129-130; Väänänen, *Introd.* 69-70.

nouns on *-orum* (instead of *-ium*): *omniorum, nepotorum, mensurum*, possibly facilitated by the fact that the genitive was gradually falling out of use.[71]

Only once do we find an archaic form, the accusative *aevom* (in no. 476), but it occurs in an inscription that is conspicuous in several other respects as well, and we will return to it later.

As to syntax, we notice *cum* with acc.: *cum Celerinum, cum virginiun sun* (= *virginium suum* instead of *virginio suo*, an unusual ending of the acc. in *-un*), probably because the accusative was gradually taking over other cases' functions after prepositions.[72] We also have some cases of errors in agreement: *archonti ... omnibus honoribus fuctus* (= *functo*). Engravers use alternatingly the ablative (*vixit annis ...*) and the accusative (*vixit annos ...*) when indicating lifetime. These are the main features to be noted for the Latin inscriptions.

Hebrew and Aramaic

As to the Hebrew and Aramaic inscriptions, most of them contain only personal names (and sometimes standard formulas) and the few that are more informative are for the most part correctly written. Hence there is no need to dwell on the grammatical aspects of these epitaphs.[73]

The vast majority of Jewish inscriptions in a Semitic language comes from Palestine and the other eastern Roman provinces (Syria, Arabia). There is little doubt that the inscriptions there are in Hebrew and Aramaic because these were the everyday languages of the deceased. The few examples elsewhere, the handful in Rome for instance,[74] should most probably not be taken to imply that there was a Hebrew or Aramaic speaking community in that city. Now

---

71 Grandgent, *Introd.* 43-44; Väänänen, *Introd.* 121-122.

72 Väänänen, *Introd.* 118-119.

73 Although we might point out some interesting spellings like זקר (*zeqer*) for זכר (*zekher*) and the frequent ה-infix in משכהבו (*mishkahvo* for *mishkavo*).

74 I leave out of account here Hebrew fixed phrases like *shalom* (*'al Yisra'el, 'al mishkavo*) at the end of Greek and Latin inscriptions; they are as little an indication of knowledge of Hebrew as the use of *Amen* in Christian inscriptions is.

and then an immigrant from Judaea who died after his arrival in Rome, may have had his epitaph engraved in his native language by his family members. But by and large Jews in the Western diaspora spoke and wrote Greek.[75] This is also confirmed by the biblical quotations.

Biblical quotations

Contrary to the practice of the Christians, who frequently referred to or quoted passages from the Bible in their funerary inscriptions,[76] Jews apparently were more reserved in this respect. Over against the wide repertoire of biblical texts in Christian epitaphs, Jews seem to have restricted themselves almost entirely to only two biblical passages, namely Proverbs 10:7 and 1 Samuel 25:29. The first passage, the favourite one, runs in the Hebrew Bible as follows: זכר צדיק לברכה (*zekher ṣaddiq livrakha*, 'the memory of the righteous one be [for] a blessing'). The Septuagint (LXX) renders rather freely: μνήμη δικαίων μετ' ἐγκωμίων (the memory of the righteous ones be with laudations). The much stricter translation of Aquila renders it as follows: μνεία δικαίου εἰς εὐλογίαν, which has the same meaning as the Hebrew. Now it is very interesting to see that our inscriptions quote both Greek versions of the text. In no. 370 (Rome) we have Aquila: μνεία δικαίου εἰς εὐλογίαν, which is, by the way, a nice illustration of the success this translation had in ousting the LXX. But in no. 201 (Rome) we have the LXX, albeit slightly modified: μνήμη δικαίου σὺν ἐγκωμίῳ (both plurals have become singulars in accordance with the Hebrew text). However, in no. 86 (Rome) we have a very interesting mixture of LXX and Aquila: μνήμη δικαίου εἰς εὐλογίαν οὗ ἀληθῆ τὰ ἐγκώμια (the memory of the righteous one, the laudations for whom are true, is

---

[75] Solin, Juden und Syrer 701-711.

[76] D. Feissel, Notes d'épigraphie chrétienne, *BCH* 108 (1984) 575-579, remarks that especially Psalm 90 was a favourite with the Christians. On the differences between Jews and Christians in this respect see Feissel's La Bible dans les inscriptions grecques, in C. Mondésert (ed.), *Le monde grec ancien et la Bible,* Paris: Beauchesne, 1984, 223-231. Cf. also L. Malunowicz, Citations bibliques dans l'épigraphie grecque, in E. A. Livingstone (ed.), *Studia Evangelica VII*, Berlin: Akademie Verlag, 1982, 333-337.

(for) a blessing). Is this a conscious harmonizing of both versions or does the engraver know both versions and does he mix them up when quoting from memory? We simply do not know. No. 731c (Crete) is a free rendering or allusion: μνήμη δικαίας εἰς αἰῶνα. Nos. 625 (Tarente) and 635 (Oria) are just an exact quotation of the Hebrew text. Interesting again are the bi- and trilingual nos. 629 (Tarente) and 661 (Tortosa), since both provide us with the Hebrew text, in free rendition, and with equally free Latin and Greek equivalents: no. 629 reads נזכר צדיק לברכה (*nizkar ṣaddiq livrakha,* 'may the righteous one be remembered for a blessing') and has on the one side *benememorius* (of blessed memory) and on the other *memoria iustorum ad benedictionem,* which is a translation of the Hebrew Bible text, although one would expect *iusti,* but the LXX also has the plural.[77] But no. 661 reads תהי לברכה זכרונה (*t^ehi livrakha zikhronah,* 'may her memory be for a blessing', adding a verb, omitting 'the righteous one'), has in the Latin part *benememoria,* and in the Greek πάμμνηστος (always to be remembered), roughly dynamic equivalents of the Hebrew quotation. We thus can see how Prov. 10:7 functions in Jewish epitaphs, in various forms and various languages, but most often in recognized Greek versions, which the engravers or those who ordered the stones probably knew from synagogue services in Greek.[78]

The other biblical text, 1 Sam. 25:29, is seldomly quoted in ancient Jewish epitaphs (but very frequently in later times[79]). The Hebrew text is as follows: והיתה נפש אדוני צרורה בצרור החיים (*w^ehaye- tah nephesh 'adoni ṣerurah biṣror haḥayim,* 'the soul/life of my lord shall be bound in the bundle of the living'). The LXX has: καὶ ἔσται

---

[77] See Frey's Appendix p. 596.

[78] See Frey, Introd. to CIJ, LXVI. G. H. R. Horsley, *New Documents Illustrating Early Christianity* 4 (1987) 23-24, thinks the inscription *IGUR* III 1240 is Jewish because of μνημοσυνῆς ἀγαθῆς, which he takes to be an allusion to Prov. 10:7 (cf. *benememorius*); that may be correct.

[79] See, e.g., the epitaphs in D. Chwolson, *Achtzehn hebräische Inschriften aus der Krim,* St. Petersburg: Akademie der Wissenschaften, 1865, esp. nos. 3-12, but their authenticity is still a matter of debate. See, e.g., O. Eissfeldt, *Der Beutel der Lebendigen,* Berlin: Akademie Verlag, 1960, 28-40; S. Szyszman, Les inscriptions funéraires découvertes par A. Firkowicz, *Journal asiatique* 263 (1975) 231-264; idem, Centenaire de la mort de Firkowicz, *Congress Volume Edinburgh 1974* (VTSuppl. 28), Leiden: Brill, 1975, 196-216.

ἡ ψυχὴ κυρίου μου ἐνδεδεμένη ἐν δεσμῷ τῆς ζωῆς. Unfortunately, no Greek epitaphs with this verse are extant. In the late inscription just discussed, no. 661 (from sixth century Tortosa in Spain), we have only the words *naphsheh biṣror haḥayim*[80] ([may] his soul/life [be] in the bundle of the living); but in the second century CE inscription from Antinoopolis in Egypt, no. 1534, we read *nuaḥ naphsho biṣror haḥayim,* 'may his soul rest in the bundle of the living); and in 665a (from Adra in Spain) we have the Latin *ligatus in ligatorium vitae.* These are interesting testimonies to the development in the understanding of this biblical text as referring to afterlife (which it certainly did not in the original biblical story).[81] But this has led us already far away from the problems of language. We will return to the question of the afterlife in one of the later chapters.

---

[80] Note the mixture of Hebrew and Aramaic.
[81] For a discussion of these inscriptions and the evidence from literary sources see, besides Eissfeldt, also K. Berger, *Die Weisheitsschrift aus der Kairoer Geniza,* Tübingen: Francke Verlag, 1989, 179-180.

III. Forms, Formulas, and Motifs

Not only in language but also in forms and genres Jewish epitaphs hardly differ from their pagan counterparts. The wide variety of forms we find in Jewish funerary epigraphy are not original creations but derive from pagan examples.[1] Whatever these forms are, all of them have as their common background the strong desire to keep the memory of the deceased alive. To most of the ancients, being remembered was immensely important since it was often the only form of 'afterlife' they believed in. In order to ensure that they would be remembered, people sometimes erected and engraved their own tombstones already during their lifetime. This is often indicated on the stones by the word ζῶν/ζῶσα/ζῶντες/ζῇ or *vivus*, etc.[2] (in our corpus e.g. nos. 681, 746, 753, 773).

We will not dwell upon the simplest form of epitaph which mentions only the name of the deceased (onomastics falls outside the

---

[1] There is also a great continuity between pagan and Christian epitaphs; see esp. R. Lattimore, *Themes in Greek and Latin Epitaphs*, Urbana: University of Illinois Press, 1942 (repr. 1962), 301-340; also G. Pfohl, Grabinschrift (griechisch), *RAC* 12 (1983) 495-510; Ch. Pietri, Grabinschrift (lateinisch), *RAC* 12 (1983) 548-586; D. Pikhaus, *Levensbeschouwing en milieu in de Latijnse metrische inscripties. Een onderzoek naar de invloed van plaats, tijd, sociale herkomst en affectief klimaat,* Brussel: Vlaamse Academie van Wetenschappen, 1978. Lattimore's book, although published half a century ago, remains an invaluable source of information on the pagan precursors of our Jewish epitaphs. A valuable short survey is G. Pfohl, Über Form und Inhalt griechischer Grabinschriften, in his *Elemente der griechischen Epigraphik*, Darmstadt: WBG, 1968, 59-83.

[2] Pfohl, *RAC* 12, 476, refers to the instances in W. Peek's *Griechische Versinschriften* I, Berlin: Akademie Verlag, 1956 (repr. Chicago: Ares, 1988), nos. 247-274. This work by Peek will henceforth be referred to by the usual abbreviation *GV*.

scope of this study[3]). We only remark in passing that the name may be either in the nominative (implying, 'here lies ...') or in the genitive (implying, 'this is the tomb of ...') or in the dative (implying, 'this stone was set up for ...').[4] As soon as we are told more than just the name, regional varieties come into the picture.

For example, in the inscriptions from Rome a large majority begin with the standard formula ἐνθάδε κεῖται (occasionally ἔνθα or ὧδε, sometimes κεῖμαι)[5] and end with ἐν εἰρήνῃ ἡ κοίμησις αὐτοῦ/αὐτῆς/αὐτῶν/σου.[6] The almost unvarying uniformity in the use of these formulas is not paralleled elsewhere and must be regarded as typically Roman Jewish. (Several Latin inscriptions of Jews in Rome start with *hic situs/a est, hic est positus/a, hic iacet, hic pausat, hic requiescit*; so there is more variety.) In Venusia (South-Italy), on the other hand, we hardly ever find this formula but rather τάφος + genitive of the name; and in Asia Minor one prefers τὸ μνημεῖον or θήκη or σωματοθήκη + genitive, or 'Α. κατεσκεύασεν τὸ μνημεῖον or some similar formula.

Terms for 'grave'

By way of digression, this allows us to expatiate upon the various terms for 'tomb' or 'grave' used in Jewish epitaphs. The most common are of course μνημεῖον and μνῆμα (note that their original meaning is 'memory, remembrance'!), but we also find:

---

3 We refer the interested reader to Leon, *Jews* 93-121 ('The Names of the Jews of Rome'); Solin, *Juden und Syrer, passim* but esp. 633-647 (with a bibliography at 636-7 n. 103); also the many contributions by Robert (see bibliography); G. Delling, Biblisch-jüdische Namen im hellenistisch-römischen Ägypten, *Bulletin de la Société d'Archéologie Copte* 22 (1974/75) [1976] 1-42; and R. Singerman, *Jewish and Hebrew Onomastics,* New York – London: Garland, 1977, esp. 38-39. For women's names see the references in note 1 to chapter VII.
4 See Kajanto, *Study* 7-8, 16-25.
5 References in Leon, *Jews* 122.
6 When quoting inscriptions I tacitly correct the misspellings and other engraver's errors unless it is necessary for some reason to retain them.

τάφος, σῆμα, οἶκος, οἶκος αἰώνιος, τόπος, τόπος αἰώνιος, ἀνάπαυσις, βωμός, ἡρῷον, σορός, ἐνσόριον, ὀστοφάγος, θήκη,
σωματοθήκη, θέσις, κοῦπα, μυστήριον, γλωσσόκομον, μημόριον,
ψυχή, ἁψίς, ἔμβασις, μάκρα, γουτάριον and γούντη (the latter
two being probably Latin terms [*guntha, guttarium*],[7] see nos. 765
and 767); *memoria, locus, domus aeterna, ara*; *mᵉnuḥa, mishkav,
nephesh (naphsha), taḥanit naphsha, qever (qᵉvurtah), beth 'olam
(beth 'alᵉma), beth ha'aṣmot*.

Not all of these 40 different terms for 'grave' require comments,
but some unusual ones may be singled out for brief explanation.[8]
The one common to all three (or four) languages is *domus aeterna,*
οἶκος αἰώνιος, בית עולם (*beth 'olam,* or Aramaic בית עלמא, *beth
'alᵉma*). The expression 'eternal home' for a grave was formerly
often said to have been of Egyptian origin,[9] but there are several
early (and late) Semitic instances, and as a matter of fact it is found
later throughout the ancient world, both in the Bible (Eccclesiastes
12:5, 'man goes to his eternal home', בית עולמו, *beth 'olamo*) and in
pagan literature and inscriptions.[10] The original background of the
term was that the dead were supposed to dwell forever in the little
home that was their tomb, but in the course of time it lost this
connotation and became just one of the common words for a tomb
and could also be used by people who firmly believed in the resurrection of the body (see e.g. Pseudo-Phocylides 112). The terms
βωμός and *ara*, actually meaning 'altar', were used to designate
tombs since in pagan antiquity tombs were often the sites where
sacrifices to the gods of the netherworld were offered. This is also
evident in the innumerable Latin epitaphs beginning with *Dis
Manibus*, mostly abbreviated to *DM* – and imitated by the Greeks in

---

[7] See MAMA VI 101 (*ad* no. 277= CIJ 765) and Waelkens, *Türsteine* 165-166
(*ad* no. 411= CIJ 767). There is some doubt about the Jewishness of nos. 765
and 767.

[8] A discussion of several terms can be found in J. Kubinska, *Les monuments
funéraires dans les inscriptions grecques de l'Asie Mineure*, Warsaw: Centre
d'archéologie méditerranée, 1968 (non vidi).

[9] See my *The Sentences of Pseudo-Phocylides*, Leiden: Brill, 1978, 194.

[10] Details in A. Parrot, *Malédictions et violations de tombes*, Paris: Geuthner,
1939, 165-189, and E. Stommel, *Domus aeterna, RAC* 4 (1959) 109-128.

Θ(εοῖς) Κ(αταχθονίοις) – which indicate by this dedication that these gods or spirits of death had to be placated.[11] But here, too, in the course of time the original meaning was lost to such an extent that we even find quite a number of Jewish and Christian inscriptions which bear this dedication *DM* without any significance (see e.g. nos. 464, 524, 531, 678, etc.).[12] A parallel process was, inevitably, the change in meaning of βωμός and *ara* from 'altar' to 'grave'. The same process of loss of the original meaning can be observed in ἡρῷον, originally 'shrine of a *heros*', but in the long run simply 'grave' (when the belief in the heroification of the dead had disappeared), just as ἥρως very often designates no more than 'dead person'.[13] Μυστήριον as designation of a tomb occurs probably only once (871, from Byblos), and it is not easy to see how it developed from the meaning 'mystery', perhaps via 'mystery of death', to 'place of the dead', but there are also a couple of Christian inscriptions where it seems to have this meaning.[14] Γλωσσόκομον originally referred to a case for keeping the tongues (γλῶσσαι) or mouth-pieces of musical instruments, then developed the wider meaning of case, casket, or chest, and finally also came to mean more specifically coffin or sarcophagus (only in no. 1008).[15] The term μάκρα is the later form of μάκτρα, kneading-trough (μάσσω = to knead), which, not completely surprisingly, became one of the

---

[11] See Lattimore, *Themes* 90-96; Pfohl, *RAC* 12, 490; Pietri, *RAC* 12, 522-524.

[12] F. Becker, *Die heidnische Weiheformel D.M. auf altchristlichen Grabsteinen,* 1881 (non vidi). C. M. Kaufmann, *Handbuch der altchristlichen Epigraphik,* Freiburg: Herder, 1917, 37. Frey, Introd. to CIJ p. CXIX, remarks that one should also take into account that stones bought at stonecutters' workshops were often already pre-inscribed with D.M. at the top. And of course one cannot wholly rule out cases of real religious syncretism in which D.M. does have its original meaning.

[13] See the many instances quoted by Lattimore, *Themes* 97-100. Schürer, *History* III 33 for literature.

[14] D. Feissel, Notes d'épigraphie chrétienne (V): Μυστήριον dans les épitaphes juives et chrétiennes, *BCH* 105 (1981) 483-488. In CIJ 651 μυστήριον must have another meaning.

[15] In the NT it means purse or money-box, John 12:6. See the sketch of the word's history in J. H. Moulton – G. Milligan, *The Vocabulary of the Greek Testament,* London: Hodder & Stoughton, 1930, 128.

words for sarcophagus.[16] (The term σαρκοφάγος itself does not occur in our inscriptions, but we do find the closely related ὀστο-φάγος, bone-eater, albeit only in Jerusalem.) The word ἔμβασις (only in 654 as corrected by Robert in *BE* 1964 no. 631) had a similar semantic development, from 'bath-tub' to 'sarcophagus'. Ἀψίς is actually the vault or room (in the catacomb) where the body is deposited (BS II 141). More often than these rare terms we come across words for 'soul', נפש (*nephesh*) and ψυχή, in the meaning 'grave' (BS I 126 and 132; CIJ 1009, 1389, 1392, 1423, etc.). Here we probably have to do with an abbreviated form for בית הנפש (*beth hanephesh*) or נוח נפש (*nuaḥ nephesh*), house or (place of) rest for the soul (569, 611, 988, etc.), although one would expect the abbreviation to be בית (house) or נוח (rest) rather than נפש (soul). One should, however, bear in mind that the semantic development of *nephesh* went from 'soul of the dead' via 'symbol of the soul of the dead' to '(marker on) the tomb of the dead'. In Talmudic litera-ture the word is also found in the sense of a tombstone or mauso-leum (e.g. m.*Sheqalim* II 5, b.*Eruvim* 53a). The Greek ψυχή in this instance is nothing but a literal translation of the Hebrew (BS II 131).[17]

Dedications and memory

So much for some of the words for a tomb. We have seen that many inscriptions are of the type 'here lies' + name in the nominative, or 'this is the tomb of' + name in the genitive. A third type is that which mentions the names of the deceased in the dative followed by the name(s) of the dedicator(s) in the nominative, sometimes with but often without a verb. If there is a verb, it usually is a form like ἐποίησεν, ἀνέθηκεν, κατεσκεύασεν, *fecit, dedicavit,* with the ob-ject added very seldomly; only occasionally do we find complete

---

[16] The term occurs only once, in one of the Beth Shearim epitaphs; see Schwabe – Lifshitz, *Beth She'arim* vol. II no. 172. From now on we will refer to the Beth She'arim inscriptions as follows: BS II 172.

[17] Schwabe – Lifshitz *ad locum* (p. 117) note several other instances of both *nephesh* and *psyche* in the meaning of 'grave' and 'stele'. See also Mazar in *BS* I p. 198 on *nephesh*.

formulas like: Στράτων Τυράννου ᾽Ιουδαῖος ζῶν τὸ μνημεῖον κατεσκεύασε ἑαυτῷ καὶ γυναικὶ καὶ τέκνοις (753), Πτολεμαῖος ... κατεσκεύασεν ἐκ τῶν ἰδίων τὸ ἡρῷον κτλ. (757; cf. 768, 770, 773 for some other instances, all of them from Asia Minor). The dedicators are for the most part close relatives, either parents (or one of them) or children, or brothers and/or sisters, sometimes a master when the deceased was a slave.[18] And it is no wonder that these relatives often state explicitly that they have made or prepared or dedicated the tombstone for the sake of the memory of the deceased: μνήμης χάριν and μνείας ἕνεκα (and variants) belong to the stock formulas of ancient funerary epigraphy, although in Jewish epitaphs they are relatively rarer than in pagan ones.[19] The Aramaic equivalent is the frequent דכיר לטב (dᵉkhir lᵉtav, 'may he be remembered for good'). Some Ephesian inscriptions explicitly state that it is the local Jewish community that takes care of the tomb: ταύτης τῆς σοροῦ κήδονται οἱ ἐν ᾽Εφέσῳ ᾽Ιουδαῖοι (745, cf. 746).

Expressions of grief

Naturally the survivors often voice their sorrow over the loss of their beloved one(s). A great variety of Greek and Latin examples for expressing grief in epitaphs lay ready at hand,[20] and again most of the Jewish instances are not innovatory. Of course the circumstance of untimely death was the chief ground for lamentation.[21] Hence the frequency of the words ἄωρος and *immaturus* in both pagan and Jewish epitaphs.[22] The word ἄωρος is especially frequent

---

[18] In 619e "the chief of her fellow-slaves" buried Quarta, the slave of Tullianus. On epitaphs for slaves see Horsley, *New Documents* 2 (1982) 52-54.

[19] Pfohl, *RAC* 12, 474.

[20] Lattimore, *Themes* 172-214, gives an excellent survey.

[21] See the pithy instance in *GV* 1665: οὐ τὸ θανεῖν κακόν ἐστιν, ἐπεὶ τό γε Μοῖρ' ἐπέκλωσεν ἀλλὰ πρὶν ἡλικίης καὶ γονέων πρότερος.

[22] E. Griessmair, *Das Motiv der Mors Immatura in den griechischen metrischen Grabinschriften,* Innsbruck: Universitätsverlag, 1966. A.-M. Vérilhac, Παῖδες ἄωροι. *Poésie funéraire,* 2 vols., Athens: Athens' Academy Press, 1978-1982, publishes, translates, and discusses some 200 metrical epitaphs with this theme. R. Garland, *The Greek Way of Death,* London: Duckworth, 1985, 77-88.

in Egypt, where it occurs in several dozens of Jewish epitaphs,[23] and although it is not attested at Rome, there are numerous Roman inscriptions that emphasize that the deceased was still νήπιος/ον, βρέφος, or *infans*.[24] (Often no such word is used, but the stated age of the deceased is significant enough.)[25] Particularly moving are instances like no. 466 (Rome) *Inpendi anima innox qui vixit annos tres dies viginti octo,* 'the innocent soul of Inpendius who lived 3 years and 28 days', and no. 1524 (Leontopolis) Δωσθίων ... ὀρφανὲ μικρὲ τραυματία, χαῖρε, ὡς ἐτῶν τριῶν, 'Dosthion, you little wounded orphan, farewell; about 3 years old'.

But the expressions of grief often go much further than the use of words like ἄωρος or νήπιος. Let us quote some illustrative examples. Still relatively restrained is no. 68, a Roman inscription in which the mother who buried her son says: *mater dulci filio suo fecit quod ipse mihi debuit facere* (his mother did for her sweet son what he should have done for me). This is one of many epitaphs in which parents protest against the fact that they have to bury their children instead of the other way round, therein using most often the verbs *debuerat, debuit, decet,* ἔπρεπεν.[26]

Quite a different instance is no. 1512 (from Leontopolis): "Look on my tombstone, passer-by, weep as you gaze; beat five times with your hands for a five-year-old. For early and without marriage I lie in the tomb. My parents suffer likewise for the son that pleased them. My friends miss their companion and playfellow. But my body lies in the place of the pious. Weeping say: untimely gone, much lamented, best of all, who were always known for all kinds of virtue".[27] This is the first instance we see of metrical funerary

---

[23] See e.g. nos. 1452, 1456, 1460-61, and almost all of nos. 1467-1486.

[24] E.g. nos. 111, 120, 122, 126, 137-8, 146, 152, 154, 161, 171, 273, 305, 326, 331, 342, 349, 359, 364, 371, 388, 396, 399, 401, 413, 418, 507, 509, and two inscriptions published by Fasola in *Riv. Arch. Crist.* 52 (1976) 49 and 56.

[25] For the problem of the age at death see Ch. 5.

[26] Many instances in Lattimore, *Themes* 187-191; Griessmair, *Motiv* 44-47.

[27] The translation is by D. M. Lewis (slightly adapted) in *CPJ* III 158. The Greek text is:

εἴσιδέ μου στήλην, παροδῖτα, κλαῦσον ἀθλήσας,
σαῖς χερσὶν κόψαι πεντάκι (πενταέτην).
ἄρτι γὰρ οὐδὲ γάμου μέτοχος κεῖμαι ἐν τύμβῳ,

poetry and also of direct address to a traveller, but we defer for the moment treatment of that aspect since we first wish to draw attention to the fact that the parents apparently saw fit to emphasize, even in the case of a 5-year-old boy, that he did not have the chance to marry. This is a major theme in funerary epigraphy: death instead of marriage.[28] The death of an ἄγαμος involves a lack of completeness; it means an unfinished life. And, as Lattimore rightly put it, "pathos is only accentuated if death intervenes just before marriage".[29] Hence the poignant mention of the fact that the deceased was μελλόνυμφος, 'on the point of getting married', e.g. nos. 106, 148, cf. 1468. (A comparable sentiment is expressed by the use of ἄτεκνος, childless; although it need not imply that the deceased had not attained (the age of) marriage, a similar sense of incompleteness is conveyed; see e.g. nos. 1461, 1476, 1485, 1500, all from Egypt.[30])

The theme is often grimly expressed by the image of death as marriage to Hades. To be the bride of Hades or Acheron is a well-known motif from Greek tragedy, especially Sophocles' *Antigone* and Euripides' *Iphigeneia in Aulis*.[31] The extensive collection of literary epitaphs with this motif in the *Anthologia Palatina* book VII[32] (ranging from the sixth century BCE to the sixth century CE) demonstrates how constant this theme has remained throughout

---

καὶ γονέες πάσχουσ᾽ ἱκέλως ἐπὶ υἱὸν ἀρεστόν,
οἵ τε φίλοι ζητοῦσιν ὁμήλικα καὶ συνέταιρον.
σῶμα δ᾽ ἐμὸν κεῖται χῶρον εἰς εὐσεβέα.
κλαύσας εἰπέ· ἄωρε, πανώδυρε καὶ πανάριστε,
ὃς πάσης ἀρετῆς πάντοτε κυδαλίμῳ.
As the editor remarks, "no kind of Greek can be extracted from the last line" (158).

[28] Lattimore, *Themes* 192-194, gives abundant references. Of special importance is the study by M. Alexiou and P. Dronke, The Lament of Jephtha's Daughter: Themes, Traditions, Originality, *Studi Medievali* (3rd ser.) 12 (1971) 819-863, esp. 832-837 on funerary inscriptions.

[29] *Themes* 192. See also Griessmair, *Motiv* 63-75.

[30] On this motif esp. Griessmair, *Motiv* 75-77.

[31] *Antig.* 653-4, 814-6, 877-82, 917-20, 944-6, 1204-5, 1240-1; *Iph. Aul.* 433-9, 460-1, 1397-9.

[32] *Anth. Pal.* VII 182, 185, 568, 604, 710-12, and many other references in Lattimore, *Themes* 194 n.62.

antiquity. And this is also made clear by the great number of inscriptions referring to death as marriage in Peek's *Griechische Versinschriften*.[33] Although these inscriptions show a fair degree of standardization, they demonstrate sufficient variation in language and style for us not to dismiss their evidence as entirely derivative from literary sources. They express the real and deep sorrow felt by the survivors when a beloved one had died before having had the chance to marry and have children. In Jewish sources we find this sentiment expressed in the dramatic lament of Jephtha's daughter as composed by the pseudo-Philonic author of the so-called *Liber Antiquitatum Biblicarum,* in which she says among other things: *factus est infernus thalamus meus* ('the netherworld has become my bridal chamber', 40:6).[34] The clearest example from Jewish funerary epigraphy is the poetic no. 1508 (Leontopolis, Egypt): "Weep for me, stranger, a maiden ripe for marriage, who formerly shone in a great house. For, decked in fair bridal garments, I untimely have received this hateful tomb as my bridal chamber. For when a noise of revellers already at my doors told that I was leaving my father's house, like a rose in a garden nurtured by fresh rain, suddenly Hades came and snatched me away. And I, stranger, had accomplished twenty revolving years".[35] The latest editor remarks, "The appearance of Hades is noteworthy, but too abstract to be called much of a concession to paganism".[36] I would rather say that this mention of Hades is hardly noteworthy since over the centuries it had become so much a literary flourish that it cannot be called in any sense a 'concession to paganism'. What is noteworthy, nevertheless, is that we find here on a Jewish tomb a perfect example of a literary epitaph in the Greek tradition.

---

[33] *GV* 68, 434, 710, 1148, 1263, 1330, 1437, 1540, 1584, 1810 through 1830, 1833, 1989, 2026; many other references in Alexiou – Dronke, Lament 833-835.

[34] See, besides Alexiou – Dronke's Lament, my essay Portraits of Biblical Women in Pseudo-Philo's *LAB*, in my *Essays on the Jewish World* 117-120.

[35] Translation by Lewis in *CPJ* III 156. Lewis' text is from Peek, *GV* 1238. I refrain from quoting the Greek since the stone is so badly damaged that widely diverging readings have been proposed (see both Frey and Lewis *ad loc*.). The motif under discussion is there, however, beyond any doubt in lines 3-4.

[36] Lewis *ibid*.

Comparable to this epitaph are those where the lamented is said to have been ἀκμαία, 'in full bloom, at prime' (1507, 1508), or to have reached the ἀκμῆς ἄνθος, the flower of youth (1510), at the moment of death. In pagan inscriptions we often find in such laments the same or similar expressions: ἄνθος ἥβης, ἀκμὴ ἡλικίας, *flos aetatis*, and the like.[37] It is a striking fact that, whereas elsewhere (in Rome, for example) the young age of the deceased is noted with grief, it is only in Leontopolis that we find this type of elaborate lament in the Greek tradition. But, as we shall see, in other respects as well Jewish inscriptions from Egypt reflect a greater measure of hellenization than those elsewhere. As a matter of fact, it is in Leontopolis that we find no less than 12 of the 15 Jewish Greek metrical epitaphs extant: nos. 1451, 1489, 1490, 1508-1513, 1522, 1530, 1530A (the other three being BS II 127 and 183 from Beth She'arim in Palestine, and no. 701 from Larissa in Thessaly; no. 476 from Rome is the only instance in Latin). As compared to the thousands of pagan Greek instances of metrical epitaphs (see the collections by Peek and Hansen), this is a very small harvest, but the significant thing is the concentration in one (or two) area(s).

Grief is also expressed by saying that the deceased left nothing but great mourning and pain to the survivors.[38] In Beth She'arim, the young Justus says on his tombstone: "I left my poor parents and my brothers in endless mourning" (BS II 127), and in Rome an 18-year-old girl, παρθένος μελλόνυμφος, says she is λιποῦσα πατρὶ πέν-θος ἀπειρέσιον, 'leaving to her father endless grief' (*Inscriptiones Graecae* XIV 1648).[39]

Epitaphs addressing the passer-by

One of the striking characteristics of many ancient epitaphs (pagan, Jewish and Christian) is that they invite or even command the stranger or passer-by to stop, to read the epitaph, and to share in the

---

[37] Lattimore, *Themes* 195-198; Griessmair, *Motiv* 30-44.
[38] Lattimore, *Themes* 179-180.
[39] Horsley, *New Documents* 4 (1987) 221-222, regards this inscription (which is not in Frey) as probably Jewish, but since he does so on the basis of names alone, this cannot be regarded as being beyond doubt.

grief.[40] Both Greek and Latin epitaphs abound in expressions de-
signed to attract the attention of the wayfarer, to make him at least
read the name on the stone, to have some value attached to that name
alive in his consciousness for a while. Most often there is the pre-
tence that the dead person, through his epitaph, addresses the traveller. The many literary parallels to this genre in the 7th book of the
Anthologia Palatina probably exhibit the influence exerted by inscriptions on literature, not the other way round. For, as Lattimore
has remarked, "the address to the traveller is a feature which is fun-
damentally appropriate to the inscribed epitaph, and to nothing else;
it could only be grounded in the fact that in classical times the dead
were buried, for reasons hygienic or religious or both, outside of
cities, and therefore the great highways became lined with tombs".[41]
And it is there that they could attract the attention of the wayfarers.
That situation is the 'Sitz im Leben' of this genre.

Again, most of the Jewish imitations of this classical model are to
be found in Leontopolis in Egypt.[42] Let us quote some characteristic
instances. CIJ 1508, of the young lady who died just before the day
of her marriage, has already been quoted. No. 1509 is another dramatic example (I quote the translation by Lewis):[43] "This is the tomb
of Horaia, wayfarer, shed a tear. The daughter of Nikolaos, who
was unfortunate in all things in her thirty years. Three of us are
here, husband, daughter, and I whom they struck down with grief.
My husband died on the third, then on the fifth my daughter Eirene,
to whom marriage was not granted. I then with no place or joy was
laid here after them under the earth on the seventh of Choiak. But,
stranger, you have already all there is to know from us to tell all
men of the swiftness of death".[44] And no. 1510:[45] "This is the grave

---

[40] Lattimore, *Themes* 230-237, with numerous references. Good examples
(with translation) in W. Peek, *Griechische Grabgedichte*, Berlin: Akademie Verlag, 1960, nos. 169-183, 319-328.

[41] Lattimore, *Themes* 230.

[42] A unique example in Aramaic is the inscription in Jason's tomb in Jerusalem
which starts with "A powerful lament make for Jason, ..."; see N. Avigad,
Aramaic Inscriptions in the Tomb of Jason, *IEJ* 17 (1967) 101-111.

[43] See also the valuable edition with translation and commentary by E.
Bernand, *Inscriptions métriques de l'Égypte gréco-romaine*, Paris: Les Belles
Lettres, 1969, 206-209.

[44] This epitaph is also in Peek, *GV* 644. Its Jewishness seems more or less

of Arsinoe, wayfarer. Stand by and weep for her, unfortunate in all things, whose lot was hard and terrible. For I[46] was bereaved of my mother when I was a little girl, and when the flower of my youth made me ready for a bridegroom, my father married me to Phabeis, and Fate brought me to the end of my life in bearing my firstborn child. I had a small span of years, but great grace flowered in the beauty of my spirit. This grave hides in its bosom my chaste body, but my soul has flown to the holy ones. Lament for Arsinoe".[47] A shorter specimen is no. 1513:[48] "Citizens and strangers, all weep for Rachelis, a chaste woman, friend of all, about 30 years old. Do not weep vainly for me. If I did live but a short allotted span of time, nevertheless I await a good hope of mercy".[49] There are also some instances in which all men are called upon to weep: κλαύσατε πάντες (1522, 1530b, 1530d).[50]

Several of the instances in which the traveller or stranger is addressed are in poetic form, either hexametric or iambic, a literary phenomenon with a long and rich tradition in the Greek world, witness the many hundreds of instances collected in Werner Peek's *Griechische Versinschriften*.[51] In the collection of Jewish epitaphs the instances of this poetic genre are almost all restricted to Egypt, as we have seen; only a couple of them occur in Rome and Beth She'arim (476, BS II 127, 183).

---

guaranteed by the combination of the fact that it was found quite near the Jewish colony in Leontopolis and of the name Eirene which occurs so frequently among Jews in Egypt and elsewhere.

[45] Peek, *GV* 643; Bernand, *Inscriptions* 196-199.

[46] Note the transition from third to first person.

[47] We will return to the eschatological ideas in these epitaphs in Ch. VIII.

[48] Bernand, *Inscriptions* 203-206.

[49] Lewis' translation (p. 158), slightly modified. The exhortation to stop useless grieving, very common in pagan epitaphs (Lattimore, *Themes* 217-220), is found in no other Jewish inscription; but see Ps-Phocylides 97f.

[50] The most simple form of 'addressing' the passer-by is, of course, the use of κεῖμαι instead of κεῖται, because it implies talking by the dead person (e.g. nos. 37, 118, 358).

[51] Unfortunately, of Peek's large scale project with 4 planned volumes (including commentary and indexes) only volume I has appeared as well as the booklet *Verzeichnis der Gedichtanfänge* belonging to this volume (1956).

Epitaphs addressing the deceased

In pagan funerary epigraphy this poetic form is also often used when not the passer-by but the deceased person himself is addressed by the survivors,[52] but in our Jewish corpus this is mostly done in prose. Of this very common type of epitaph some instances may suffice by way of illustration: no. 123 (Rome), "Be of good courage, Julia Aemilia, aged 40 years. You lived a good life with your husband. I am grateful to you for your thoughtfulness and your soul" (transl. Leon). No. 1451 (Leontopolis), "Mikkos, (...), farewell, you friend of all, excellent one, untimely dead". No. 1514 (Leontopolis), "O Marion, of priestly descent, excellent one, friend of all, you who caused pain to no-one and were a friend to your neighbours, farewell". It may be noticed that in this type of epitaph the farewell greeting χαῖρε is extremely common, again especially in Egypt.

Sometimes, however, it is the deceased himself who bids the traveller farewell by saying χαῖρε. It is noteworthy that the Jews of the Thessalonian city of Larissa had developed their own variant of this greeting: 12 epitaphs end with τῷ λαῷ χαίρειν (699-708c), in which λαός is to be understood in the sense of 'the local Jewish community'.[53] An interesting mixed form of addressing the dead one, addressing God, and having the deceased address the stranger, is the Roman inscription no. 358: "Would that I, who reared[54] you, Justus, my child, were able to place you in a golden coffin. Now, o Lord, (grant) in thy righteous judgement (that) Justus, a peerless child, (may) sleep in peace. Here I lie, Justus, aged 4 years and 8 months, sweet to my foster father. Theodotus the foster father to his most sweet child" (transl. Leon, slightly adapted; for the Greek text see our Ch. 10).

Another form of addressing the deceased person, but formally akin to the greeting formula χαῖρε, is the type in which the dead one

---

52 Peek, *Grabgedichte,* nos. 184-207 and 329-347

53 For this sense of λαός see esp. Robert, *Hellenica* III (1946) 103-104, XI-XII (1960) 260-262; *BE* 1976 no. 333.

54 The stone reads θεψάμενος. Frey hesitates between emending to θαψάμενος or to θρεψάμενος, Ferrua and Leon opt for θρεψάμενος, Schwabe and Lifshitz for θαψάμενος, less likely in view of τροφεύς (some lines further).

is encouraged by means of formulas like θάρσει (most often θάρσει, οὐδεὶς ἀθάνατος), εὐμοίρει, εὐψύχει, εὐφρόνει. These imperatives occur very often, with a remarkably high frequency in Beth She'arim and Leontopolis.[55] We will have to return to the problem of the meaning of these imperatives in the chapter on afterlife (Ch. VIII).

By way of finale to this paragraph on epitaphs which address either the passer-by or the deceased, let me quote a very curious and fascinating metrical inscription from Leontopolis which presents, in Doric dialect, a fine specimen of a genre not uncommon in pagan epitaphs, namely dialogue between the passer-by and the deceased.[56] It is CIJ no. 1530:[57] "The speaking tombstone: 'Who are you who lie in the dark tomb? Tell me your country and birth.' – 'Arsinoe, daughter of Aline and Theodosius. The famous land of Onias reared me.' – 'How old were you when you slipped down the dark slope of Lethe?' – 'At twenty I went to the sad place of the dead.' – 'Were you married?' – 'I was.' – 'Did you leave him a child?' – 'Childless I went to the house of Hades.' – 'May earth, the guardian of the dead, be light on you.' – 'And for you, stranger, may she bear fruitful crops'." (Στάλα μανύτειρα. – τίς ἐν τύμβῳ κεῖσαι; καὶ πάτραν καὶ γενέτην ἔνεπε. – Ἀρσινόα, κούρα δ' Ἀλινόης καὶ Θηδοσίοιο: φαμισθὰ δ' Ὀνίου γᾶ τροφὸς ἀμετέρα. – ποσσαέτης δ' ὤλισθας ὑπὸ σκοτόεν κλίμα Λάθας; – ἰκοσέτης γοερὸν χῶρον ἔβην νεκύων. – ζευγίσθης δὲ γάμους; – ζεύχθην. – κατελίνπανες αὐτῷ τέκνον; – ἄτεκνος ἔβαν εἰς Ἀΐδαο δόμους. – ἴη σοὶ κούφα χθὼν ἁ

---

[55] Beth She'arim: e.g. BS II 2-7, 29, 39-41, 43, 47, 52, 57, 59, 84, 87-89 102; Tell el-Yehudieh: e.g. 1452, 1454, 1458, 1460, 1464, 1467-1471, 1476-1477, 1480-1488, 1493-1497, 1501-1504, 1514, 1519, 1524-1527. See M. Simon, ΘΑΡΣΕΙ, ΟΥΔΕΙΣ ΑΘΑΝΑΤΟΣ. For pagan parallels see Pfohl, RAC 12, 482.

[56] Good instances with translation can be found in Peek, Grabgedichte, nos. 424-440. D. C. Kurtz and J. Boardman, Greek Burial Customs, London: Thames and Hudson, 1971, 266, quote the following nice example: "Chariton, how are things below? – All dark. – And what about the way up? – A lie. – And Pluto? – A myth. – Then we are done for."

[57] Also Peek, GV 1861; Bernand, Inscriptions 199-203. See also A. Momigliano, Un documento della spiritualità dei Giudei Leontopolitani, Aegyptus 12 (1932) 171-172. Peek, GV 1831-1887, is a whole collection of dialogue-epitaphs.

φθιμένοιο φυλάκτωρ. – καὶ σοί, ξεῖνε, φέροι καρπὸν ἀπὸ
σταχύων.)

Sit tibi terra levis

The final remark of the passer-by in this epitaph, εἴη σοι κούφα
χθών, 'may earth be light on you', brings us again to another well-
known topic of ancient funerary epigraphy, namely the *sit tibi terra
levis* motif.[58] I give here the Latin wording because in Latin
epitaphs the formula in this (metrical) form has become so common
that it is very frequently abbreviated to *s.t.t.l.*[59] (Roman Africa
developed its own stereotyped formula: *ossa tibi bene quiescant
[o.t.b.q.].*) In Greek epitaphs it never became such a fixed formula,
even though the source of the expression is a passage from
Euripides' *Alcestis* 463-4 κούφα σοι χθὼν ἐπάνωθε πέσοι (cf.
Meleager in *Anthologia Palatina* VII 461), a phrase that underwent
all kinds of variations especially in Latin poets like Propertius,
Ovid, and Martial.[60] Besides the Jewish epitaph already quoted, we
note only 4 other instances: BS II 167 (κούφα γῆ), CIJ 1484 and
1488 (both γῆς ἐλαφρᾶς τύχοις), and 1530a (γαῖαν ἔχοις
ἐλαφράν). It is noteworthy that of the extremely popular Latin
formula no Jewish instances have been recovered and also that the
Greek formulas are again found only in Leontopolis and Beth
She'arim.

Curses

We now turn to a very different genre of epitaphs, those comprising
a threat and malediction or curse against the ones who do not leave
the tomb untouched. This form – common among pagans, Jews, and
Christians – occurs mainly, though not exclusively, in Asia Minor,
most of the instances coming from Phrygia (some from Pisidia,
Lycia, and Caria) and dating to the second and third centuries CE.[61]

---

58 Lattimore, *Themes* 65-70; Pietri, *RAC* 12, 535-536.
59 Lattimore, *Themes* 68 n.354, gives dozens of examples.
60 Lattimore, *Themes* 70.
61 A. Parrot, *Malédictions et violations de tombes,* Paris: Geuthner, 1939,

There is ample evidence for the presence of a special attitude towards the tomb in Asia Minor. The widely attested use of tombs in the shape of a house or of gravestones with the representation of doors ('Türsteine') in Anatolia seems to be indicative of a belief that the dead body continued living in some sense. Therefore, "it was considered tremendously important that the grave should be untouched save by those for whom it was meant. Furthermore, there must have been a widespread belief that such defensive curses would work, that the religious awe of the public in general would correspond to the intense concern felt by those who built the tomb".[62] Always the sanctity and exclusivity of the tomb are stressed. This may be done by simple formulas like 'do not open this tomb'[63] or 'it is not permitted to bury here anyone else'. Or, to quote a more elaborate pagan example: "You who pass by, do not injure my sacred grave, lest you incur the sharp anger of Agesilaos and Persephone, maiden daughter of Demeter. But as you go by, say to Aratius: may you have light earth upon you".[64] This epitaph (from first century Crete, incidentally) already refers to the gods' anger which was to play such a large role in the later cursing formulas. This anger is often said to result in bodily sufferings, a terrible

---

103-139; Lattimore, *Themes* 106-125; W. Speyer, Fluch, *RAC* VII (1969) 1160-1288, esp. 1198-1201; L. Robert, Malédictions funéraires grecques, *CRAI* 1978, 241-289 (253: "En effet la Phrygie est le domaine par excellence des imprécations funéraires"). Although more than half a century old, Parrot's survey of the various formulas is still most useful; but see now also J. H. M. Strubbe, *Arai Epitymbioi. Een uitgave en studie van de heidense vervloekingen tegen eventuele grafschenners in de Griekse funeraire inscripties van Klein-Azië,* 3 vols., diss. Gent 1983, with the author's own valuable summary in the article Vervloekingen tegen grafschenners, *Lampas* 16 (1983) 248-274; see also his "Cursed be he that moves my bones", in C. A. Faraone – D. Obbink (edd.), *Magika Hiera,* Oxford: OUP, 1991, 33-59.

[62] Lattimore, *Themes* 109. A. D. Nock, Tomb Violations and Pontifical Law, in his *Essays on Religion and the Ancient World* II, Oxford: OUP, 1972, 527-533 (532: "We must not minimize ancient fears of being disturbed in the grave"). For the 'Türsteine' see M. Waelkens, *Die kleinasiatischen Türsteine* (1986).

[63] In Palestine often *la´ lemaphteaḥ* (nos. 1300, 1334, 1359, etc.); see Parrot, *Malédictions* 61.

[64] Peek, *GV* 1370. Peek has numerous poetic examples, although most other instances are in prose.

death, and punishment after death of the tomb-violator (and his relatives).

Let us quote some Jewish examples, first from Acmonia in Phrygia (third cent. CE): CIJ 770, "Titus Flavius Alexander prepared this tomb during his lifetime for himself and his wife Gaiana, for the sake of remembrance. He was a council-member and an archon, he led a good life without causing grief to anyone. If someone[65] opens this tomb after the interment of me, Alexander, and my wife, Gaiana, all the curses that have been written against his eyes, his entire body, his children, and his life will befall him; etc."[66] The 'written curses' referred to are not specified, but in another Phrygian epitaph from the same place this riddle is solved: no. 760, "Aurelius Phrougianus (...) and his wife Aurelia Juliana have built (this tomb) during their lifetime for Makaria, (his/her) mother, and Alexandria, their very sweet daughter, for the sake of remembrance. If, after they have been deposited here, someone buries another dead person here or commits injustice by buying (the place), the curses that are written in Deuteronomy will befall him" (see Robert, *Hellenica* X 249; cf. MAMA VI 335: "... whosoever dares to inter here someone else, (...), such a one will be accursed, and may all the curses that are written in Deuteronomy befall him and his children and his descendants and all his family (relatives)"[67].) There can be no doubt that the curses referred to are those in Deuteronomy 28, esp. vv. 22 and 28-29: (22) πατάξαι σε κύριος ἀπορίᾳ καὶ πυρετῷ καὶ ῥίγει καὶ ἐρεθισμῷ καὶ φόνῳ καὶ ἀνεμοφθορίᾳ καὶ τῇ

---

[65] For the wide variety of 'if someone' formulas see Parrot, *Malédictions* 127-129.

[66] Τ. Φλ. ᾿Αλέξανδρος ζῶν ἑαυτῷ καὶ Γαιανῇ γυναικὶ τὸ μνημεῖον κατεσκεύσεν μνήμης χάριν, βουλεύσας, ἄρξας, ζήσας καλῶς, μηδένα λυπήσας. μετὰ δὲ τὸ τεθῆναι ἐμὲ τὸν ᾿Αλέξανδρον καὶ τὴν σύμβιόν μου Γαιανήν, εἴ τις ἀνοίξῃ τὸ μνημεῖον, ἔσονται αὐτῷ κατάραι ὅσαι ἂν γεγραμμέναι εἰσὶν εἰς ὅρασιν καὶ εἰς ὅλον τὸ σῶμα αὐτῷ καὶ εἰς τέκνα καὶ εἰς βίον, κτλ.

[67] This epitaph, not in CIJ, is adduced by Horsley, *New Documents* 1 (1981) 101 (no. 61); cf. also *New Documents* 3 (1983) 123-125 (no. 96). Parrot, *Malédictions* 134-135, lists a variety of curses in which family members of the perpetrator are involved. Three inscriptions from Acmonia (Phrygia) state that the curse will be extended to the τέκνα τέκνων (763, 765, 767); for this LXX expression see Exod. 34:7; Prov. 17:6.

ὤχρᾳ, καὶ καταδιώξονταί σε ἕως ἂν ἀπολέσωσίν σε. ... (28) πατάξαι σε κύριος παραπληξίᾳ καὶ ἀορασίᾳ καὶ ἐκστάσει διανοίας, (29) καὶ ἔσῃ ψηλαφῶν μεσημβρίας ὡσεὶ ψηλαφήσαι ὁ τυφλὸς ἐν τῷ σκότει, καὶ οὐκ εὐοδώσει τὰς ὁδούς σου. καὶ ἔσῃ τότε ἀδικούμενος καὶ διαρπαζόμενος πάσας τὰς ἡμέρας καὶ οὐκ ἔσται σοι ὁ βοηθῶν ('May the Lord smite you with distress, fever, cold, inflammation, murder, blighting and paleness, and they shall pursue you until they have destroyed you. ... May the Lord smite you with insanity, blindness and astonishment of mind; and then you will grope at midday, as a blind man would grope in the darkness, and you will not prosper in your ways; and then you will be unjustly treated and plundered all your days, and there will be no helper'). This grim picture of divine vengeance could of course be evoked only in the minds of those who knew what 'the curses written in Deuteronomy' were. So one might infer that the imprecations were directed primarily at the coreligionists of the dedicators. Or did they assume their pagan fellow Phrygians to have knowledge of the Bible as well? One feels inclined to believe so in view of the formulation of no. 774: "No one else may be put here, but if some-one burics here (another person), he knows the Law of the Jews" (to be sure, this epitaph is not from Acmonia, but from Apameia). The fact that here the law referred to is so explicitly identified as 'the Law *of the Jews*' might indicate that the writer, when formulating the epitaph, had non-Jews in mind. (Cf. also no. 650, from Sicily, where the husband of the deceased says: *adiuro vos (...) per legem quam Dominus dedit Iudaeis, ne quis aperiat memoriam ...*).[68]

Another interesting variant is exemplified by no. 769 (Acmonia, Phrygia): "...; if someone inters here another body, he will have to reckon with God Most High, and may the sickle of the curse enter his house and leave no one alive" (..., ἔσται αὐτῷ πρὸς τὸν θεὸν τὸν ὕψιστον, καὶ τὸ ἀρᾶς δρέπανον εἰς τὸν οἶκον αὐτοῦ [εἰσέλθοιτο καὶ μηδένα ἐγκαταλείψαιτο]).[69] The curious formula

---

68 W. M. Ramsay, *The Cities and Bishoprics of Phrygia*, II, Oxford: Claren-don Press, 1897, 538, does the implausible suggestion that "the law of the Jews cannot here be the law of Moses (...). It seems to be a special law peculiar to Apameia, apparently some agreement made with the city by the resident Jews for the better protection of their graves".

69 Partly reconstructed on the basis of no. 768 which has a very similar text (=

ἔσται αὐτῷ πρὸς τὸν θεόν[70] occurs frequently in Christian inscriptions from Eumenia (Phrygia), which may but need not have influenced the formulation of the Jewish epitaph here (it was never exclusively Jewish or Christian).[71] It certainly implies an eschatological threat. Τὸ ἀρᾶς δρέπανον can hardly be anything else than an allusion to the LXX version of Zech. 5:2-4, where, in the Hebrew text, the prophet sees in a vision a scroll (*megillah*) flying around, but where the LXX has δρέπανον for *megillah,* obviously because *maggāl* (= sickle) was read. This sickle could be taken to be an instrument of God's curse and of divine vengeance by the Phrygian Jews who engraved the stone since the biblical text itself interprets the sickle as ἡ ἀρὰ ἡ ἐκπορευομένη ἐπὶ πρόσωπον πάσης τῆς γῆς (5:3), that will punish every thief and perjurer with death; and cf. also Joel 4:13 LXX! (In parentheses, this is again an interesting testimony to the use of the LXX which differs here so much from the Hebrew text).

These biblical references are of course meant to warn the potential tomb-violator of God's anger. A straightforward mention of the ὀργὴ θεοῦ is found in only two inscriptions, in MAMA VI 325: "... after they have been deposited here, whosoever will open this grave (...) or demolishes its inscription, God's wrath will destroy his entire family"; and in an Asia Minor type inscription found in Rome with an almost identical closing phrase, "God's wrath will destroy his whole family" (like the previous one not in CIJ, but published by L. Moretti in *Riv. Arch. Crist.* 50 [1974] 213-219). In pagan and Christian epitaphs threats with the anger of the gods or God are much more frequent.[72]

MAMA VI 316).

[70] Frey translates: "il aura à compter avec Dieu"; Robert, *Hellenica* XI-XII 399: "il aura affaire à Dieu". W. M. Calder, The Eumeneian Formula, in W. M. Calder – J. Keil (edd.), *Anatolian Studies Presented to W. H. Buckler*, Manchester: Manchester University Press, 1939, 15-26, 20: "he shall have to reckon with God".

[71] See on this problem A. R. R. Sheppard, Jews, Christians and Heretics in Acmonia and Eumenia, *AS* 29 (1979) 169-180; Robert, *Hellenica* XI-XII 398-413; more lit. in Strubbe, 'Cursed be he that moves my bones' 48 n.17.

[72] Survey of formulas in Parrot, *Malédictions* 131; see also Robert, *Hellenica* XI-XII 407. If Robert, *ibid.* 436-439, is right, there is also a third century Jewish inscription from Phrygia that states that the tresspasser "will receive from

Quite different is an epitaph from mainland Greece, no. 719 (Argos): "I, Aurelius Justus, adjure by the divine and great powers of God and by the powers of the Law and by the honour of the patriarchs and by the honour of the ethnarchs and by the honour of the sages and by the honour of the worship that is offered daily to God, that no one will destroy this grave-monument that I have made with so much labour".[73] Although there is no curse here, both heavenly and earthly powers are called upon to prevent violation of the tomb. This can also be seen, albeit in quite a different form, in an epitaph from Beth She'arim (BS II 134), where it is said that no one should open the grave, κατὰ τὴν ὁσίαν, κατὰ πρόσταγμα, 'in accordance with the holy (commandment), in accordance with (imperial) decree'.[74]

A duality of religious and worldly sanctions is also apparent from the fact that in the inscriptions from Asia Minor often a double fine to be paid by the violator is stipulated, e.g. no. 741 from Smyrna (= *Inschriften von Smyrna* I, ed. G. Petzl, Bonn: Habelt, 1982, 295): "Rufina, a Jewish woman, head of the synagogue, prepared this tomb for her freedmen and slaves; and no one else has the authority to bury here anyone else. If someone dares to do so, he will have to give 1500 *denaria* to the most sacred treasury and 1000 *denaria* to the Jewish community. A copy of this inscription has been deposited in the public archives". This is one of the many instances in which not divine vengeance but a double financial penalty is the threat that is supposed to deter tomb-violators. Cf. also the following inscription from Lydian Thyatira, no. 752 (=*TAM* V [2], ed. P. Hermann, Vienna: Oesterreichische Akademie der Wissenschaften, 1989, 1142): "Fabius Zosimus, who had this sarcophagus made, placed it on a sacred spot before the city, beside the *Sambatheion* [= synagogue] in the Chaldaean quarter, along the public road, for himself, in order that he be deposited there, and also for his very sweet wife Aurelia Pontiane. No one else has the right to deposit someone in

---

the immortal God eternal flagellation" (μάστιγα αἰώνιον).

[73] Cf. no. 650 (Sicily) *adiuro vos per honores patriarcharum, item adiuro vos per legem quam Dominus dedit Iudaeis, ne quis aperiat memoriam ...*

[74] After τὴν ὁσίαν probably ἐντολήν is to be suppleted; πρόσταγμα probably refers to an imperial edict such as the famous Nazareth inscription (on which see below in Ch. 10).

this sarcophagus. But if someone dares to do so or act contrary to these (rules), he will have to pay 1500 silver *denaria* to the city of the Thyatirans and to the most holy treasury 2500 silver *denaria*, and, moreover, he falls under the law on tomb-violation [τῷ τῆς τυμβωρυχίας νόμῳ][75]. Two copies of this inscription have been written, one of which has been deposited in the archives".[76] Sometimes the fine is said to be due to 'the most sacred synagogue', as two inscriptions from Greece have it.[77]

Let us finally quote a characteristically Jewish threat in one of the Beth She'arim epitaphs, BS II 162: "Anyone who removes this woman, He who has promised to bring back to life the dead, will Himself judge him". We will dwell on the implied belief in the resurrection of the dead in a later chapter (Ch. VIII).

---

[75] See E. Gerner, Tymborychia, *Zeitschrift der Savigny-Stiftung für Rechtsgeschichte, Romanistische Abteilung* 61 (1941) 230-275.

[76] For the Greek text see below, Ch.10, no.VII. More examples could be quoted but we refer the reader to the nos. 757, 761-763, 765, 767-768, 773-776, 778-779, 786. For literature see Schürer, *History* III 106 n. 68. Sometimes the fines stipulated were much heavier.

[77] Robert, *Hellenica* XI-XII 391-392.

IV. Epithets

Before we discuss the epithets – that is, the virtues ascribed to the deceased either by means of adjectives or by means of participial or relative clauses – we will first have to raise the question of the sincerity of these epithets. As in modern times, so in antiquity as well, there was a venerable tradition which had developed and fixed the laudatory words and phrases suitable to the deceased. The result of this process was that in the long run a whole stock of standard expressions of praise was available to the survivors who decided to erect and inscribe a tombstone for their beloved deceased. Some scholars have assumed that there even existed manuals of stock phrases and epithets or stonemasons' catalogues which either the family of the deceased or the engraver himself could draw upon when having to formulate an epitaph.[1]

Sincerity

This of course raises the problem of the authenticity, in the sense of sincerity, of the laudatory formulations in the epitaphs. If epitaphs were most of the time no more than copies of readily available models in the manuals of the engraver or stonemason, then the sincerity of the epitaph itself comes under strong suspicion, that is, in the eyes of the adherents of the manual-theory. But, in spite of the continual recurrence of the same or similar formulas over a long period and over a wide area, really hard and unambiguous evidence for the existence of such manuals has never been brought forward. It is relatively seldom that a formula is often repeated literally or

---

[1] Lattimore, *Themes* 18-19; Pietri, *RAC* 12, 518-519; Pikhaus, *Levensbeschouwing* 31-33.

verbally; and verbal agreements can easily be explained in other ways. Moreover – and this is not unimportant – even a certain amount of inevitable plagiarism does not imply that the sincerity of the feelings expressed has to be doubted. When I inscribe a tombstone with the words 'To my beloved father/mother', then the sheer fact that there are millions of tombstones with exactly the same formula does not in the least detract from the authenticity of the feeling expressed by the word 'beloved'. Standard formulas often come into existence precisely because they express so exactly what people feel. This, of course, is not to deny that flattery and exaggeration to the point of insincerity do occur in epitaphs, as they do in *laudationes funebres*. But the familiar *de mortuis nil nisi bonum* does not imply that there is a need for excessive scepticism in dealing with the epithets. "For tombstones were set up in public places for all members of the community to see and read, and the survivor who made a blatantly false and exaggerated claim on behalf of the dead would bring ridicule upon himself without in any way benefiting the reputation of the person commemorated".[2]

Epithets in common with pagan epitaphs

Jewish laudatory epitaphs have very much in common with pagan Greek and Latin epitaphs. We will first discuss these common elements before we turn to the specifically Jewish epithets. The most frequently occurring epithets in pagan Greek and Latin epitaphs are the following:[3]

ἀγαθός, ἀείμνηστος, ἄλυπος, ἄξιος, ἀσύγκριτος, ἄωρος, γλυ-κύτατος, εὐσεβής/-έστατος, καλός, μείλιχος, μόνανδρος, πασίφι-λος (or πάντων φιλός), σεμνός, σώφρων, τιμιώτατος, φιλάδελφος, φίλανδρος, φιλάνθρωπος, φιλογείτων, φιλόθεος, φιλομήτωρ, φιλο-

---

[2] M. N. Tod, Laudatory Epithets in Greek Epitaphs, *Annual of the British School at Athens* 46 (1951) 184.

[3] The epithets are here enumerated in alphabetical order and in the form in which they are found in the dictionaries. See Lattimore, *Themes* 290-299; Kajanto, *A Study of the Greek Epitaphs* 30-39; Pietri, *RAC* 12, 525-528; Tod, Laudatory Epithets 182-190.

πάτωρ, φιλότεκνος, φιλόφιλος, φίλτατος, χρηστός (note the frequency of adjectives with φιλ-);[4] *benemerens, benemeritus, carissimus, castus/-issimus* (almost always in the feminine form), *decens, dignus/-issimus, dulcis/-issimus, fidelis/-issimus, incomparabilis, optimus, pius/piissimus/pientissimus, pudicus* (mostly in the feminine), *rarissimus, sanctus/-issimus, univira* (note the much higher frequency of superlatives in the Latin register).[5]

These adjectives have been listed in alphabetical order, not in the order of frequency, because as yet there is no comprehensive statistical survey of all the relevant evidence. But even so it is clear that these epithets reveal a certain scale of values and that these values were not exactly the same among Greeks and Romans. But this is a matter that we cannot go into in this connection.[6]

Of all these epithets not one is absent from the Jewish epitaphs, which shows to what extent the Jews borrowed traditional terminology from their pagan neighbours in this respect.

---

[4] See Tod, Laudatory Epithets 189, on the many compounds with φιλ-. At p. 186 Tod remarks that χρηστός, which is by far the most popular epithet, is much more frequent than ἀγαθός because "ἀγαθός may represent an 'abstract' virtue of the human soul, while χρηστός may denote goodness in action, goodness which finds an outlet in the service of those in the home or the community, helpfulness".

[5] In the Semitic epitaphs virtually no epithets are to be found.

[6] Kajanto, *Study* 30-39, notes that what is the most frequent Latin epithet in Rome, *benemerens*, lays emphasis upon the performance and reward of duty, whereas the most frequent Greek epithet in Rome, γλυκύτατος, emphasizes the joy people have experienced with one another. Tod, Laudatory Epithets 189-190, summarizes the results of his investigation of the Greek epithets as follows: "We see the portrait of one who respects religion, but in whose life it does not play a leading part, one for whom virtue is in the main related to the family and the circle of friends and neighbours, consisting above all in a friendly helpfulness and the avoidance of all that might cause pain or annoyance to others, one whose affections are warm, but normally restricted, and who claims no special loyalty to city-state or sovereign lord, one who values honesty, fidelity, probity and all the qualities which help the wheels of social intercourse to run smoothly". For a good comparison of the epithets in epitaphs with those in Plutarch's ethical writings see C. Panagopoulos, Vocabulaire et mentalité dans les *Moralia de Plutarque*, *Dialogues d'histoire ancienne* 3 (1977) 197-235.

Other laudatory epithets which occur in both pagan and Jewish epitaphs, but much less frequently, include:
ἀβλαβής, ἀγαπητός, αἰνόμορος, ἄμεμπτος, ἀμίαντος, ἄμωμος, ἀτυχής, δίκαιος, δύσμορος, ἡδύς, λαμπρός/-ότατος, μακάριος/μακαρίστατος/μακάρτατος, ὅσιος, παρθενικός, ταλαίπωρος, and finally the expression καλῶς βιώσας/ζήσας, which frequently appears on Jewish tombs in the form of a finite phrase, καλῶς ἔζησεν. We also find once καλῶς συμβιώσας ('who lived a good marriage life', 28), the nice combination καλῶς βιώσας καὶ καλῶς ἀκούσας ('who lived a good life and had a good reputation', 119), and the profound variant καλῶς ἀποθανών ('who died a good death', 79); unique is the expression καλῶς βιώσασα ἐν τῷ Ἰουδαϊσμῷ (537). For the Latin we may add: *bonus, desiderantissimus, innocens*.[7]

There are some general comments to be made on these lists. First, the high frequency in both pagan and Jewish epitaphs of composite adjectives with the stem φιλ- indicates that warm relationships, especially in the family but also between friends and neighbours, were highly esteemed in both traditions; and, as we shall see below, the register was firmly extended by the Jews by means of new word-formations with φιλ-. Secondly, there was a high regard for all virtues of correct behaviour, e.g. justice, gentleness, worthiness, self-control, decency, chastity, faithfulness, piety, and not grieving or causing harm to anyone; in brief: to live as a good human being (which is actually what the formula καλῶς βιώσας implies). The words used in the Latin inscriptions suggest a heavier emphasis on duties of children towards parents and of wives towards husbands, and on the merits earned by these when they had fulfilled these duties. It may be noted in passing that, in contradistinction to several Christian inscriptions, virginity is nowhere praised. Anyone who dies as a virgin, either male or female, is to be lamented.[8]

---

[7] Many instances in inscriptions from Europe may be found via the index in vol. I of Frey's CIJ. Unfortunately, the posthumously published vol. II was not indexed, but hopefully the Cambridge and Tübingen projects will soon remedy this.

[8] See Frey's Introd. CXII-CXVIII; Leon, *Jews* 128-134; both sketches are limited to Rome. A comprehensive study of the epitheta in all Jewish inscriptions (not only funerary) is a real desideratum. A good study of terms for gentleness

Typically Jewish epithets

We now turn to the few exclusively (or almost exclusively)[9] Jewish laudatory epithets. Let us first list them alphabetically and then discuss them briefly one by one.

benememorius (639, 630, 670), *colens legem* (72), *eruditus* (Le Bohec no. 10);[10] εὐδίδακτος (190), εὐλογημένος (Le Bohec nos. 31 and 32), πενιχρός (BS II 99 and 206), φιλέντολος (132, 203, 482, 509; cf. φιλεντόλιος in the Maltese inscription published by Ferrua in *Civiltà Cattolica* 1949, 513[11]), φιλογόνευς (Fasola p. 46), φιλόλαος (203, 509), φιλόνομος (111, Fasola p. 17, Horsley, *New Documents* 1 no. 74), φιλοπένης (203), φιλοσυνάγωγος (321). (Note again the predominance of compounds with φιλ, also in these typically Jewish epithets.)

To begin with the Latin ones, *benememorius* is of late occurrence (no. 670 being in fact the latest inscription in our corpus, it is from the year 688). It is of interest in that two of the three inscriptions are Latin-Hebrew bilinguals of which the Hebrew part quotes or alludes to Prov. 10:7 (*zekher ṣaddiq livrakha*). The Latin part paraphrases this concept of blessed memory with a new adjective which in its first half looks strikingly like the traditional pagan *benemerens*, but is in fact the free dynamic equivalent of a biblical and Jewish expression.

Eruditus ('well instructed, learned') should be dealt with together with εὐδίδακτος and with the *discipulina bona* in no. 215 (but also with the female proper name Eumathia in BS II 113). They may reflect the typically Jewish concept of the religious value of learning

---

in Greek inscriptions in general is J. de Romilly, *La douceur dans la pensée grecque*, Paris: Les Belles Lettres, 1979, Ch. 15.

[9] There may be some occasional parallels in later Christian epitaphs, but these are almost always due to the common scriptural background of both religious traditions. See e.g. Horsley, *New Documents* 3 (1983) 105-106 (no. 89).

[10] Y. le Bohec, Inscriptions juives et judaïsantes de l'Afrique romaine, *Antiquités Africaines* 17 (1981) 165-207.

[11] See now R. S. Kraemer, A New Inscription from Malta and the Question of Women Elders in the Diaspora Jewish Communities, *HTR* 78 (1986) 431-438.

and study.[12] This implies that the epitaphs containing these epithets should probably be read as glorifying the deceased not only as intellectuals but also as 'religious virtuosi' (to use Weberian terminology). The intriguing fact that two of the three are females (a μαθητής and a *discipulina*) and that Eumathia is only attested as the name of a woman, will be discussed in the chapter on women.

Colens legem is a testimony to the high regard the Torah was held in among diaspora Jews (cf. also *legis observantia* in 476) and should be considered together with φιλόνομος and φιλέντολος, the latter two being in fact the most frequently used exclusively Jewish epithets. The centrality of Torah for diaspora Judaism, albeit it not necessarily in its rabbinic interpretation, cannot be doubted; we have literary evidence for it in all of Hellenistic-Jewish literature and, apart from the epithets under discussion, there are also quite a number of other terms which testify to that, e.g. νομομαθής, νομοδιδάσκαλος, σοφοδιδάσκαλος, *observantia legis*; and also the whole range of titles for synagogue or community officials (see the next chapter) are clear evidence that the religious congregation and the synagogue formed the backbone of Jewish life in the diaspora. Since synagogue implies Torah, hearing and reading and studying the Torah, it cannot surprise us that φιλόνομος and φιλέντολος were favourite epithets in Jewish epigraphy.[13] Φιλοσυνάγωγος and φιλόλαος (in the sense of 'lover of the [Jewish] community')[14] belong to the same conceptual sphere. It requires little imagination that in sometimes inimical surroundings the feeling of togetherness and the experience of mutual support and warmth created a deeply felt bond or even love of the individual Jews for the synagogual community they belonged to. That is what these adjectives clearly express.[15] The epithet φιλογόνευς highlights the value of a loving

---

[12] On which see B. T. Viviano, *Study as Worship*, Leiden: Brill, 1978. Both Frey's translation of εὐδίδακτος ('docile') and Leon's ('easily taught') are too minimalistic; 'well educated' or 'with good training' is nearer the mark.

[13] Lieberman, *Greek in Jewish Palestine* 72, suggests that *philentolos* is a literal translation of the Aramaic epitheton *raḥem miṣwᵉta*, meaning 'lover of charity'.

[14] For this sense of λαός see Robert, *BE* 1976 no. 333, and *Hellenica* III 103-104, XI-XII 260.

[15] Perhaps ὁμοφροσύνη in 1489 should be interpreted in this same context,

relationship between parents and children, which was cherished so much in Jewish families.

The epithet εὐλογημένος is most probably a translation of the Hebrew passive participle ברוך, *barukh*, 'blessed', deriving from one of the Greek translations of the Hebrew Bible. Applied to humans it implies gratefulness to God for the blessings he bestowed on the deceased man or woman (in fact both times it is said of women in our two inscriptions). The same sentiment is also expressed in Jewish names like Eulogia, Eulogētos, Eulogistos, and Benedicta.[16]

Finally, we have φιλοπένης and πενιχρός, 'lover of the poor' and 'poor'. The first is an adjective that could hardly be expected to be laudatory in the classical world of Greece and Rome. In his great work, *Wohltätigkeit und Armenpflege im vorchristlichen Altertum* (1939), the Dutch historian of antiquity Hendrik Bolkestein demonstrated that care for the poor was not regarded as a virtue in Greco-Roman antiquity.[17] It was Judaism that put this virtue into the centre, and Christianity followed suit. So in the adjective φιλοπένης we see that a Jew wanted to express that he, who as an *archōn* was a lover of his community and also a lover of God's commandments (he is called both φιλόλαος and φιλέντολος in the inscription, no. 203), gave concrete shape to this love by performing deeds of loving-kindness (*gemiluth ḥasadim*) to the poor. As to πενιχρός, it is actually not said of the dead persons themselves but of their fathers ('Samuel, son of Isaac the poor' and 'Samuel, son of Germanus the poor', BS II 99 and 206), who probably had already died as well. It may just be the case that their fathers were poor men. It may, however, also be a sort of honorary title, comparable to the use of *'evyon* in late-biblical and post-biblical Hebrew, where 'poor' often came close to meaning something like 'being God's favourite'. (In this light we may also see the inscription of the Jerusalemite Abba who calls himself "the oppressed, the pursued", certainly with religious overtones; cf. Is. 58:7).[18] Being used as epithets in an

---

but the stone is too damaged for us to be sure of this interpretation.

[16] See Frey, vol. I, index *s.vv.* for references, and also the *index nominum* of Solin's *ANRW* contribution.

[17] See also P. Veyne, *Le pain et le cirque. Sociologie historique d'un pluralisme politique,* Paris: Seuil, 1976, 236-238.

[18] This Aramaic epitaph was published by E. S. Rosenthal in *IEJ* 23 (1973)

epitaph these can hardly have been meant as non-laudatory. But this must remain purely speculative.[19]

Be that as it may, this brief survey has demonstrated that, in spite of all the laudatory terminology that the Jews borrowed from their pagan neighbours, we can clearly see a highly distinctive strand of epithets which express central Jewish values. But it cannot be denied that the number of inscriptions in which these distinctive epithets are used is very small as compared to the overwhelmingly great numbers in which the traditional 'pagan' epithets occur. So it would be completely unwarranted to say that central Jewish values play a major role in Jewish epitaphs. In fact they do not.

Ioudaios, prosēlytos, theosebēs

By way of appendix a paragraph on the use of Ἰουδαῖος, προσή- λυτος and θεοσεβής may be added here. At first sight the meaning of the word Ἰουδαῖος/Iudaeus seems unproblematic: it means 'Jew'. Nevertheless, the question 'what is a Ἰουδαῖος/Iudaeus?' cannot be easily answered. In his great survey of Jewish settlements in the Western Empire, Heikki Solin states that these terms practically always denote membership of a Jewish religious community, whereas it is never or hardly ever an indication of ethnic or geographic origin.[20] Very recently, however, Ross Kraemer has argued that the term Ἰουδαῖος/Iudaeus may have *four* different meanings in the 35 occurrences in the inscriptions:[21] *a*) Jew; *b*) pagan adherent to Judaism (not: proselyte); *c*) someone from Judaea (not necessarily a Jew); *d*) a name (possibly a hellenized form of Yehuda, like Judas). That the word cannot only have the first meaning ('Jew'), says Kraemer, is apparent from the fact that in the vast majority of the inscriptions Jews do not identify themselves as such; so there must be a special reason to add the qualification Ἰουδαῖος. There certainly is

---

72-81.

[19] See Lifshitz in *RB* 68 (1961) 411. E. Bammel, art. πτωχός in *TWNT* 6 (1959) 888-902.

[20] Solin, *ANRW* II 29, 2 (1983) 647-651.

[21] R. S. Kraemer, On the Meaning of the Term "Jew" in Greco-Roman Inscriptions, *HTR* 82 (1989) 35-53; at p. 37 n. 6 a survey of the occurrences is given.

a great measure of truth in that argument, but nevertheless Kraemer has somewhat overstated her case. Let us briefly review the evidence.

The meaning of 'Jew' is of course obvious and needs no discussion. We will begin with her fourth category, Ἰουδαῖος as a name. There can be no doubt about that simply because we have two inscriptions (not funerary) in which it is explicitly stated that Ἰουδαῖος was a man's name (nos. 710 and 711, from Delphi). But I see no compelling reason whatsoever to follow Kraemer's suggestion to regard the following epitaphs as instances of Ἰουδαῖος/ *Iudaeus* as a name: no. 296 ἔνθα κεῖται Ἀμμίας Ἰουδαῖα ἀπὸ Λαοδικίας, no. 678 *Septimae Mariae Iudaeae quae vixit annis xviii*, no. 680 *Aurelius Dionysius Iudaeus Tiberiensis annorum xxxx, filiorum trium pater* (actually written in Greek letters),[22] no. 697 Βουκολίουν τοῦ υἱοῦ Ἑρμίου καὶ Ποντιανῆς τῆς Ἰουδαίας, and no. 715i Δημήτριος Δημητρίου Ἰουδαῖος. All of these are perfectly regular examples of the meaning 'Jew', in the sense of member of a Jewish religious community. I cannot see a problem in the fact that only a small minority of the Jews indicated their religious affiliation in such a way. Others did it by means of Jewish symbols (*menorah, shofar, aron,* etc.), or by exclusively Jewish epithets such as φιλοσυνάγωγος, φιλέντολος, or by mentioning their typically Jewish functions (ἀρχισυνάγωγος, γερουσιάρχης, often with the name of the synagogue added, in Rome at least); many did not see any reason to indicate their Jewishness either because they were buried in an exclusively Jewish burial place (such as the catacombs in Rome and Beth She'arim)[23] or simply because they did not find it important enough to be recorded.

Kraemer's third category, indication of Judaean provenance, is difficult to prove. One cannot rule out the possibility that there are some instances with the meaning 'Judaean',[24] but since this original

---

[22] Αὐρη(λ)ιους Διονυσιους Ἰουδεους Τιβε(ρ)ιηνσις ἀν(νωρουν) XXXX φι(λ)ιωρουν τριουν πατερ.

[23] P. J. Tomson, The Names Israel and Jew in Ancient Judaism and in the New Testament, *Bijdragen* 47 (1986) 131, rightly remarks that "in inner-Jewish circumstances, ethnic identification is superfluous".

[24] Perhaps no. 742 (Smyrna, 2nd cent. CE), οἱ ποτὲ Ἰουδαῖοι, as interpreted by A. T. Kraabel in *JJS* 33 (1982) 455 ('perhaps immigrants from Pale-

meaning of the word seems to have practically faded out by the end
of the Hellenistic era, it is not very probable. Solin rightly stresses
that, when the place of origin of a Ἰουδαῖος is mentioned, it is
never (in) Judaea, and that too many *Iudaei* have Latin cognomina to
make a Judaean origin probable.[25] Kraemer's argument that in no.
741 (Smyrna),ʹΡουφῖνα Ἰουδαῖα ἀρχισυνάγωγος, the word Ἰουδαῖα could be taken as a 'geographic indicator'[26] since the word
ἀρχισυνάγωγος makes sufficiently clear that Rufina is Jewish, is
not valid, for ἀρχισυνάγωγος can also be used for a pagan official.[27] In the case of the word *Hebraeus*, however, which occurs 5
times as a self-designation in Rome (354, 370, 379, 502, 505), it
would seem to me that we have to do with an ethno-geographical
designation. "It indicates that one's place of birth was in Syro-Pale-
stine from which the individual emigrated to Rome".[28]

   Kraemer's second category, Ἰουδαῖος as an indication of pagan
sympathizers with Judaism, is a fascinating possibility. Dio Cassius
says in his *Roman History* (37, 17, 1)[29] that the name Ἰουδαῖος was
also borne by people who were not Jews but who, although of other
ethnicity, lived according to the laws of the Jews. If that is correct, it
implies that pagan 'sympathizers' called themselves 'Jews' in some
general sense, or were called so by others (probably the latter since
one can very well imagine that it started as a nickname; cf. Acts
11:26). And if it could be proven that no. 748, the famous theatre-
inscription from Miletus, τόπος Ειουδέων τῶν καὶ θεοσεβίον (sic),
is to be interpreted as 'place of (those) Jews who (are) also (called)
Godfearers',[30] then we would have epigraphic evidence that

---

stine'), is an exception.
25 Solin, *ANRW* II 29, 2, 648. He regards no. 21 as a possible exception but
the interpretation of this hardly translatable inscription is so uncertain (see below
in the text) that one cannot base any conclusions upon it.
26 Kraemer, *HTR* 82 (1989)45.
27 See Robert, *BE* 1954, no. 24 (*ad no.* 744).
28 J. Z. Smith, Fences and Neighbors: Some Contours of Early Judaism, in
W. S. Green (ed.), *Approaches to Ancient Judaism* II, Chico: Scholars Press,
1980, 19.
29 See M. Stern, *Greek and Latin Authors on Jews and Judaism* II, Jerusalem:
Israel Academy of Sciences, 1980, 349-350.
30 Thus H. Hommel, Juden und Christen im kaiserzeitlichen Milet, in his
Sebasmata II, Tübingen: Mohr, 1984, 200-230. But this interpretation is admit-

sympathizers were also called – or called themselves – Jews.[31] But, to be sure, the evidence is meagre and does not enable us to tell these 'would-be' Jews from 'real' Jews in the funerary inscriptions.

The Miletus inscription brings us to the θεοσεβεῖς. Solin categorically states that all inscriptions which record the dead as θεο- σεβεῖς or *metuentes* should be removed from the corpus of Jewish inscriptions since these so-called Godfearers were not Jews in the strict sense of the word.[32] (These are nos. 5, 202, 285, 500, 524, 529, 619a, 642, 731e, 754.)[33] *Metuentes* is an abbreviated translation of the Hebrew *yir'e shamayim* ('fearers of heaven') or of φοβούμενοι τὸν θεόν ('Godfearers'), commonly regarded as the equivalent of σεβόμενοι or θεοσεβεῖς. The dispute during the last decade over whether or not such a thing as a distinct class of 'Godfearers' had ever existed at all, has now been settled – thanks to the discovery of a new and revealing inscription – in favour of the traditional point of view: the new inscription from Aphrodisias[34] makes a clearcut distinction between Jews, proselytes, and Godfearers, the third (large) category obviously being pagan sympathizers, no doubt with varying degrees of adherence to Judaism.[35]

---

tedly controversial; see e.g. L. Robert, *Nouvelles inscriptions de Sardes*, Paris: Maisonneuve, 1964, 41-45; G. Delling, *Die Bewältigung der Diasporasituation durch das hellenistische Judentum*, Berlin: Evangelische Verlagsanstalt, 1987, 62-63 n. 425.

[31] One might also refer to the remark in Revelation 3:9 on "those who say that they are Jews but are not".

[32] Solin, *ANRW* II 29, 2, 655.

[33] Other instances are the above-mentioned Miletus inscription (748) and, outside of CIJ, the inscriptions of Capitolina *theosebēs* and Euphrosyna *theosebēs* mentioned by L. Robert, *Études anatoliennes,* Paris: Boccard, 1937, 409-412.

[34] J. Reynolds – R. Tannenbaum, *Jews and Godfearers at Aphrodisias*, Cambridge: Cambridge Philological Society, 1987, where all the relevant literature about the Godfearers debate may be found. A good survey is M. Simon, Gottesfürchtiger, *RAC* XI (1981) 1060-1070. See now also L. H. Feldman, Proselytes and 'Sympathizers' in the Light of the New Inscription from Aphrodisias, *REJ* 148 (1989) 265-305. Very useful is the recent survey by Fergus Millar in E. Schürer, *A History of the Jewish People in the Age of Jesus Christ* III 1, Edinburgh: Clark, 1986, 150-176.

[35] Feldman, *REJ* 148 (1989) 282-297, has a good survey of "factors that attracted non-Jews to Judaism", of which he enumerates 28!

This entitles us to take the 10 inscriptions of θεοσεβεῖς and *metuentes*[36] as referring to pagans who, however far they went in adopting a Jewish way of life, never took the final step of becoming converts. So Solin is right that they should not be part of a *Corpus Inscriptionum Judaicarum* in the strict sense of the term. (Nonetheless, we should be grateful that Frey included them in CIJ.)

Inscriptions of proselytes do belong in such a corpus, for these pagans did take the final step. There are no less than 14 or 15 inscriptions of proselytes: nos. 21, 37 (?), 68 (*Iudaeus proselytus*, to rule out all misunderstandings), 202, 222, 256, 462, 523, 576, 1385; *Dominus Flevit* nos. 13, 21, 22, 31;[37] Lifshitz in *RB* 68 (1961) 115 no. 2; that is, seven or eight from Rome, one from Venosa, five from Jerusalem and one from Caesarea Maritima. The donors' inscription from Aphrodisias has added another three proselytes. The fact that in absolute terms this is not a very high number should not deceive us. The total number is about 1% of our Jewish inscriptions. If we take into account the lacunose nature of our archaeological evidence and the fact that many proselytes, who had after all become 100 % Jewish, would not have seen fit to record for eternity that they were proselytes, we may surmise that the actual number of proselytes may have been much higher than 1%. (The fact that during the greatest part of the Imperial period, from Hadrian onwards, conversion to Judaism was regarded as a capital crime,[38] certainly did not encourage people to divulge such a conversion, not even on a tombstone.) From other sources we know that Jewish religious propaganda was very successful in the Imperial period.[39] To this success our stones testify in a modest but undeniable way.

---

[36] The fact that we find in Latin inscriptions transcriptions like *teuseues* (= θεοσεβής) already indicates that we have to do here with a *terminus technicus* as does also the fact that in *metuentes* the object of worship is not indicated.

[37] P. B. Bagatti – J. T. Milik, *Gli scavi del Dominus Flevit (Monte Oliveto – Gerusalemme)* I, Jerusalem: Franciscan Press, 1958, 70-100.

[38] Reynolds-Tannenbaum, *Jews and Godfearers* 43-44.

[39] See esp. M. Simon, *Verus Israel*, Oxford: Blackwell, 1986 (orig. French ed. 1948).

V. Age at Death

In the entire collection of ancient Jewish epitaphs (ca. 1600) approximately one third (ca. 540) indicate the age at death of the deceased. The average age at death turns out to be 28.4 years, that is, for men ca. 29 years, for women ca. 27 years. At first sight these are shocking figures when compared to the average life expectancy in our own time (for both sexes above 70, in western countries). But the scholar who has a demographic interest in antiquity should ask the question: what is the value of these figures? This apparently simple question is in fact extremely difficult to answer, as will become clear in the following paragraphs.

Representativeness

Demography of the ancient world constantly has to struggle with the problem of the scarcity and the questionable representativeness of the sources.[1] Of the various classes into which ancient Greek and

---

[1] There is an abundance of literature on this topic. I list here only some of the most influential studies in a chronological order: A. G. Harkness, Age at Marriage and at Death in the Roman Empire, *TAPA* 27 (1896) 35-72; A. R. Burn, Hic breve vivitur. A Study of the Expectation of Life in the Roman Empire, *Past & Present* 4 (1953) 2-31; L. Moretti, Statistica demografica ed epigrafia: durata media della vita in Roma imperiale, *Epigraphica* 21 (1959) 60-78; B. Blumenkranz, Quelques notations démographiques sur les Juifs de Rome des premiers siècles, *Studia Patristica* IV 2 (ed. F. L. Cross), Berlin: Akademie Verlag, 1961, 341-347; H. Nordberg, *Biometrical Notes. The Information on Ancient Christian Inscriptions from Rome Concerning the Duration of Life and the Dates of Birth and Death*, Helsinki: Academia Scientiarum Fennica, 1963 (see also the instructive review of this work by A. R. Burn in *JRS* 55 [1965] 253-257); I. Kajanto, *On the Problem of the Average Duration of Life in the Roman Empire,* Helsinki: Academia Scientiarum Fennica, 1968; M. Clauss,

Latin inscriptions fall, by far the largest numerically is that of epitaphs. In many tens of thousands of these inscriptions the age at
death is mentioned. But, as a specialist in the epigraphy and demography of the Roman Empire recently calculated,[2] even so we only
know the age at death of ca. 0,015 % of all people in the first 5
centuries of the Empire. (He made the calculation on the basis of the
assumption that in 500 years there are approximately 16 generations, each of which on average counted some 20 million people; this
total of some 320 million divided by the total number of inscriptions
with age indication yields 0,015%). Even if these numbers needed to
be substantially corrected, the overall picture would hardly change.
We will always remain far below 1% of the total population. This
fact raises the acute problem of how representative this less than 1%
is for the population of the Empire as a whole. As a matter of fact
that completely depends upon whether or not we can clearly get into
the picture the possibly distorting factors in the data at our disposal.
There are several distorting factors, although to what extent they
really distort our picture is a matter of ongoing debate. Let us review here only the most important of them and then try to find out
whether these factors also influenced the Jewish material.

Distorting factors: general

First, there is a great unevenness in the geographical distribution of
the evidence. Roman Africa is by far our richest quarry of material,
and in Europe the Danube provinces yield more for our purpose
than other areas. In some geographical areas it seems to have been
standard procedure to mention the age at death in an epitaph, where-

---

Probleme der Lebensalterstatistiken aufgrund römischer Grabinschriften, *Chiron*
3 (1973) 395-417; B. Boyaval, Remarques sur les indications d'âges de
l'épigraphie funéraire grecque d'Egypte, *ZPE* 21 (1976) 217-243; B. Boyaval,
Tableau général des indications d'âge de l'Egypte gréco-romaine, *Chronique
d'Egypte* 52 (1977) 345-351; B. Frier, Roman Life Expectancy: The Pannonian
Evidence, *Phoenix* 37 (1983) 328-344. More literature can be found in M.
Clauss, Ausgewählte Bibliographie zur lateinischen Epigraphik der römischen
Kaiserzeit, *ANRW* II 1 (1974) 814, also in Clauss' essay mentioned above,
Chiron 3 (1973) 412-414, and in Frier's article in *Phoenix*.
[2] Clauss, *Chiron* 3 (1973) 411.

as in others it was an exception. The resultant over- and under-representation is not so equally distributed over the Empire that one can say that they cancel each other out. In addition, in cities it was much more usual to erect tombstones with inscriptions than in the countryside. Tombstones tend to be an urban institution; many peasants were either too poor or too illiterate (or both) to afford an inscribed stone.

Second, the distribution in time is uneven. In spite of the many difficulties in assigning an exact date to an inscription, it is clear that the first two centuries of our era yield much more material than the third through fifth centuries, due primarily to the impoverishment of so many people after the early third century.

Third, there is the very great problem of the under-representation of young children and especially of infants. At some ancient cemeteries an enormous proportion of infant interments has been discovered, whereas materials for actual statistics of infant mortality, which must have been very high, are simply not available due to the fact that infants were very rarely given tombstones. So the actual rate of infant mortality does not appear from the epitaphs. For instance, in the Numidian cities of Celtianis and Quattuor Coloniae we find only one out of 1258 and six out of 1596 inscriptions for a baby respectively. "These low figures cannot possibly be credited".[3] The estimate of a recent authority that less than half of those born reached the age of five[4] seems reasonable, and this would tend to make the average life expectancy in the Roman Empire much lower than is often assumed. And it should be borne in mind that this scholar made this statement in criticism of another expert who had stated that the average length of life in Imperial Rome was less than 25 years![5] Be that as it may, our lack of knowledge of the rate of infant mortality is a serious complication in determining the actual life expectancy in the Empire. On the other hand, in areas where children who died as ἄωροι did receive tombstones, one often sees that it is their inscriptions, rather than those of adults, that mention the age at death. The reason for that is partly that the young age of the deceased added an extra dimension of pathos to the epitaph, and

---

[3] Kajanto, *Problem* 6.
[4] Burn, *JRS* 55 (1965) 254.
[5] Nordberg, *Biometrical Notes* 41.

partly that it was much easier to keep accurate track of the age of a young person than of an old one. In the present context that implies that sometimes and at some places young children tend to be somewhat over-represented in epitaphs containing age-indication.

Fourth, there is an under-representation of women. For instance, in five large Egyptian necropoles with Greek epitaphs indicating life-time, we find some 450 inscriptions, 265 of which are for men and 185 for women.[6] In other places the situation is still worse, sometimes men being 20 times as numerous as women in epitaphs indicating age.[7] This is a very serious problem because from the material extant, however limited, we do know that women had a higher mortality rate than men. On average, it seems, men lived some five years longer than women, because many more women than men died in the so-called 'reproductive period', that is, between 12 and 38 years. This may have been partly the result of deaths in childbirth but partly (perhaps even in greater part) the result of general exhaustion, as modern parallels in Third World countries seem to suggest.[8]

Fifth, there is the problem of the imprecision in the indication of age. Far too many tombstones give ages ending in 0 or 5, especially for those above 20 years; after the age of 70 virtually all end in 0.[9] This is simply the result of lack of knowledge of the exact age. There was no absolute chronology in the ancient world, which made it extremely difficult to determine one's exact age. Those who were good in ancient relative chronology (or who had easy access to consular lists or *fasti*) could make a relatively precise count of their or others' ages. But in most provinces acquaintance with the Roman system of time-reckoning will have been less than adequate. Hence the many age-indications rounded off at 5 or 0. These can hardly be trusted. But, since knowledge of one's exact age was hard to ascertain, we cannot trust either the many epitaphs in which not only the number of years, but also the number of months, days, hours (and even minutes [*CIL* VI 36122!]) is recorded. These are nothing but

---

6 Boyaval, *ZPE* 21 (1976) 228-229. The numbers are slightly rounded off.
7 Clauss, *Chiron* 3 (1973) 405-406.
8 Burn, *Past & Present* 4 (1953) 10-13.
9 On this phenomenon see R. P. Duncan Jones, Age-Rounding, Illiteracy and Social Differentiation in the Roman Empire, *Chiron* 7 (1977) 333-353.

specimens of guesswork. Although hours and minutes are not often mentioned, months and days are, and they pretend an exactitude of knowledge which simply was often not available. An epitaph of someone who lived 51 years, 4 months and 13 days, looks impressive but has a good chance of having to be discredited.[10]

Sixth, related to this is the inexactitude, in the sense of exaggeration, in indications of age of elderly people. Especially in Roman Africa we find "an incredible number of very old people".[11] More than 5% of the people there, both men and women, are said to have died at an age above one hundred. There are records of persons of 120 and 125; and elsewhere we find some people of 160 and 170 years. It stands to reason that these are absurd exaggerations, parallels for which are, however, still to be found among peoples or tribes in developing countries. The incredibility of these numbers is apparent especially when, for instance, a woman of 105 years old is said to be the mother of children of 20, 12 and 8, or when a man of 100 years old is elsewhere said to have died at 83.[12] In his *Natural History* (VII 162-164), Pliny the Elder tells us that during a census held by Vespasian in the year 74 in northern Italy, three persons claimed 120 years at Parma and one at Brescello; two at Parma 125; one man at Piacenza and one woman at Faenza 130; one man at Bologna 135; at Rimini a woman 137 and a man 140 years; in Veleia six claimed 110 years, four 120, one 140; and, Pliny adds, the census registered in the eighth region of Italy fifty-four persons of 100 years, fourteen of 110, two of 125, four of 130, four of 135, and three of 140. Although Pliny gives credit to these numbers,[13] there can be little doubt that we should discard them, the more so since (with one exception) all figures reported end in 5 or 0. Pliny's report does make clear, however, that there was a marked tendency to ascribe to old people very exaggerated (and round) numbers of years, exactly as we see it in the inscriptions. This leaves us with the

---

[10] Clauss, *Chiron* 3 (1973) 396-397.

[11] Kajanto, *Problem* 19.

[12] Kajanto, *Problem* 19. Of course, children may have predeceased their old mothers.

[13] See the whole of his discussion of the problem of longevity in *Nat. Hist.* VII 153-164. In antiquity stories about μακρόβιοι were a favourite literary topos.

fact that most data in epitaphs about the longevity of persons cannot be trusted and so add to the problem under consideration.

Seventh, there is the problem of the very great divergences between the averages of age at death from city to city and from region to region. Sometimes the differences even within one and the same country are great. For example, in Egypt epitaphs in Tell el-Yehudieh show an average age of 26 years; in Alexandria 28.2 years; in Kom Abu Billu 32.7 years; in Tehneh 34.4 years; and in Akhmim 40.4 years.[14] But over the Roman Empire as a whole the divergencies are much larger.[15] For example, the average age at death (calculated on the basis of tomb inscriptions, that is) in Ostia is 16.8 years; in Rome 22.2; in Tibur 22.6; in Burdigala (Bordeaux) 35.7; in Spain 37.4; in Noricum and Pannonia 43.5; in North-Africa 46.7 (but within North-Africa the score of Carthago is 33.3 years, of Quattuor Coloniae 46 years, and of Celtianis 60.2 years). So we see averages varying from 16 to 60 years! Again one feels these figures cannot be trusted. Of course people in Ostia lived on average more than 16 years and people in Celtianis less than 60 years, however much more healthy it may have been to live in the climate of North Africa than in a harbour town like Ostia or an overcrowded metropolis like Rome. We have already seen that the very high averages in Roman Africa are due partly to the incredibly large numbers of people of over a hundred years and partly also to the fact that infants did not have tombstones there. In Rome, where the average is so much lower, many children received tombstones with records of their age at death, whereas such records of adults were far less common there than in Africa. Whereas in Africa these were the rule, in Rome only a third of the epitaphs give this indication. These two factors explain to a large extent why the recorded average in Africa is more than twice as high as in Rome. And so for every other region or country or city all factors like under-representation, over-representation, exaggeration, inexactitude, etc., have to be taken into account when assessing the value of epigraphical data on age at death.

---

[14] Boyaval, *ZPE* 21 (1976) 217-243.
[15] Burn, *Past & Present* 4(1953) 20-29; Clauss, *Chiron* 3 (1973) 408-417; Kajanto, *Problem*.

Representativeness of the Jewish epitaphs

All this having been said, the reader may have the feeling of being left in a quandary, and the writer must confess that he shares in this state of perplexity and doubt. There seems to be no way to make sense of the data on duration of life in less than 550 inscriptions from the ancient Jewish world. It may be tempting to draw some comfort and confidence from the fact that in a recent Belgian dissertation, covering almost the same period as ours and by and large the same geographical area, but dealing with a completely different corpus of inscriptions, *scil.* only pagan and Christian metrical epitaphs in Latin, the average duration of life comes very close to our Jewish average, namely 29.1 years (as compared to our 28.4 years).[16] But it would be premature and unmethodical to build any confidence upon that coincidence. We will first have to establish in how far the caveats mentioned above affect our data.

To begin with the number of inscriptions as compared to the number of Jews in our period, we have to concede that it is indeed only an extremely tiny minority of whom we know the age at death. If we take our period, spanning a thousand years, to have comprised about 33 generations (30 years for one generation, for the sake of convenience), and if we take a generation as averaging 5 million Jews, then we have 550 inscriptions for 165 million Jews: that is to say, one inscription for every 300,000 Jews. Even if the average number of Jews per generation had to be drastically reduced, we would not even reach 0,001%. (As is well-known, estimates of the number of Jews in the Hellenistic and Roman periods are notoriously difficult and vary from 2 million to 10 million;[17] for safety's sake I take a lower middle course for my average of 5 million because in the early Hellenistic period the number of Jews was of course considerably lower than in the later Roman Empire; but even if we were to take 2 million as a safer minimum, the percentage of Jews

---

[16] Pikhaus, *Levensbeschouwing* 361-437, lists all of the 861 inscriptions dealt with in her work, 613 of which record the age at death. She has not calculated the average; the 29.1 years is based upon my own count.

[17] See S. W. Baron, *A Social and Religious History of the Jews* I, Philadelphia: Jewish Publication Society, 1952, 370-372; and idem, *Encyclopaedia Judaica* XIII (1972) 870-872 (*s.v.* Population).

whose tombstones with a record of age have been preserved, would still remain below 0,001%).

But let us look at a situation of a smaller scale. From Rome a relatively large number of Jewish epitaphs is known to us, 163 of which record the age at death (with an average of 26 years). All these date from the first five centuries of our era. Now the estimates of the number of Jews in Rome in the first century have been a matter of much debate and they vary from 10,000 to 60,000.[18] Let us take, again for safety's sake, a lower middle course and assume a Jewish presence of 25,000 persons in the first century. Even if we neglect the factor of growth in the following centuries, then we still have a total of at least 400,000 Jews in Rome in the first five centuries (16 to 17 generations of ca. 25,000 persons). That is to say that we have one inscription with age indication for every 2,500 Jews, *i.e.* 0.04%. This situation, which would be the most favourable we can reach, is still unmanageable from a statistical point of view, if only because the other distorting factors prevent us from taking this small sample as representative. It would seem that, for statistical and other reasons, we have to drop the whole enterprise of drawing demographic conclusions from our small corpus of data. Nevertheless, there are some small elements in that corpus that may perhaps save us from total despair. In order to find these elements we have to recall again the seven factors of distortion and see how far these can be proved to have played a significant role in our material.

Distorting factors in the Jewish evidence

First, the imbalance in geographical distribution. We have already mentioned the unevenness in the distribution of the inscriptions in our introductory chapter (in the paragraph on 'geographical spread'). This picture changes, however, when we now limit ourselves to epitaphs containing records of age. It appears that ca. 55% of the evidence comes from Roman Africa, including Egypt; 30% comes from the city of Rome; the remaining 15% comes from all

---

[18] For references see Solin in *ANRW* II 29, 2 (1983) 698-9 n. 240, and R. Penna, Les Juifs à Rome au temps de l'apôtre Paul, *NTS* 28 (1982) 341 n. 53.

the other areas, including Palestine and Asia Minor, which have yielded about half of the funerary inscriptions. This picture fits in well with the general situation in the Roman Empire, especially in the predominance of African evidence, followed by that from Rome. In this respect there is no marked difference between Jewish and non-Jewish material.

Second, a certain unevenness in the chronological distribution is apparent also in the Jewish material. The Hellenistic period is underrepresented, the first three centuries CE yield the bulk of the material, the fourth through seventh centuries show a decline, although probably slightly less than in non-Jewish funerary epigraphy.

Third, there is the under-representation of infants and little children. This phenomenon, too, can be observed in Jewish tomb inscriptions, but here we find a first sign of deviation from common pagan practice in that it would seem that Jewish epitaphs mention the age at death of little children relatively more often than pagan ones. This can be seen most clearly in Africa, where the underrepresentation of children in pagan epitaphs is very striking, whereas from the almost 300 Jewish age indications from Africa including Egypt some 55 are of children under 10 years. This is a relatively high score as compared to other material, even though this much higher percentage still conceals the probably very high rate of death among babies. In Rome we see something similar: almost 25% of the Jews whose age is mentioned had died between birth and 5 years of age.[19] We cannot but conclude that apparently Jews did not conform fully to the pagan practice of denying very young children stones with epitaphs. Whether we can also conclude from this, as Bernard Blumenkranz does, that Jews had greater parental love for their children than pagans (see previous note), is uncertain. But it is a noteworthy phenomenon indeed, which most probably has something to do with Jewish beliefs or values.

Fourth, there certainly is an under-representation of women in Jewish epitaphs. Rome has 43% women against 57% men, and elsewhere the situation is not very different.[20] But on the whole the

---

[19] Blumenkranz, *Stud. Patr.* IV 2 (1961) 343.

[20] R. S. Kraemer, Non-Literary Evidence for Jewish Women in Rome and Egypt, *Helios* 13 (1986) 87, presents statistics for Italy, Asia Minor, Beth She'arim, Leontopolis, and Roman Africa: of 931 dead persons in total 473 are

picture is not as bad as in pagan inscriptions. We nowhere have a situation in which men are in an overwhelming majority. There is a certain imbalance, but always within the margins of 40% (for women) and 60% (for men). We will return to the subject of women in chapter 7.

Fifth, the lack of precision in age indications. There can be little doubt that the custom of giving round numbers of years to people above a certain age was also practised by Jews. Of about 300 people who died over the age of 20, some 165 have an age ending in 5 or 0. From a statistical point of view 20% could have died at ages ending in 5 or 0, but 165 out of 300 is 55%. This makes abundantly clear that the practice of attributing round numbers for reasons of ignorance concerning the exact age was very common among ancient Jews. Below 20 years, the data are more precise and here we find relatively few round numbers. The number of those who died under the age of 20 is ca. 230 out of some 540, that is slightly over 40%, but the many tombstones for νήπιοι whose age is not indicated, makes one surmise that their number may have gone up to over 50%. Of those who died before reaching the age of 5 we have 75 epitaphs, that is 14%. In reality this percentage will have been much higher, both because many νήπιοι are recorded without age indication and because the probably numerous infants who died within a couple of months or weeks or even days after their birth did not receive epitaphs, even among the Jews. How many did not reach the age of five we will never know, but it was certainly far above 25%. Be that as it may, in respect to precision in age indication and the use of round numbers Jewish inscriptions did not differ from others.

However – and this is the sixth point – the numerous cases of exaggerated longevity have no parallel in Jewish epitaphs. There is only one case of a person who is asserted to have reached the age of 110, a Roman 'father of the synagogue' (no. 509); another person is said to have died at 102, a man from Leontopolis (no. 1458); and one person in the Cyrenaica is said to have reached 100 (Lüderitz no. 63). These are isolated cases, with far lower numbers than in many pagan epitaphs (see above). And the figures are not incredible.

---

male (51%), 348 are female (37,5%), 110 of unknown sex (12,5%). That is to say that most probably some 58% are male and some 42% female.

This remarkable restraint may give us some confidence that on the whole indications of age in Jewish epitaphs, especially for elderly people, may be somewhat more reliable than those in their pagan counterparts.

Seventh – and this is a final point that may inspire some confidence in the reliability of the age records in Jewish tomb inscriptions – the enormous divergences between the average ages of various cities and countries, which we have observed in the pagan evidence, do not occur in Jewish epitaphs. As has already been said in the opening paragraph of this chapter, the average age in the Jewish epitaphs with records of age is 28.4 years. When we look at Rome only, the average is 26 years, and when we look at Africa only, the average is 29.4 years. When we compare this to 22 years for Rome and 47 for Africa (or 60 for Celtianis) in pagan inscriptions, the impression we get is decidedly that the Jewish numbers are closer to reality. The difference between Rome and Africa in the Jewish evidence is so much smaller than in the pagan material that one can only conclude that here again the Jewish epitaphs are more reliable. The difference between Rome and Africa of almost 3.5 years may easily be explained by a combination of epigraphical habits and a more healthy life in the African countryside than in the overcrowded city of Rome. That the average age for Jewish Rome (26) is four years higher than for pagan Rome (22) is a fact for which I do not have a satisfactory explanation, although I presume that some of the distorting factors have made the pagan average much too low. To speculate that the Jews lived more healthily than pagans is unwarranted, although it cannot be completely ruled out that it may be part of an explanation. When we look at Greco-Roman Egypt, we see that the average in five large necropoles is 32.3 years and the average of the country as a whole is 30 years (according to the epitaphs, that is),[21] whereas the Jewish average in Egypt is 31. Here the Jewish figure shows no significant difference from the pagan one. So we should be careful in looking for explanations for these differences.

In general it may cautiously be suggested that Jewish indications of age are in some respects somewhat more to be credited than

---

[21] Boyaval, *ZPE* 21 (1976) 217-243, and *Chron. d'Eg.* 52 (1977) 345-351.

pagan ones. It may also be said that Jews shared with pagans both the fate of a short life expectancy – the average length of life having been perhaps about 30 years or even less[22] – and the fate of a high infant and child mortality, probably not half of those born reaching adulthood.[23]

---

[22] Frier, *Phoenix* 37 (1983) 329 n.3, remarks that "the now prevalent scholarly view that Roman life expectancy at birth must have been ca. 20-30 years seems in accord with evidence emerging on pre-Industrial Europe".
[23] Frier, *Phoenix* 37 (1983) 328, suggests that about two-thirds of all liveborn children were dead by the age of 30.

VI. Functions and Professions

Conspicuous in Jewish epitaphs is the fact that functions in the religious community are mentioned much more often than secular occupations and professions. This is a clear indication of the fact that the synagogal community played a major role in the Jewry of the Roman period. It is only from the inscriptions from Rome that, besides data on the various community officials, we also get information on the various congregations themselves. Due to the wealth of epitaphs from Rome we know of the existence and the names of at least ten different Jewish communities in the first three centuries of imperial Rome, which were organized independently.[1] We will first devote some attention to these congregations and then deal with their officials.[2]

---

[1] That the Roman communities were organized as independent and autonomous units, in contradistinction to e.g. the Alexandrian Jewish community where a central overseeing and coordinating body exercised authority, is now recognized by most scholars. See Frey, Introd. LXVIII-LXXXI; Leon, *Jews* 135-194; R. Penna, Les Juifs de Rome au temps de l'apôtre Paul, *NTS* 28 (1982) 326-327; Schürer, *History* III 1, 87-106 (one of Emil Schürer's earliest publications already pointed in the right direction: *Die Gemeindeverfassung der Juden in Rom in der Kaiserzeit nach den Inschriften dargestellt*, Leipzig: Hinrichs, 1879).

[2] Leon's chapter on the synagogues in Rome is still the best treatment. Following Leon (139) I use 'congregation' and 'synagogue' interchangeably. Ancient synagogue buildings have never been found at Rome. On the various terms for the synagogue building – προσευχή, συναγωγή, ἅγιος τόπος – see S. Applebaum, The Organization of the Jewish Communities in the Diaspora, in Safrai – Stern (edd.), *The Jewish People in the First Century* I 490. On the different terms for local Jewish communities – λαός, ἔθνος, σύνοδος, πολί-τευμα, κατοικία, συναγωγή, *universitas* – see Schürer, *History* III 1, 87-91.

Congregations

First there are three synagogal communities which derived their names from prominent persons, who may or may not have been patrons of these congregations. The συναγωγὴ Αὐγουστησίων (nos. 284, 301, 338, 368, 416, 496) was no doubt named after the great first Emperor, who is known to have befriended the Jews; and the συναγωγὴ ᾿Αγριππησίων (365, 425, 503) was very probably named after Augustus' son-in-law and adviser Marcus Agrippa, who was also a real friend of the Jews, as we know from literary sources.[3] The συναγωγὴ Βολουμνησίων (343, 402, 417, 523) was named after a certain Volumnius, presumably its patron, who is however completely unknown to us. We have no way of knowing whether or not these congregations remained in existence after the death of their patrons, although it seems very likely that they did.

Three other communities were named after the district or area of the city where the members lived or where their house of worship was situated (or probably both). There is a synagogue of the Καμπήσιοι (nos. 88, 319, 523, perhaps 433), named after the Campus Martius; a synagogue of the Σιβουρήσιοι (nos. 18, 22, 67, 140, 380, 35a, perhaps 37), named after the Subura, "one of the most populous quarters of ancient Rome, well-known as a trading area".[4] Probably also the synagogue of the Καλκαρήσιοι (nos. 304, 316, 384, 504, 537, perhaps 433) belongs here: *calcar(i)enses* are lime-burners, and it seems reasonable to assume that this name derives from the quarter where the lime-burners lived and worked and where the Jewish synagogue building was situated. Now, it is well-known that in Roman antiquity there were many associations (*collegia*) of people working in the same profession whose members also observed

---

[3] Evidence for both persons in Leon, *Jews* 11. Fergus Millar, in Schürer's *History* III 96, defends the thesis that these communities "may have originally consisted of slaves and freedmen of Augustus or of Agrippa", and he refers to οἱ ἐκ τῆς Καίσαρος οἰκίας in Phil. 4:22. This cannot be wholly ruled out. The less probable thesis that the *Agrippēsioi* named themselves after the Jewish king Agrippa I (or II) is proposed, for example, by K. Galling, Die jüdischen Katakomben in Rom als ein Beitrag zur jüdischen Konfessionskunde, *Theologische Studien und Kritiken* 103 (1931) 353.
[4] Schürer, *History* III 1, 97.

the same cult. So it cannot be ruled out that we are concerned here with a community of Jewish lime-burners. But, as Leon remarks, "it seems hardly credible that enough Jews were engaged in this occupation to form a separate congregation, nor does it appear to have been a Jewish custom for members of the same occupation to form a separate religious group and to name their congregation after it".[5] The fact, however, that we do know of the existence of pagan religious associations of lime-burners and that we do not know of a city quarter named after the *calcarienses* should make us very careful in making too certain statements in this matter.[6]

Further there are two synagogues named after the cities where their members originally came from: a συναγωγὴ Τριπολιτῶν (390, 408), probably Tripolis in Phoenicia but possibly Tripolis in Libya being meant here; and a συναγωγὴ Ἐλέας or Ἐλαίας (281, 509), probably not the 'synagogue of the olive tree' (which does not make sense), but the synagogue of Elea, although it must remain quite uncertain which one of the various towns named Elea can be meant here.[7]

Finally, there are two synagogues named after characteristics of their members. There is a συναγωγὴ Ἐβραίων (291, 317, 510, 535; cf. no. 718: a 'synagogue of the Hebrews' in Corinth, and also one in Lydian Philadelphia, no. 754), the nature of which is much debated. Does it designate a synagogue of Hebrew speaking persons (but their inscriptions are in Greek!), or a synagogue where the liturgy was in Hebrew, or the synagogue of those recently immigrated from Palestine, or does it simply mean: congregation of the Jews, 'Hebrews' being the self-identification of what was possibly the first community of Jews in Rome by which they distinguished themselves from other (i.e., pagan) religious or ethnic groups (note that συναγωγή was not an exclusively Jewish term![8]). This last possibility seems to be favoured by the fact that Jewish communities in Greece and Asia Minor also designated themselves as συναγωγὴ (τῶν) Ἐβραίων

---

[5] Leon, *Jews* 145.
[6] See esp. Schürer, *History* III 1, 97 n. 32.
[7] See the various possibilities discussed by Frey, Introd. LXXVII-LXXVIII, and Leon, *Jews* 146-147.
[8] See Schürer, *History* II 430-1 nn. 13-14 and 436 n. 40, on non-Jewish συναγωγαί.

(nos. 718 and 754). But this, too, remains an educated guess. Equally debated is the nature of the συναγωγὴ Βερνακλησίων or Βερνα-κλώρων, 'of the *vernaculi*' (nos. 318, 383, 398, 494). It has been argued that *vernaculus* means δοῦλος οἰκογενής, houseborn slave, and that this is the synagogue "der im kaiserlichen Hause geborenen jüdischen Kaisersklaven".[9] It would be very fascinating if there had been a separate synagogue of imperial slaves and/ or freedmen, comparable perhaps to the συναγωγὴ Λιβερτίνων in Jerusalem according to Acts 6:9. But it is highly doubtful whether this is the right explanation, for, as Leon has correctly noted, *vernaculus* "regularly means 'native' or 'indigenous' with no connotation whatever of servitude. (...) In fact the word *verna* itself means 'native-born' and etymologically has nothing to do with slaves, but it came to be used of slaves born in the house of the master in contrast with those that were purchased".[10] So most probably this synagogue consisted, at least originally, of native-born Romans, i.e., of indigenous Jews, as opposed to the 'Hebrews'.

There has further been speculation about synagogues of the Σεκηνοί (no. 7), of the Arca of Lebanon (no. 501), of the Herodians (or Rhodians, no. 173), of Calabria (no. 290), *et al.*, but all of this is based either upon very uncertain readings or restorations of the inscriptions or upon highly dubious interpretations.[11]

The above list is certainly not complete, for there will have been more synagogues in Rome, a city which had a very large Jewish population. Moreover, not all of these 10 synagogues may have been in existence at the same time. Nevertheless, more than in any other ancient city we get here a glimpse of the variety of independently organized Jewish communities in a large metropolis. And not only

---

[9] Müller – Bees, *Inschriften* 99. They continue, "Die Existenz einer organisierten Synagogengemeinde jüdischer Kaisersklaven in Rom ist (...) von hohem Interesse für die Erwähnung der οἱ ἐκ τῆς Καίσαρος οἰκίας durch Paulus in Phil. 4,22". Cf. the reference to the same NT text by Millar in connection with the Augustesians, above n. 3.

[10] Leon, *Jews* 155 with n. 2.

[11] See Leon, *Jews* 159-166, and Schürer, *History* III 98. P. Lampe, *Die stadt-römischen Christen in den ersten beiden Jahrhunderten*, Tübingen: Mohr, 1989, 367-368, is too optimistic in finding 14 synagogues mentioned in the inscriptions.

that, the inscriptions also reveal to us something about the internal organization of these communities, about the various officials and their titles. That is what we will turn to now.

Officials

It has to be said at the start that, unfortunately, the inscriptions which mention the titles of the communities' officials do not give us any clue as to what may have been the functions or exact tasks of these dignitaries in their congregations. Even with such a function as that of ἄρχων, which occurs more frequently than any other title (48 times), the epitaphs do not offer us the slightest hint as to the duties and responsibilities of this office.[12] The title is vague ('ruler'), but it is clear that the ἄρχων was a leading official who probably was elected annually; the fact that δὶς ἄρχων occurs repeatedly (125, 289, 316, 397, 505; τρὶς ἄρχων only in 494) indicates that a person could be re-elected (twice?). We do not know for sure if each community had only one or more *archontes*, although a plurality of archons seems more likely.[13] It is curious that in the case of an office for a fixed period we nevertheless find several times the formula διὰ βίου, referring to lifelong archonship (266, 398, 416, 503, 561, 575). Probably we are concerned here with an honorary title rather than with one involving active service. Even more problematic is the phenomenon of the ἄρχων νήπιος ('child archon', 88, 120), the δὶς ἄρχων of 13 years (505), and the 2 or 8 or 12 year old future archon or archon elect, μελλάρχων (85, 284, 325, 402, 457, 483). We can probably only explain this on the assumption that "the title of ἄρχων was conferred on small children as a mark of honour, apparently in view of the distinction of the family".[14] The high status of some families ensured that their children would some day become archons and by way of anticipation these (sometimes very young) children were already designated as such. It goes without

---

[12] See Leon, *Jews* 173-176, Schürer, *History* III 98-100, and Krauss, *Synagogale Altertümer* 146-149.

[13] See S. Applebaum, The Organization of the Jewish Communities in the Diaspora, in Safrai – Stern (edd.), *Jewish People* I 487.

[14] Leon, *Jews* 179.

saying that such a practice undermined the 'democratic' nature of the annual elections of archons.[15] (This phenomenon has a pagan analogy in the child *decuriones* [governing body of a Roman municipality] and a Christian parallel in the child *lectores* in some church communities).[16] Additional phrases that signify a higher dignity occur in ἄρχων πάσης τιμῆς (85, 216, 324, 337)[17] and in *archon alti ordinis* (470),[18] but we do not know what this higher honour implied. Finally, ἐξάρχων (317, 465) has been taken to be an equivalent of ἄρχων, but it would seem "unlikely that there should be an alternative to so familiar and traditional a title".[19] In the light of terms like ἔξαθλος, ἔξηβος, *exconsul, exduumvir*, it seems probable that ἐξάρχων means 'former archon' (but why then only 2 *exarchontes* and almost 50 *archontes*?). Frey guesses that the archons formed the executive committee of the council of elders, and Leon thinks that they were probably concerned with secular affairs exclusively,[20] but, as has already been said, the exact nature of this office remains elusive.

---

[15] Solin, *ANRW* II 29, 2 (1983) 697-698: "Trotz der scheinbar demokratischen Struktur lag die exekutive Macht in den Händen der einflussreichsten Familien, was u.a. daraus gut hervorgeht, dass neben der Wahl auf bestimmte Zeit auch die Wahl auf Lebenszeit vorgekommen zu sein scheint, wenn der Titel διὰ βίου wirklich lebenslängliche Archonten meint; ein noch weiterer Schritt zur aristokratischen Verfassungsform war es, wenn schon Kinder aus angesehenen Familien zu künftigen Archonten designiert wurden (sie wurden ἄρχων νήπιος und μελλάρχων genannt)."

[16] Schürer, *History* III 100 n. 47; Leon, *Jews* 179-180.

[17] No. 216 has *archon pases tessimen* (in a Latin inscription), most probably a garbled form of the Greek πάσης τιμῆς (Leon 176 n. 2). Krauss' suggestion that this official was "der Chef der ganzen Judenheit zu Rom" (*Synagogale Altertümer* 138) is unlikely.

[18] I. Di Stefano Manzello, L. Maccius Archon, centurio alti ordinis. Nota critica su *CIL* VI, 39084 = *CII* I, 470, *ZPE* 77 (1989) 103-112, argues that no. 470 has always been incorrectly read and is not Jewish. His argument that an *archon alti ordinis* never existed deserves consideration but does not seem to be conclusive.

[19] Leon, *Jews* 189, *pro* Müller and *contra* Bees in Müller-Bees, *Inschriften* 4 and 20.

[20] Frey, Introd. LXXXVII, and Leon, *Jews* 176; see also Penna, *NTS* 28 (1982) 329-330, who follows Frey.

If the *archontes* were the executive committee of the γερουσία,[21] the γερουσιάρχης was its president or perhaps the chairman of this executive board. We find this designation in 16 Roman inscriptions, none of which assigns it to a child (9, 95, 106, 119, 147, 301, 353, 368, 405, 408, 425, 504, 511, 533, 733b; Ferrua, *Riv. Arch. Crist.* 59 [1983] 329). On the functions of the *gerousiarches* and those of the *gerousia* over which he presided we can only speculate, although probably their duties were "not unlike those of modern congregational boards, that is, exercising general supervision over both religious and secular matters including the congregational properties, charities, care of the sick, burials, " etc.[22]

Recently a new epitaph from Rome was published in which an ἀρχιγερουσιάρχης is mentioned.[23] This new term rekindled the old discussion about whether or not the Jewish communities of Rome were, after all, organized centrally, as in Alexandria, with an ἀρχι-γερουσιάρχης acting as the head of all the γερουσιάρχαι.[24] But this single occurrence of the word ἀρχιγερουσιάρχης is too weak a basis to build such a hypothesis upon, the more so since there are other compounds as well in which the element ἀρχι- does not have the sense of 'leading ...'.[25] The other members of the γερουσία were called 'elders', πρεσβύτεροι (only once in Rome, 378; outside of Rome, e.g. 650c, 650d, 653b, 663, 731f, 800, 803, 829, 931, 1277, 1404, etc.).[26]

Each congregation also had a γραμματεύς. Twenty-five inscriptions mention this function, which makes it second in frequency after *archon* (see nos. 7, 18, 24, 36, 53, 67, 99, 102, 122, 125, 142, 145, 146, 148, 149, 177, 180, 221, 225, 284, 318, 351, 433, 456; Fasola, *Riv. Arch. Crist* 52 [1976] 19); two inscriptions (121, 279)

---

[21] The term γερουσία does not occur in the Roman inscriptions, but the existence of a council of elders can be inferred from the frequently occurring title γερουσιάρχης.

[22] Thus Leon, *Jews* 183.

[23] U. M. Fasola, Le due catacombe ebraiche di Villa Torlonia, *Riv. Arch. Crist.* 52 (1976) 36; Horsley, *New Documents* I (1981) no. 76.

[24] See above, n.1.

[25] See Solin in *ANRW* II 29, 2 (1983) 696 n. 239.

[26] Schürer, *History* III 102 n. 56. In CIG II 3417 a γερουσία is also called συνέδριον τῶν πρεσβυτέρων; see G. A. Deissmann, *Bibelstudien*, Hildesheim: Olms, 1977 (= Marburg 1895), 155.

mention a μελλογραμματεύς, a secretary designate; and four (99, 146, 180, 284) mention a γραμματεὺς νήπιος, a child secretary. "Secretary" is the correct designation, for the *grammateus* certainly was not the learned scribe (*sopher*) mentioned in the NT and rabbinic literature, as was formerly thought.[27] There was great variety in the social roles, functions and status of γραμματεῖς, but in our inscriptions they are almost certainly subordinate officials, probably the clerks who kept membership lists up to date, conserved the archives and wrote marriage contracts. In one exceptional inscription the *grammateus* is also said to have been ψαλμῳδός, probably a kind of *hazzan* during the services.[28] The child secretaries possibly received their title as a tribute to their families, which would indicate that "in some families at least there was a sort of presumptive right to this office",[29] as in the case of the archons. Nos. 145, 146, 149 show us indeed three consecutive generations of *grammateis*.[30]

Another important function is that of ἀρχισυνάγωγος, head of the synagogue (mentioned in nos. 265, 282, 336, 383, 504; outside of Rome 584, 587, 596, 638, 741, 756, 766, 991, 1404, etc.). Again, none of the epitaphs gives any detail about the functions of this official, but here literary sources are of some help. Both the New Testament (Mk. 5:22. 35-6. 38; Lk. 8:49; 13:14; Acts 13:15; 18:8. 17) and Talmudic literature (m. *Sotah* 7:7-8, *Yoma* 7:1; b.*Pesahim* 49b) indicate that the ἀρχισυνάγωγος or *ro'sh ha-keneseth* was not the head of the congregation but the one responsible for the cult.[31] He presided over the meetings in the synagogue, regulated the services there, for instance by designating the men who were to read from the Torah or to recite prayers or to deliver a sermon. According to some sources he was also responsible for the construction and repairs of the synagogue building.[32] Inscriptions like nos. 584

---

[27] Leon, *Jews* 184-185, and esp. A. J. Saldarini, *Pharisees, Scribes, and Sadducees in Palestinian Society*, Wilmington: Glazier, 1988, 272-273.

[28] This is the new inscription published by Fasola in *Riv. Arch. Crist.* 52 (1976) 19.

[29] Leon, *Jews* 185.

[30] Saldarini, *Pharisees* 241-276, is the best study of the *grammateis* to date.

[31] See Krauss, *Synagogale Altertümer* 114-121, still the best treatment.

[32] See e.g. nos. 722, 766, 1404.

and 1404 seem to indicate that ἀρχισυνάγωγοι sometimes came from the same family and were father, son and grandson of an ἀρχισυνάγωγος, which suggests a hereditary principle. There is also one inscription of a νήπιος ἀρχισυνάγωγος of three years of age (no. 587). We do not know whether this official, *if* he was chosen, got the function for a fixed period. We have no inscription with δὶς ἀρχισυνάγωγος, but we do have two with an ἀρχισυνάγωγος διὰ βίου (744, 766, from Asia Minor). There can be no doubt that this was a very honoured position.[33]

The head of the synagogue was assisted during the service by a ὑπηρέτης ('helper, assistant', see Luke 4:20), of which we have only one mention in the inscriptions (172; likewise only one of a διάκονος, which indicates the same function, see no. 805), probably because "the office was not a sufficiently exalted one to be regarded as ordinarily worthy of mention on one's epitaph".[34] *Inter alia*, he brought out the sacred scroll from the ark and replaced it after the Torah portions had been read.[35] He probably also administered corporal punishment, like the forty strokes save one (see 2 Cor. 11:24), when it was inflicted by the community court.[36]

Further there is the title πατὴρ συναγωγῆς (88, 93, 319, 494, 508, 509, 510, 535, 537, and many times outside of Rome).[37] Although again the inscriptions yield no information on his tasks, most

---

[33] The identification of the ἀρχισυνάγωγος with the ἄρχων which is implicit in the synoptic comparison of the Jaïrus story (Mt. 9:18. 23; Mk. 5:22. 35-6. 38; Lk. 8:41. 49) is probably either a mistake or a case of loose use of terminology, as is correctly argued by B. J. Brooten, *Women Leaders in the Ancient Synagogue*, Chico: Scholars Press, 1982, 29-30.

[34] Leon, *Jews* 190.

[35] See P. Billerbeck, Ein Synagogengottesdienstdienst in Jesu Tagen, *ZNW* 55 (1964) 143-161; also the excursus in his *Kommentar zum NT* IV 1, 115-188, esp. 147-149; Schürer, *History* II 438. The ὑπηρέτης is called חזן (*ḥazzan*) in Talmudic literature (m. *Sotah* 7:7-8, *Shabbath* 1:3, *Sukkoth* 4:6.11, *Ta'anith* 1:14). See no. 805, where an ἀζζανα [sic!] explains this designation as διάκονος. Nowadays he would be called *shammash*.

[36] See S. Gallas, "Fünfmal vierzig weniger einen ..." Die an Paulus vollzogenen Synagogalstrafen nach 2 Kor 11, 24, *ZNW* 81 (1990) 178-191, esp. 188-189.

[37] With the *mater synagogae* (166, 496, 523) we will deal in our chapter on women.

scholars assume that this was "purely a honorary one, probably involving no active duties",[38] whereas some have assumed he was the
organizer of the charitable activities of the community. There is no
supporting evidence for either opinion; we simply do not know. We
do know, however, that the *Codex Theodosianus* XVI 8, 4 states that
the *patres synagogarum*, together with other synagogue officials,
were exempt from certain compulsory services on the basis of their
functional role in the synagogue. The fact, however, that this Codex
mentions *hiereis* (see below) in the same context, indicates that this
role may have been minimal. Anyhow, it certainly cannot be doubted that it must have been a position of very high honour. When one
inscription informs us that the deceased was the wife of a man who
was the brother of another man who was the 'father of a synagogue'
in Rome (319), we may certainly infer from this roundabout way of
putting it that it was considered important to emphasize a relationship with a person of such distinction. Moreover, we find that one of
those *pateres* is said to have been ἄρχων three times and φροντιστής
twice (494; on φροντιστής see below), one is said to have been
μαθητὴς σοφῶν (508), and one epitaph calls a father of the synagogue a lover of the community and of the commandments, who
lived a good life for no less than 110 years (509). There can be little
doubt about the high dignity and status of these 'fathers'.

The above-mentioned φροντιστής[39] (lit. 'one who takes care') is
only listed twice for Rome (337, 494) but he was probably a very
prestigious official, since on both occasions the title comes at the end
of a series of very important offices. One was twice *archon*, also
archon pases times, and *phrontistes*, the other was father of the synagogue, thrice *archon*, and twice *phrontistes*. The latter seems to imply that the office was an elective one. Inscriptions from Alexandria
(918), Side (781), and Porto (*BE* 1982, 499) also reveal little about
the function except that one (781) states that the φροντιστής made
repairs to the synagogue building. Whether we can infer from that,

---

38 Leon, *Jews* 186; cf. Schürer, *History* III 101, and Krauss, *Synagogale
Altertümer* 166.
39 On which see, besides Leon, *Jews* 191, also Robert, *Revue de philologie*
1958, 36-38, *BE* 1968 no. 560, and *BE* 1982 no. 499. For φροντισταί outside
of Rome see SEG XX 462 (Caesarea), CIJ 781 (Side) and 918 (Alexandria).

as Frey did,[40] that this official was the business manager or curator of the community, must again remain uncertain. What is certain, however, is that the φροντιστής was a dignitary of high standing.

We now come to the προστάτης (100, 365).[41] Frey assumed that this was the "défenseur et protecteur légal" of the community; others regard him as the *patronus* of the congregation. Προστάτης can mean in general either the presiding officer or leader of a political body or the patron or representative of a group. Maybe he was "the official who defended the interests of the congregation in the community at large, especially in its relations with the political authorities".[42] A legal representative of the community to the government will certainly not have been a superfluous luxury for a Jewish congregation, especially in the later Roman Empire when the legal status of the Jews worsened. But again we cannot reach certainty.

Although μαθητὴς σοφῶν (508) looks like an exact translation of the rabbinic term חכמים תלמיד (*talmid ḥakhamim,* 'pupil of the sages'), it need not necessarily imply that the bearer of this designation was a rabbi in the traditional sense of the word (see also below). Like the two νομομαθεῖς in nos. 193 and 333, he certainly was a student of Jewish law and lore, but there is no historically reliable evidence for the existence of a rabbinic school in Rome. The fact that the νομομαθής of no. 333 is also called διδάσκαλος indicates, however, that one or more of the communities did have their own Jewish school where Torah was taught (cf. perhaps also no. 201, if νομοδιδάσκαλος is to be read there).[43] The μαθητὴς σοφῶν may, of course, have come from Palestine or Babylon, but as we shall see presently, there is little or no evidence to support the traditional view that in the Imperial period rabbis dominated or strongly influenced diaspora communities in the West. We do not know whether a μαθητὴς σοφῶν or a νομομαθής had an official position or function in the Jewish communities of Rome.

---

[40] Frey, Introd. XCI; see also Applebaum in *Jewish People* I 1, 497.
[41] Frey, Introd. XCV; Leon, *Jews* 191-192; Penna, *NTS* 28 (1982) 330.
[42] Leon, *Jews* 192.
[43] See Applebaum in *Jewish People* I 1, 498. Talmudic reports about a rabbinic school in Rome in the second century are of very doubtful historicity; see the references in [H. L. Strack -] P. Billerbeck, *Kommentar zum Neuen Testament aus Talmud und Midrasch* III, München: Beck, 1926, 23-24.

Finally we find five references to a ἱερεύς (346, 347bis, 355, 375) and one to a ἱερίσσα (315). Almost all scholars agree that we are not concerned here with real priests and a priestess. Most probably these were *kohanim* in the sense of 'descendants of Aaron' or 'persons of Levitical descent' (cf. the Λευίτης in 902). As in the modern synagogue, they had no official function in the community at all, "but because of their hereditary distinction they had a minor part in the cult, especially that of pronouncing certain benedictions",[44] which was the only priestly task left after 70 CE. Apparently their distinction was still so great that in the third/fourth century catacombs of Beth She'arim a special room was reserved for *kohanim* (BS I 4, II 66 *et al*.).[45] In Beth She'arim we also find once the designation χωην (= *kohen*, BS II 148).

This concludes the material from Rome. It must be conceded that the picture remains vague. We would like to know many more details about the various tasks and the interrelatedness of the several functions within the communities, but the evidence is not very helpful in this respect. Perhaps some light may be shed on this problem by the fact that there is a striking terminological agreement between the political organization of cities in the Hellenistic and Roman world and the organization of these synagogues. In both we find *archontes, grammateis, prostatai, pateres, gerousiai*; in both we also find child-magistracies and the going together of elections with the maintenance of a hereditary principle.[46] It seems that the city has served as a model for the Jewish religious community. This is an aspect of the matter that will not be dealt with here but that certainly deserves further investigation.

Most of the titles mentioned recur in other Jewish inscriptions throughout the ancient world, from Spain to Mesopotamia, as we have already seen. Outside of Rome we find, however, only very few new titles. For instance, in Emerita (Spain) we find a *super orans* (665a), a chief cantor; in Athens we find a πρόσχολος (715b),

---

[44] Leon, *Jews* 192.
[45] B. Lifshitz, Fonctions et titres honorifiques dans les communautés juives, *RB* 67 (1960) 63.
[46] See, e.g., A. H. M. Jones, *The Greek City from Alexander to Justinian*, Oxford: Clarendon Press, 1940, 211-258. For child officials now especially M. Kleywegt, *Ancient Youth,* Amsterdam: Gieben, 1991, 247-272.

perhaps the head of a Jewish school;[47] in Nicomedia (Bithynia) we find an exceptional ἀναγνώστης (798 = *TAM* IV [1], ed. F. K. Doerner, Vienna: Oest. Akad. der Wiss., 1978, 374), apparently a reader of the Torah portion (בעל קורא, *ba'al qore'*), although the inscription has often been (unnecessarily) judged to be Christian because the ἀναγνώστης *(lector)* seemed to be such a typically Christian institution;[48] in Bithynia we also find an ἐπιστάτης τῶν παλαιῶν (800 = *SEG* XXXVII 1035), probably a local variant for gerousiarch, but curiously enough the same man was also *grammateus*, although he need not necessarily have had both functions at the same time; and finally we frequently find *rabbi*, a term to which we have to devote some attention now.

Rabbi

In a recent article Shaye Cohen has collected 57 'epigraphical rabbis',[49] 50 of which are from ancient Palestine. He shows that it is very difficult to ascertain in which cases the word *rabbi* designates an ordained Rabbi and in which cases it means just an individual of rank or an important person (which is a well established meaning of both *rabbi* and *biribbi* and variants, also in rabbinic literature[50]). This non-technical, popular use of the term never fell into complete desuetude. In addition, of the 50 epigraphical rabbis from Palestine not one can *with certainty* be identified with a Palestinian Rabbi

---

[47] Robert, *BE* 1964 no. 146

[48] Frey, *CIJ* II 50-51 *ad loc.*

[49] S. J. D. Cohen, Epigraphical Rabbis, *JQR* 72 (1981/82) 1-17. For an addendum see P. W. van der Horst, 'Lord, Help the Rabbi'. The Interpretation of SEG XXXI 1578b, *JJS* 38 (1987) 102-106, now also in my *Essays on the Jewish World* 182-186. Cohen notes the following orthographical variants in the inscriptions: ραββι, ραβι, ραββη, ριββι, ραβ, ριβ, βηρεβι, *rebbi*, רבי, רב, בירבי, רבי בירבי, רבן, רבנו; sometimes the abbreviations ρ or ר are used.

[50] See now also L. I. Levine, *The Rabbinic Class of Roman Palestine in Late Antiquity*, Jerusalem – New York: Yad Izhak Ben-Zvi – The Jewish Theological Seminary of America, 1989, 15: "In antiquity this title was applied to anyone of high standing in the community". Cf. also E. R. Goodenough, *Jewish Symbols in the Greco-Roman Period* I, New York: Pantheon, 1953, 90. For *birabbi/biribbi* meaning 'important man' see M. Sokoloff, *A Dictionary of Jewish Palestinian Aramaic of the Byzantine Period*, Bar Ilan University Press, 1990, *s.v.*

known to us from rabbinic literature. The names are often the same, but "obviously a secure identification requires some other data, e.g. identical name of offspring or identical area of activity, to supplement a similarity in nomenclature".[51] Some identifications are possible but none is really certain. 'Rabbi' was not a protected title and there was no central registry of persons who were ordained Rabbis. "Who could prevent various communities from bestowing the title 'rabbi' on their prominent citizens regardless of their practices and beliefs? Hence it makes no sense to assume that all rabbis in antiquity were Talmudic scholars".[52] The inscriptions make clear that the real leaders of the communities were the *archontes*, the *archisynagōgoi*, the *gerousiarchai*, etc. Nowhere do the inscriptions support "the notion of Rabbinic dominance"; epigraphical rabbis "appear as donors, not as leaders of the synagogues".[53] The negligibly few rabbis mentioned in the more than 1500 inscriptions outside the Land of Israel indicate that, even if *rabbi* were to mean 'Talmudic Rabbi', rabbinic presence in the diaspora was very meagre. It seems that "not only did diaspora Jewry have no Rabbis of its own, it also did not look to Israel for Rabbinic leadership".[54] Cohen concludes that most of the epigraphical rabbis were not Rabbis in the strict sense of the word, and that most synagogues in both Israel and the diaspora were not led by Rabbis. We cannot but concur with these conclusions.[55]

---

[51] Cohen *JQR* 72 (1981/82) 11.

[52] Cohen, *ibid.* 13.

[53] Cohen, *ibid.* 14.

[54] Cohen, *ibid.* 15.

[55] Out of over 700 inscriptions from Italy only 2 mention *rebbites*, nos. 568 and 611. It is only no. 611 (from Venosa) which might suggest that Rabbis were leading the community. Part of the text runs as follows: "Here lies Faustina (...), 14 years and 5 months, who was her parents' only child. Two *apostuli* and two *rebbites* spoke lamentations over her. Her death caused very great grief to her parents and tears to the community". The *apostuli* (ἀπόστολοι), however, can hardly be anything else than the envoys from the Jewish patriarch (*sheluḥim*, on which see, e.g., S. Krauss, Die jüdischen Apostel, *JQR* 17 (1905) 370-383, and A. David in *Enc. Jud.* 14 [1972] 1358-1368), and this suggests that the two rabbis may also have been merely dignitaries from the outside; see H. J. Leon, The Jews of Venusia, *JQR* 44 (1953/54) 273. On the very limited power and influence of the patriarch's 'apostles' see also Goodenough, *Jewish Symbols* I 12.

Secular professions

As has been said at the beginning of this chapter, functions in the religious community are mentioned in the epitaphs in a considerably higher frequency than secular professions or occupations. Only some dozens of tombstones record the employment of the deceased and we cannot draw any valid sociological conclusions from them, unless one would conclude *e silentio* that most people did not see fit to mention their jobs because they were of low social status. Be that as it may, the professions we find are those of painter (109), butcher (210), teacher (333, 594, 1158c, 1266, 1268, 1269), soldier (79 and Scheiber nos. 4 and 6, not all of them completely certain[56]), slave (556, 619e),[57] *patēr kai patrōn tēs poleōs* (619b,c,d)[58] or just *pater* (676, see previous note), wine-seller (681b), physician (600, 745),[59] purple-dyer (777), boot-seller (787), city-councillor (788, 985),

---

[56] See A. Scheiber, *Jewish Inscriptions in Hungary From the Third Century to 1686,* Budapest: Akadémiai Kiadó – Leiden: Brill, 1983, 33-37.

[57] G. Fuks, Where Have All the Freedmen Gone? On an Anomaly in the Jewish Grave-Inscriptions from Rome, *JJS* 36 (1985) 25-32, draws attention to the curious fact that the names of at least 10% of the Roman Jews in the inscriptions indicate that they were probably freedmen (ex-slaves) but that is made nowhere explicit. He explains this deliberate avoidance of any mention of the fact that they were formerly slaves from religious motives: they refrained from calling their former owners 'masters' since these were heathens and members of a hated nation, and only God could be called 'master'.

[58] Ch. Roueché, *Aphrodisias in Late Antiquity,* London: Roman Society, 1989, 77, demonstrates that a 'father (or patron) of the city' was "the local official responsible for undertaking building works for the city with the city's own funds" (cf. *Anth. Pal.* IX 662!). It was often abbreviated as *pater*; cf. Robert, *Hellenica* IV (1948) 130-132.

[59] The term used is not *iatros* (for which see no. 1100) but *archiatros*, 'chief doctor' (no. 745 now re-edited in *Inschr. von Ephesos* V, ed. C. Börker – R. Merkelbach, Bonn: Habelt, 1980, 1677), which "may imply that the man was among the doctors recognized by a city (...); they enjoyed immunity from all obligations", Schürer, *History* III 23 (with lit.). See on *archiatroi* also Horsley, *New Documents* 2 (1982) 10-19. The *iatros* in 1419 is perhaps not Jewish, see Bloedhorn *apud* Hengel in *JSS* 35 (1990) 65. R. Kudlien, Jüdische Ärzte im römischen Reich, *Medizinhistorisches Journal* 20 (1985) 36-57, deals with the inscriptions at pp. 42-47 (see especially 43-44 on the γερουσιάρχων ἀρχίατρος of no. 600).

silk-manufacturer (873), huckster (881), baker (902, 940), seller of small wares (928), fuller (929), linen-seller (931), goldsmith (1006), perfume-seller (BS II 79), cloth-dyer (BS II 188), cloth-merchant (BS II 189), and potter (Naveh, *IEJ* 20 [1970] 35 no. 2). (In the new Aphrodisias inscription we find Jews involved in the production of food, and there are a bronze-smith, a gold-smith, a dealer in horse fodder, a poulterer, a confectioner, a shepherd, and a rag-dealer.[60]) So we see that Jews were engaged in a broad range of occupations, ranging from the lowest to the highest social echelon, from slave to city-councillor. We even have 2 cases of Jewish πρωτοπολῖται, 'first citizens' (Lifshitz, *Euphrosyne* 6 [1973/74] 44-45, and Le Bohec, *Antiquités Africaines* 17 [1981] no. 79), an honorary title of the highest order designating the most prominent notables of a city or a community (compare the Jewish *maiores civitatis* in Venusia, no. 611).[61] Although this list is not very revealing, it does at least make clear that Jews were present in all strata of ancient society, certainly not only on the lower levels.[62] It is especially interesting to notice that in the third and fourth centuries some Jews occupied positions as high as city-councillor, which is a leading function in the municipal administration that could hardly be fulfilled without some involvement in pagan rites. It is noteworthy that the Mishna tractate on idolatry, *Avodah Zara*, does not deal with such a situation, apparently because the rabbis did not even envisage such a possibility, whereas the contemporary treatise by Tertullian, *De idololatria,* does deal with the problem of Christians as city officials.[63]

The scarcity of data concerning secular professions as compared to what we learn about the Jews' functions within their religious

---

[60] Reynolds – Tannenbaum, *Jews and Godfearers at Aphrodisias* 116-124.

[61] Robert, *BE* 1958 no. 105; Lifshitz, *Euphrosyne* 6 (1973/74) 46.

[62] See the more extensive survey by S. Applebaum, The Social and Economic Status of the Jews in the Diaspora, in Safrai – Stern (edd.), *Jewish People* II 701-727.

[63] This contrast is noticed by A. R. R. Sheppard, Jews, Christians and Heretics in Acmonia and Eumeneia, *Anatolian Studies* 29 (1979) 169-170. For other Jewish city-councillors than those mentioned above see J. H. M. Strubbe, Joden en Grieken: onverzoenlijke vijanden?, *Lampas* 22 (1989) 192-193, who notices that Jews began to exercise the functions of magistrates and city-councillors only from the end of the second century CE onwards.

communities highlights once again the central role of the synagogue in Jewish life throughout the ancient world.[64] As has been rightly remarked, "the most basic self-definition of these Jews is in terms of relationship to, membership in, and service for the synagogue".[65]

---

[64] Naveh, *IEJ* 20 (1970) 33-34, publishes a Jerusalem inscription of 'Simon, a builder of the sanctuary' (that is, the Jerusalem temple). Although a secular profession, it obviously has religious overtones.
The only epitaphs which can be related directly or indirectly to persons known from other sources, are the ossuary inscriptions of the sons of Nikanor of Alexandria, who donated the doors of one of the gates of Herod's temple (no. 1256) and one of the granddaughter of the high priest Theophilus (published by D. Barag and D. Flusser in *IEJ* 36 [1986] 39-44).
[65] J. Z. Smith, Fences and Neighbors: Some Contours of Early Judaism, in W. S. Green (ed.), *Approaches to Ancient Judaism* II, Chico: Scholars Press, 1980, 17.
The only tomb-inscription that mentions Jewish feasts is no. 777 from Hierapolis (Phrygia), where ἡ ἑορτὴ τῶν ἀζύμων and ἡ ἑορτὴ πεντηκοστῆς are referred as the occasions for certain distributions.

VII. Women

Women are underrepresented in Jewish epitaphs, but less so than in pagan funerary epigraphy. At least 40% of the Jewish epitaphs are of women. In previous chapters some remarks have already been made with regard to epithets and age at death of women.[1] In this chapter we will deal with some loose ends of that material and we will try to glean from the inscriptions some other information that is specific to women.

Epithets

In the chapter on epithets we saw that some adjectives indicating chastity, decency and modesty, were almost exclusively applied to women. That these virtues were deemed far more important for women than for men is well-known from other sources as well.[2] It is often recorded of girls or young women that they were παρθένοι when they died (45, 168, 320, 381, 588, 733, etc.). Although this term need not necessarily imply virginity – παρθένος can mean 'girl of marriageable age' – nonetheless it very often has the notion of virgin.[3] Virginity of a girl on the day of marriage was regarded

---

[1] Onomastics falls outside the scope of this study, but for women's names we refer the interested reader to G. Mayer, *Die jüdische Frau in der hellenistisch-römischen Antike*, Stuttgart: Kohlhammer, 1987, 33-42 and 103-127; T. Ilan, Notes on the Distribution of Jewish Women's Names in Palestine in the Second Temple and Mishnaic Periods, *JJS* 40 (1989) 186-200.

[2] See e.g. L. J. Archer, *Her Price is Beyond Rubies. The Jewish Woman in Graeco-Roman Palestine*, Sheffield: Sheffield Academic Press, 1990, *passim*.

[3] G. Delling, *TWNT* VI 824-835 (825: "Meist handelt es sich in diesen Zusammenhängen [sc., the general popular usage] um *tatsächlich* unberührte Mädchen").

as of paramount importance for the honour of the family.[4] The fact that occasionally παρθένος or παρθενικός (*virginius*) is used of men in our inscriptions (e.g. 81, 242) does not, however, *per se* indicate that virginity was seen as a desirable quality in men; it just means that the deceased was not married or had not been married before.

The adjective μόνανδρος or *univira* is, of course, also typical of women (81, 158[?], 392, 541, all of them in Rome; it has no masculine equivalent[5]). There has been some debate about the meaning of this term. Frey said that in Christian epitaphs it indicates a widow who did not remarry, whereas in pagan and Jewish tomb-inscriptions it means that the woman never had a divorce and so had only one husband.[6] Others objected to this interpretation and took μόνανδρος-*univira* in Jewish epitaphs to imply that the deceased woman did not remarry after the death of her husband.[7] "Since it was a common practice among Jews for widows to remarry, it was apparently regarded as a noteworthy mark of devotion to her dead husband if a widow did not take another husband".[8] This fits in with a tendency discernible in the later Empire among pagans (especially Romans), Christians and Jews not to engage in a second marriage.[9] Whether μόνανδρος-*univira* refers to not-remarrying or to not-divorcing, at any rate it is clear that it was regarded as especially praiseworthy among (Roman) Jews if a woman had had only one husband during her lifetime. No such thing is ever said of a man, however.

For Jewish women – as for women in antiquity generally – marriage was often entered into early. We do not have many inscriptions recording the age at which women were married, but the

---

4 Archer, *Price* 101-122.
5 Cf. μιᾶς γυναικὸς ἀνήρ in 1 Tim. 3:2.12, where this is a requirement for clerical functions. Note that a one-word equivalent for this requirement never developed.
6 J. B. Frey, La signification des termes ΜΟΝΑΝΔΡΟΣ et Univira, *Recherches de science religieuse* 20 (1930) 48-60.
7 See e.g. B. Kötting, Univira in Inschriften, in his *Ecclesia peregrinans* I, Münster: Aschendorff, 1988, 345-355.
8 Leon, *Jews* 129-130.
9 See esp. Kötting, Univira 351-354, for references.

few who record it mention ages varying from 12 to 18 years. Fifteen probably was an average age for a girl to marry (see e.g. nos. 105, 136, 242, 268, 527, etc.).[10] The number of years the marriage lasted is seldom recorded, neither are there data on the size of the families. Most probably many children were born[11] but only a minority of them survived. The grief over so many dead infants must have put a great emotional strain upon women. We know that a high percentage of women died in the so-called 'reproductive period', that is between 12 and 38 years.[12] There can be little doubt that many of these women died in childbirth. Some inscriptions indeed mention this fact explicitly, for instance the pathetic poem of no. 1510: "This is the grave of Arsinoe, wayfarer. Stand by and weep for her, unfortunate in all things, whose lot was hard and terrible. For I was bereaved of my mother when I was a little girl, and when the flower of my youth made me ready for a bridegroom, my father married me to Phabis; and Fate brought me to the end of my life in bearing my first-born child. I had a small span of years, but great grace flowered in the beauty of my spirit. This grave hides in its bosom my chaste body, but my soul has flown to the holy ones. Lament for Arsinoe". And, by way of contrast, the sober no. 1515 (from the same time and place, Leontopolis in the beginning of the Imperial period): "Dosarion, about 25 years, in childbirth". But, apart from childbirth, general physical exhaustion may also have played a great part in the high death rate of women in this period.[13] Nevertheless, as we already saw in our chapter on age at death, the average life duration of Jewish women as recorded in the epitaphs is only two years lower than that of men; the difference in pagan

---

10 See Horsley, *New Documents* 4 (1987) 222-227, on age at marriage. He states that the few data we have seem to suggest a higher marriage age for Jewish than for pagan girls.

11 The Jews were known in antiquity as a people that – contrary to usual practice in the ancient world – did not practise abortion or exposure; see my *Sentences of Pseudo-Phocylides* 232-234, with the additions in my *Essays* 58; and Stern, *GLAJJ* III, Index s.v. infanticide.

12 Leon, *Jews* 229, presents statistics showing that out of 164 Roman Jews the age at death of which is recorded, 49 died between 10 and 30 years: 22 of these were men (out of 93 men) and 27 were women (out of 69 women). See further our Ch. 5.

13 Burn, *Past & Present* 4 (1953) 10-13.

inscriptions is greater. But we should realize how careful we have to be in drawing conclusions from our scanty evidence.

Leadership

One of the most interesting aspects of our epitaphs as far as women are concerned is that of the titles or functions assigned to women in the religious communities. There are some 20 inscriptions in which women bear titles like 'head of the synagogue', 'mother of the synagogue', 'elder', or 'leader'. Until recently most scholars assumed that women had no positions of leadership in the ancient synagogue. Therefore, they interpreted such titles borne by women as purely honorific and not functional. Over the last decade opinions have begun to change on this subject.[14]

Let us begin with women as ἀρχισυνάγωγος or ἀρχισυναγώγισσα (nos. 731c, 741, 756). This title designates one of the main synagogue officials, as we have already seen in the previous chapter (and as is also apparent from *Codex Theodosianus* XVI 8, 4.13.14). The main 'argument' for regarding the title as honorific is that women received this title because their husbands – not they themselves – held this office. However, this is a completely unfounded assertion, because in none of the three inscriptions are husbands mentioned! Let us take for instance no. 731c (from Crete): "Sophia of Gortyn, elder and leader of the synagogue of Kissamos, (lies) here. The memory of the righteous (woman) be forever, amen".[15] Brooten writes on this inscription: "There is no *internal* reason for believing that Sophia of Gortyn received the titles through her husband. If her husband were the source of her titles, why is she not called Sophia the wife of X?".[16] And it is very significant that in those instances where wives of ἀρχισυνάγωγοι are mentioned, they

---

[14] It was especially B. J. Brooten's monograph *Women Leaders in the Ancient Synagogue* (1982) that advocated a different approach. But she was not the only one; see my The Jews of Ancient Crete, in my *Essays on the Jewish World* 163-4 with nn. 59 and 64. For some justified criticisms of some aspects of Brooten's thesis see Horsley, *New Documents* 4 (1987) 213-220.

[15] See on this inscription also my essay mentioned in the previous note, 163-164.

[16] Brooten, *Women* 12.

do *not* bear this title. This seems to make it highly probable that in some places in the diaspora women were indeed leaders of the synagogue. Parallels in the contemporary pagan world would make this only more likely. In Greek and Latin inscriptions one can find many instances of women in the offices of *prytanis, gymnasiarchos, agōnothetēs, mater collegii,* etc. Women are also often found as actual officials of religious associations.[17] Although the use of such titles as honorary designations is well-known – also in the case of ἀρχισυνάγωγος, as is apparent from the νήπιος ἀρχισυνάγωγος in no. 587 – these pagan parallels are certainly relevant to the problem in that they suggest at least the possibility that women could indeed hold this high office.

Further we have an epitaph of a woman who is called ἀρχηγίσσα, the feminine equivalent of ἀρχηγός (696b).[18] The word is a rather general term for leader and it seems impossible to be specific about what function(s) this singular title implied. More helpful are 8 inscriptions of female elders (πρεσβυτέρα, πρεσβυτέρισσα; nos. 581, 590, 597, 692, 731c [see above]; SEG XXVII, 1977, no. 1201; Le Bohec no. 4; Kraemer, *HTR* 78 [1986] 431).[19] These inscriptions have often been interpreted as referring to 'aged women', a possible meaning of πρεσβυτέρα. But, as Brooten has argued,[20] nothing is against taking the word as a feminine equivalent of πρεσβύτερος, and there is no doubt that πρεσβύτεροι (the *z^eqenim* of the rabbinic sources) is the technical term for the official members of the council of elders in each congregation (see the previous chapter). Here again it is more natural to take the designation πρεσβυτέρα as implying real and active membership of the council of elders of the religious community. Absolutely nothing in their epitaphs suggests that women derived this title from their husbands. And it would be unsound methodology to assume that the term means one thing when

---

17 References in Schürer, *History* III 107 with nn. 69-71; see also R. van Bremen, Women and Wealth, in A. Cameron – A. Kuhrt (edd.), *Images of Women in Antiquity*, London: Croom Helm, 1983, 223-242.

18 An inscription on a Jewish gold medallion mentions a Ἰακὼβ ἀρχηγός (731g).

19 No. 400 is a dubious case.

20 Brooten, *Women* 41-55.

applied to a man and another when applied to a woman.[21] The new
epitaph from Malta, which runs: "[X], *gerousiarchēs*, lover of the
commandments, and Eulogia, the elder, his wife",[22] is interesting
for our purpose in that here the female elder is the wife of the head
of the council of elders. Since none of the 5 other epitaphs mentioning wives of gerousiarchs attributes titles to these women, it is
clear that wives of gerousiarchs were not routinely given titles of
their own. This suggests that the Maltese epitaph "reflects a marriage in which both husband and wife were active in the synagogue
on Malta".[23] As long as there is no unambiguous evidence that honorific titles were applied to adult women in the ancient synagogue, we
have no compelling reason to assume that, if Jewish women bearing
titles were in fact wives of synagogue officials, this implied that they
themselves had no function.

Finally, we have four inscriptions mentioning the titles of μήτηρ
συναγωγῆς or *mater synagogae* (nos. 166, 496, 523, 639), one inscription mentioning only a μήτηρ (619d), and one very curious
inscription recording a *pateressa* (606). No. 523 is interesting in that
it calls the deceased 'mother of synagogues': "Veturia Paulla, con-
signed to her eternal home, who lived 86 years (and) 6 months, a
proselyte (since) 16 years, named Sara, mother of the synagogues of
Campus and Volumnius. In peace be her sleep". The plural 'synagogues' is paralleled in no. 508: "Here lies Mniaseas [Manasseh?],
disciple of the sages and father of synagogues". These are the only
two known instances of persons who had been actively involved in
two synagogues (although not necessarily simultaneously). We have
seen in the previous chapter that the father of the synagogue was
possibly a functionary that had something to do with the administration of the synagogue, although our knowledge remains very
vague. The *matres synagogarum* were their female colleagues. For,
again, nothings compels us to assume that this was an honorific title.
It is possible that the single μήτηρ (619d) is just an abbreviation of

---

[21] Kraemer, *HTR* 78 (1986) 433-434. But it has to be admitted that it can
never be completely ruled out that *presbytera* means 'elderly woman' in some
instances. That possibility is unduly neglected by both Brooten and Kraemer.
[22] Kraemer, *ibid.* 431.
[23] Kraemer, *ibid.* 437.

the fuller title, although in this case the fact that the woman is the wife of Auxanius, a πατὴρ καὶ πάτρων τῆς πόλεως may rather indicate that she shares in her husband's titulature. But this remains uncertain. *Pateressa* (606), 'fatheress', is unparalleled and it is therefore impossible to be sure about its meaning or about the function implied. But it is a not unreasonable guess that the deceased woman received this novel title to designate her as a female 'father', *i.e.* mother, of the synagogue. But, since *pater* can also designate a municipal official, "the question of whether *pateressa* implied a synagogue function or a civic one, must remain open".[24]

Scarce though the evidence for female functionaries in the ancient synagogue may be, the inscriptions make it very probable indeed that in some diaspora situations women could rise to high positions and even to leadership in Jewish communities.[25]

It accords well with the picture of women in leading positions in early Jewish communities that in three out of four epitaphs in which the intellectual capacities of the deceased are praised, it is women who receive this praise. In no. 215 (Rome) the husband of the deceased woman calls her not only a good wife but also a *discipulina bona*, a good student. In no. 190 (Rome) a woman is called μαθητής and εὐδιδάκτη, a student and well instructed or well trained. And in Beth She'arim, BS II 113, we find the female proper name Eumathia, certainly an expression of expectation on the side of her parents that she will learn well. From most literary sources we do not at all get the impression that learned women were anything of an ideal in

---

[24] Brooten, *Women* 62. At pp. 73-99, Brooten discusses the inscriptions in which women are called ἱέρισσα or ἱερεία (315, 1007, 1514). Although she leaves open the possibility that women were called priestess because they had a cultic function, either in a temple (no. 1514 is from Leontopolis) or in a synagogue, it seems to me that it is less improbable that, as in the case of male ἱερεῖς (see above in the previous chapter), they were only of Aaronitic descent, *kohanim*.

[25] On the basis of a literary document, the *Testament of Job*, I reached the same conclusions as Brooten did on the basis of epigraphic evidence; see my The Role of Women in the Testament of Job, in my *Essays on the Jewish World* 94-110. Note that the phenomenon of female functionaries is not confined geographically to any one area as a local idiosyncrasy (although one does not find it in Roman Palestine).

early Judaism.[26] In real life, however, talented and intelligent women may sometimes really have got chances to develop their capacities and climb higher on the social ladder in their communities.
With due caution these few inscriptions may be regarded as evidence
pointing in that direction. It is at least a surprise that what is viewed
as an almost exclusively male prerogative in the vast corpus of early
Jewish literature, turns out to be also a female quality in the small
corpus of early Jewish inscriptions.[27]

Proselytes and Godfearers

It has often been noticed that there is a relatively high percentage of
women among the epigraphical proselytes and Godfearers. Of the
14 epitaphs mentioning proselytes at least 7 are women (nos. 21,
202, 222, 462, 523; Dominus Flevit no. 31; Lifshitz, RB 68 [1961]
115 no.2).[28] Of course these numbers may be due to chance, but in
view of the under-representation of women in our corpus of inscriptions, they may indicate that relatively more women than men
converted to Judaism. And when we look at the Godfearers, this
impression seems to be corroborated, for out of 12 inscriptions no
less than (9 or) 10 are of women (202, 285, 500, 524, 529, 642,
731e; Robert, Études Anatoliennes 409-412, Nouvelles inscriptions
de Sardes 44, and BE 1977, 332).[29] As a matter of fact we know
from literary sources that there were more female than male proselytes and Godfearers, probably because "it was easier for a woman
to adopt all the Jewish rites required of women than it was for an
adult male to take over all that was incumbent on a man who became
a Jew",[30] especially circumcision of course. Women even continued

---

[26] Archer, Price 69-100. Note that no. 132 Κρισπῖνα ... σπουδαῖα φιλέντολος certainly implies religious zeal for the Law.

[27] For pagan and Christian parallels see Horsley, New Documents 2 (1982)
55-56, and 4 (1987) 257-258.

[28] Frey, Introd. LXIII, also takes no. 72 as mentioning a proselyte woman,
but the epitaph records nothing of the sort.

[29] It should be noted, however, that no. 202 is of a προσήλυτος θεοσεβής.
Here theosebēs may have the meaning of 'pious'.

[30] Leon, Jews 256.

to convert to the Jewish faith after Constantine, as is apparent from a law in the *Codex Theodosianus* (XVI 8, 6, from August 339):[31] "In so far as pertains to the women who were formerly employed in our imperial weaving establishment and who have been led by the Jews into the association of their turpitude, it is our pleasure that they shall be restored to the weaving establishment. It shall be observed that Jews shall not hereafter unite Christian women to their villainy; if they should do so, however, they shall be subject to the peril of capital punishment".[32] Also John Chrysostom's strong appeal to Christian husbands, half a century later (386/7), not to allow their wives to attend synagogue services, is a strong indication that many women felt at least very much attracted to aspects of the Jewish religion (*Adversus Iudaeos* 2:4-6; 4:3).[33] And three centuries earlier, Josephus writes that of the (pagan) women of Damascus in his own time the vast majority had become converts to Judaism (*Bellum* II 560). Exaggerated though this report may be, there can be little doubt that it must have contained a kernel of truth to the effect that it was especially women who felt attracted to Judaism. So the literary sources confirm the picture suggested by the epitaphs that relatively more women than men were either Godfearers or proselytes.[34] That women converts to Judaism could rise to high positions in the Jewish community is clearly implied by an epitaph from Rome, no. 523 (already quoted above) about Veturia Paulla, who became a proselyte when 70 years old and became mother of two synagogues before she died at the age of 86.

There is one young Roman proselyte girl whose epitaph is notoriously difficult, no. 21: Εἰρήνη τρεζπτη (= θρεπτή) προσήλυτος πατρὸς καὶ μητρὸς Εἰουδέα (= Ἰουδαία) Ἰσδραηλίτης ἔζησεν ητ (= ἔτη) γ' μ (= μῆνας) ζ' ημρ (= ἡμέραν) α'. It is clear that Irene was a foster-child that died at the age of 3 years, 7 months and 1 day. But how to construct and translate the words in between: προσήλυτος πατρὸς καὶ μητρὸς Ἰουδαία Ἰσραηλίτης?

---

31 Brooten, *Women* 145.
32 Translation by C. Pharr, *The Theodosian Code and Novels and the Sirmondian Constitution*, Princeton: Princeton University Press, 1952, 467.
33 *Patrologia Graeca* 48:860-1, 881.
34 See also Schürer, *History* III 162-163.

Leon translates: "Irene, foster-child, proselyte, her father and mother Jewish, an Israelite, lived ...".[35] And he remarks: "Possibly the baby girl, born of Jewish parents, had first been reared in a non-Jewish household, then adopted by a Jewish family and formally received into Judaism. Thus the epitaph emphasizes the child's Jewish origin. It seems incredible that so young a child should have been regarded as a proselyte".[36] Kraemer, in her extensive discussion of this inscription, presents five different translations, of which she thinks one of the least improbable is: "Irene, foster-child, proselyte by her father and her mother, a Jewish Israelite [that is, the mother]".[37] This translation, too, hardly seems to do justice to the Greek text. Kraemer suggests that Irene's conversion to Judaism as an infant was forced upon her by her foster-parents of whom the mother was also a proselyte. Now it has to be conceded that the syntax of the inscription leaves much to be desired in clarity. Nonetheless, it goes without saying that the least forced solution is to take all the nominatives as referring to Irene:[38] she is a proselyte, an uncommon technical term which for the sake of clarity is elucidated as 'Jewish, member of the people of Israel'. But since Irene, as a very young child, did not herself take the decision to become Jewish – her foster-parents imposed it upon her – she is called a 'proselyte of her father and her mother'.[39]

---

[35] Leon, *Jews* 267. On the various meanings of *threptos* see now B. Levick in *MAMA* IX (1988) lxiv-lxvi (foster-child; adoptive child; slave, either house-born or child of free status exposed and brought up as slave).

[36] Leon, *Jews* 255.

[37] Kraemer, *HTR* 82 (1989) 38-41; apart from the two translations quoted in the text, she notes the following three suggested translations: "I., foster-child, her father a proselyte, her mother Jewish, an Israelite [that is, the mother]"; "I., foster-child, Israelite, her father a proselyte and her mother a Jew"; and Frey's translation: "I., pupille, prosélyte par son père et sa mère, Juive Israélite".

[38] This is in fact Frey's solution (see previous note). Kraemer's objection that "there are enough spelling errors in the inscription to make the determination of cases questionable" (39) is not very convincing. Galling, *Theol. Stud. und Krit.* 103 (1931) 358, takes 'Israelite' to mean 'belonging to the laity', as opposed to priests and Levites, but this is improbable.

[39] Greg Horsley suggests to me the following alternative: 'May the text not be attesting the conversion of the parents, and *ergo* of the foster-child? At the death of the latter she is the one who is the focus of attention and so is the only one

Let us conclude this chapter with a full quotation of what is both the most famous and one of the most beautiful Jewish epitaphs we have, a 13 line Latin laudatory poem on Regina, a young Jewish woman in Rome who died at the age of 21 years and whose husband glorifies her faithfulness, her piety, her love of the Jewish people and her observance of the commandments. It is CIJ 476:[40]

> Here lies Regina, covered by such a tomb, which her husband set up as fitting to his love. After twice ten years she spent with him one year, four months and eight days more. She will live again, return to the light again, for she can hope that she will rise to the life promised, as a real assurance, to the worthy and the pious, in that she has deserved to possess an abode in the hallowed land. This your piety has assured you, this your chaste life, this your love for your people, this your observance of the Law, your devotion to your wedlock, the glory of which was dear to you. For all these deeds your hope of the future is assured. In this your sorrowing husband seeks his comfort.[41]

This is the most elaborate *laudatio* of a woman in Jewish funerary epigraphy. All central Jewish values are praised in this woman.[42]

---

called proselyte.'

[40] The poem is in dactylic hexameters. The translation is by Leon (*Jews* 335), but slightly corrected on the basis of the critical remarks by Lifshitz (Prolegomenon to CIJ I 38), who also convincingly refutes Ferrua's thesis that the poem is Christian. Lifshitz' claim that *amor generis* (in line 10) does not mean 'love of the (Jewish) people' but 'love of (her) family' seems unfounded; cf. φιλόλαος.

[41] *Hic Regina sita est tali contecta sepulcro*
    quod coniunx statuit respondens eius amori.
    haec post bis denos secum transsegerat annum
    et quartum mensem restantibus octo diebus.
    rursum victura, reditura ad lumina rursum,
    nam sperare potest ideo quod surgat in aevom
    promissum quae vera fides dignisque piisque.
    quae meruit sedem venerandi ruris habere.
    hoc tibi praestiterat pietas, hoc vita pudica,
    hoc et amor generis, hoc observantia legis.
    coniugii meritum cuius tibi gloria curae.
    horum factorum tibi sunt speranda futura,
    de quibus et coniunx maestus solacia quaerit.
For the grammatical problems in this poem see Müller – Bees, *Inschriften* 133-136.

[42] Kraemer, *Helios* 13 (1986) 90.

The fact that her husband seeks comfort in his expectation of Regina's resurrection from the dead provides us with a smooth transition to the next chapter, on the afterlife.[43]

---

[43] Several inscriptions concerning Jewish women can be found in translation in R. S. Kraemer's book *Maenads, Martyrs, Matrons, Monastics. A Sourcebook on Women's Religions in the Greco-Roman World*, Philadelphia: Fortress, 1988 (see Index, p. 420).

VIII. Death and Afterlife

The epitaph quoted at the end of the previous chapter is exceptional in its clear expression of resurrection belief. Most of our epitaphs yield disappointingly little information concerning the ideas of either the survivors or the deceased about life after death. What information there is, will be collected in this chapter, but we will see that the evidence often defies interpretation.[1]

As a preliminary step we will briefly mention the various terms for death and dying in the epitaphs.[2] Apart from the usual ἀποθνῄσκειν (e.g. 79, 418), very few words for dying are found. In 89 we find ἀπεγ(ένετο); in BS II 127 the poetic expression φάος λιπεῖν (to

---

[1] See H. C. C. Cavallin, *Life After Death. Paul's Argument for the Resurrection of the Dead in 1 Cor. 15. Part I: An Enquiry into the Jewish Background*, Lund: Gleerup, 1974, 99-101, 166-170. Idem, Leben nach dem Tode im Spätjudentum und im frühen Christentum, I: Spätjudentum, *ANRW* II 19, 1, Berlin – New York: W. de Gruyter, 1979, 321-323. G. Delling, Speranda Futura. Jüdische Grabinschriften Italiens über das Geschick nach dem Tode, in his *Studien zum Neuen Testament und zum hellenistischen Judentum*, Göttingen: Vandenhoeck & Ruprecht, 1970, 39-44. E. Dinkler, Schalom – Eirene – Pax. Jüdische Sepulkralinschriften und ihr Verhältnis zum frühen Christentum, *Riv. Arch. Crist.* 50 (1974) 121-144. U. Fischer, *Eschatologie und Jenseitserwartung im hellenistischen Diasporajudentum*, Berlin – New York: W. de Gruyter, 1978, 215-254. H. Kosmala, *Hebräer – Essener – Christen*, Leiden: Brill, 1959, 417-428. Leon, *Jews* 244-250. B. Lifshitz, La vie de l'au-delà dans les conceptions juives, *RB* 68 (1961) 401-411. S. Nagakubo, *Investigation into Jewish Concepts of Afterlife in the Beth She'arim Greek Inscriptions*, (unpubl.) diss. Duke University, Durham (N.C.), 1974. M. Simon, Θάρσει, οὐδεὶς ἀθάνατος. Étude de vocabulaire religieux, reprinted in his *Le christianisme antique et son contexte religieux* I, Tübingen: Mohr, 1981, 63-81.

[2] For surveys of the pagan evidence see Pfohl and Pietri in *RAC* 12 (1983) 473 and 572-5; Lattimore, *Themes* 21-86; Pikhaus, *Levensbeschouwing, passim*.

leave the light) occurs; in 1510 the deceased girl says, 'my soul went
to the holy ones' (line 10); and in several epitaphs from Tell el-
Yehudieh we see the Greek mythological figure of Hades symbo-
lizing death (1508, 1511, 1530, 1530a).[3] In Latin inscriptions we
find, besides the common *mortuus* (e.g. 614, 616), also *defunctus*
(482, 635), *recessit* (460), and *obdormivit* (526). Words for the
state of being dead show scarcely more variety. There is an overwhelming predominance of terms meaning 'sleep' or 'rest': nouns
like κοίμησις, ἀνάπαυσις, *dormitio* and נוח (*nuaḥ*) are very frequent, as are verbs like κοιμᾶσθαι, *requiescere*, and *pausare*. Especially κοίμησις has a high frequency in Rome where almost 300
epitaphs end with the typically Jewish formula ἐν εἰρήνῃ ἡ κοίμησις αὐτοῦ/αὐτῆς/αὐτῶν/σου.[4]

Sleep

This apparently simple formula, 'may his/her/their/your sleep be in
peace', has given rise to much debate concerning its meaning. Some
scholars interpret it as having an eschatological content. 'Peace'
should then be taken in the sense of the biblical *shalom* but with the
added notion of eschatological salvation.[5] And if the word 'sleep' is
taken to imply 'awakening, rising' after sleep, then the eschatological salvation is the bodily resurrection of the dead followed by
eternal bliss. Other scholars, however, soberly point out that the

---

[3] Horsley, *New Documents* IV p. 23, quotes *IGUR* 1240 (Rome) as a
possibly Jewish inscription where the expression ἀνέλυσα εἰς οἶκον, 'I
departed home', is used (cf. Phil. 1:23!); but the Jewishness of the epitaph is not
beyond doubt.

[4] Frey, Introd. CXXXIII: "Cette dernière acclamation est pour ainsi dire
classique chez les Juifs; elle se lit à Rome d'innombrables fois sur les inscriptions juives, tandis qu'elle ne se rencontre jamais chez les chrétiens". On the
metaphor see the valuable study by M. B. Ogle, The Sleep of Death, *Memoirs of
the American Academy in Rome* 11 (1933) 81-117, who provides ample
documentation of the metaphorical use of 'sleep' throughout pagan, Jewish, and
Christain antiquity, but who remarks that it is much more widespread among
Jews and Christians than among pagans (see also his useful index of sources at
pp. 114-117).

[5] So Frey, *ibid.*, and Dinkler, Schalom 131-134.

formula may equally well mean undisturbed rest of the body in the tomb without implying any form of afterlife whatsoever.[6] There is no way of knowing whether the formula implies anything more than O.T. phrases such as 'you will go to your fathers in peace' (Gen. 15:5) or 'he enters into peace, they rest on their beds' (Is. 57:2)[7] or 'he went to sleep with his fathers' (frequent in the books of Kings and Chronicles; cf. Acts 13:36). Even if the formula did imply some form of belief in afterlife, it certainly does not point to a specific form of post-mortal existence, either bodily or spiritually. Some scholars have drawn attention to the fact that the formula is a wish with the force of an imperative. Hence in some epitaphs the formula is rephrased with a verb – not in the indicative but – in the imperative: ἐν εἰρήνῃ κοιμάσθω (365, 390, etc.). This imperative should be taken as an implicit prayer to God who is to grant the deceased a peaceful sleep. This prayer character is made explicit in no. 126, προσεύχοιο ἐν εἰρήνῃ τὴν κοίμησιν αὐτοῦ (sc. εἶναι), and especially in no. 358, where God is invoked with the words, "Now, o Lord, (grant) in your righteous judgement that Justus, an incomparable child, may sleep in peace" (νῦν, δέσποτα, ἐν εἰρήνῃ κοίμησιν αὐτοῦ, Ἰοῦστον νήπιον ἀσύγκριτον, ἐν δικαιώματί σου).[8] Even though the syntax of this phrase is not very clear, there can be little doubt that God is asked here to grant (some form of δίδωμι, e.g. δῴης, or a similar verb has to be supplied) a peaceful sleep to this little child.[9] But that still does not necessarily imply a blissful post-mortal existence of any sort. It may just mean that God is asked to prevent the tomb from being violated.

However, there are a number of epitaphs where the formula is

---

6 So e.g. Cavallin, *Life* 168-169.

7 LXX: ἔσται ἐν εἰρήνῃ ἡ ταφή αὐτοῦ (!).

8 This is one of the very rare instances where God is mentioned at all in our epitaphs; see also nos. 72, 671, 677. In view of the ancient Jewish tendency to avoid not only pronouncing God's Name but even using the word 'God', this is not as surprising as it might seem at first sight.

9 Fischer, *Eschatologie* 217-218. This interpretation is confirmed, it would seem to me, by the text of a probably Jewish curse tablet from Carthage, which contains the phrase, ὁρκίζω σε τὸν θεὸν τὸν τὴν κοίμησίν σοι δεδωρη- μένον καὶ ἀπολύσαντά σε ἀπὸ δεσμῶν τοῦ βίου (ed. A. Audollent, *De- fixionum Tabellae*, Paris: Fontemoing, 1904 [repr. Frankfurt: Minerva, 1967], no. 242, 29-31).

significantly expanded. We find in no. 55 ἐν εἰρήνη ἡ κοίμησις
αὐτοῦ μετὰ τῶν ὁσίων, in 526 *in pace dormitio eius cum iustis,*
in 632 צדיקים עם בשלום (*beshalom 'im ṣaddiqim,* 'in peace with the
righteous ones'),[10] and in 210 the curious formulation *dormitio tua
inter dicaeis* (= δικαίοις). The desire to sleep in peace among the
holy or righteous ones is certainly more than a wish to be as a dead
person in the same place as the patriarchs are. That it is the biblical
patriarchs that the words δίκαιοι/*iusti*/צדיקים (and ὅσιοι) refer to
can hardly be doubted. In literary sources, Abraham, Isaac, and
Jacob are represented as the just who receive the deceased in their
bosom and provide them with a celestial banquet.[11] If the epitaphs
refer to this notion, which seems indubitable, then indeed 'sleep' has
to be interpreted in a very 'non-sleepy' sense, as a term for a blissful
existence in paradise. Corroborative evidence may be found in
formulas such as *dormitio tua in bonis* (212, 228, 250), in which *in
bonis* can be taken to mean 'among the good ones', but it may also be
neuter, 'in good things', *i.e.* in happiness, in bliss. Again, no clear
picture arises of what this post-mortal existence among the
righteous patriarchs was thought to look like, but in view of the (not
explicitly mentioned) associations between being-with-the-patri-
archs and the heavenly banquet, a bodily component in that existence
can hardly be ruled out. Further support for the existence of a
resurrection belief among our epigraphical Jews is the occurrence
of the name Anastasius/-ia (211, 298, 364, 516, 576, 598[?], 732,
787, 1123, etc.). This name, which is never met with in pagan

---

[10] Cf. 981 (Chorazin) צדיקים עם חולק לה יהי (*yehi leh ḥoleq 'im tsaddiqim*).
Expressions of the desire to share the post-mortal company of the righteous ones
occur also without the prayer for peace: 78, 110, 118, 193, 281, 340, 1510.
[11] See 4 Macc. 13:17; *Test. Abr.* (rec. A) 20:14; Mt. 8:11; Lk. 16:22; *Agadat
Shir ha-Shirim* p. 20 ed. Schechter (see Frey, Introd. CXXXV); other rabbinic
references in Billerbeck, *Kommentar* IV 2, 1163-1165. Note also that in the
Targum to Ruth 2:12 it is said by Boaz to Ruth: "May you be saved from the
judgement of Gehinnom, so that your destiny will be with Sarah, Rebekkah, Ra-
chel and Leah", *i.e.,* the matriarchs. R. Meyer, art. κόλπος, *TWNT* III (1938)
825-826, remarks that the motif of lying in Abraham's bosom, which is known
from Jewish literary sources and the NT, does not occur in Jewish epitaphs but
does so frequently in Christian ones. For examples see Horsley, *New Documents* 3 (1983) 106-107.

sources (but was later taken over by Christians), is a clear testimony to a belief in the resurrection, at least among some Jews.

Beth She'arim

But there is more. In Beth She'arim there are a few inscriptions that indicate a belief in some form of afterlife. Very laconic is BS II 194, εὐτυχῶς τῇ ὑμῶν ἀναστάσει, 'good luck with your resurrection!'[12] In spite of its almost humorous brevity, it is most unambiguous in its expression of belief in the resurrection. In much more lofty but also more ambiguous language the author of the poem in BS II 183 expresses herself as follows:

> "This tomb contains the dwindling remains of noble Karteria, preserving forever her illustrious memory. Zenobia brought her here for burial, fulfilling thus her mother's request. Your offspring whom you bore from your gentle womb, your pious daughter, erected this monument for you, most blessed of women, for she always does actions praiseworthy in the eyes of mortals, so that even after the end of life's term you may both enjoy again new and indestructible riches".[13]

That both mother and daughter will enjoy 'new and indestructible riches', evidently as a reward for 'praiseworthy actions', cannot be interpreted otherwise than as meaning that their good works on earth earn them a blissful life in the hereafter.[14] Whether this postmortal existence is thought of in bodily or in spiritual terms is not stated. The same vagueness is met with in BS II 184, κύριε, μνήσθη-τι τῆς δούλης σου, κύριε, μνήσθητι τοῦ δούλου σου. This is surely more than just a request to God to recall the deceased now and then. It has rightly been remarked that the word μνήσθητι could be interpreted in the light of the usage in Luke 23:42-43, where the repentant criminal on the cross beseeches Jesus, 'Remember (μνή-

---

[12] B. Lifshitz, Beiträge zur palästinischen Epigraphik, ZDPV 78 (1962) 74, says that this epitaph comprises in fact two exclamations: a) 'good luck'; and b) '(may you share in) the resurrection', in which the dative ἀναστάσει has its parallel in congratulatory expressions like πολλοῖς ἔτεσι in Attic inscriptions. For our purpose this does not make any difference.

[13] For the Greek text see Ch. 10, no. IX.

[14] Kosmala, Hebräer 422-425, notes that also in the NT πλοῦτος often refers to eschatological blessings (cf. the 'treasure in heaven' in Mt. 6:20).

σθητι) me when you come in your kingdom', to which Jesus an-swers, 'Today you will be with me in Paradise'. This passage makes perfectly clear what eschatological overtones the word μνήσθητι could have.[15] Exactly the same eschatological note is struck by the author of the recently published Wisdom treatise from the Cairo Genizah when he says about those who have turned away from God and are the slaves of their pleasures that "they will certainly be forgotten by the Lord" (VI 10;[16] to be forgotten is the equivalent of not being remembered; and the frequent דכיר לטב (d^ekhir l^etav), 'may he be remembered for good', in Aramaic inscriptions proba-bly has the same eschatological intention: may God remember him for the ultimate good in the hereafter[17]). There are several early Jewish texts that connect being remembered by God with the (escha-tological) idea of a Book of Life.[18] So there can be no doubt about the eschatological connotations of the notion of 'being remem-bered', but again we are given no clue as to the nature of life after death in this inscription, although it implies at least being with God.

BS II 130 states: "May your soul cling to immortal life";[19] here the words 'soul' and 'immortal life' strongly suggest that the dedi-cator believed *not* in a bodily resurrection but in the immortality of the soul. BS II 129 states: "... May anyone who dares to open (the grave) above us not have a portion in eternal life". This unique threat against tomb-violators implies that the one who set up this stone believed in a judgement and in eternal life, but the nature of this life remains unspecified. BS II 162, however, leaves the reader in no doubt: "Anyone who removes this woman, He who promised

---

15 Kosmala, *Hebräer* 418-421. That Kosmala takes these and other inscrip-tions from Beth She'arim to be of Essene origin, is untenable; they date from the third to fourth century.

16 K. Berger, *Weisheitsschrift* 260, 263.

17 No. 496 (Rome) says of the deceased woman: μνησθῇ, 'may she be remem-bered', *i.e.* by God in the eschaton.

18 The relevant evidence has been collected in W. C. van Unnik, The Back-ground and Significance of Acts X 4 and 35, in his *Sparsa Collecta* I, Leiden: Brill, 1973, 213-258.

19 Lifshitz (*ad loc.*) translates: "May your soul be bound (in the bundle) of eternal life"; he sees here a free rendering of 1 Sam. 25:29. The Greek, ἔσηται ἡ ψυχὴ ὑμῶν ἐχομένη ἀθανάτου βίου, does not seem to me to refer to that biblical text. The verb ἔχεσθαι with gen. means 'to cling to, to border on'.

to revive the dead will Himself judge him" (ὁ ἐπαγγειλάμενος ζῳοποιῆσαι τοὺς νεκροὺς αὐτὸς κρινεῖ). To 'revive' (ζῳοποιῆσαι) is as clear a reference to the resurrection as εὐτυχῶς τῇ ὑμῶν ἀναστάσει in BS II 194. The fact that we have a couple of unambiguous statements on resurrection of the body should, however, not seduce us to assume that the other references to life after death have to be interpreted in the same sense, for it is well-known that throughout the Hellenistic-Roman period a wide variety of notions concerning afterlife existed side by side in Judaism.[20]

That belief in a blissful afterlife was strong among the pious believers who had themselves buried in the holy soil of Beth She'a-rim, may probably be inferred also from the very frequent occurrence of the formula εὐμοίρει (lit. 'have a good share/portion') with which the deceased is bid farewell (also the adjective εὔμοιρος occurs). To be sure, the formula is not of Jewish origin; it is found often in pagan Hellenistic epitaphs, where it wishes the dead a happy hereafter.[21] In a Jewish context, the formula took on a new value.[22] In an early credal formula in the Mishna treatise *Sanhedrin* 10:1 we find: "All Israelites have a share in the world to come" (כל ישראל יש להם חלק לעולם הבא, *kol Yisra'el yesh lahem ḥeleq le'olam hab-ba'*). 'Share', *ḥeleq*, became a technical term for a happy afterlife (see no. 981, quoted above). The associations with *ḥeleq* (share) evoked by the (pagan) wish εὐμοίρει, in which the element μοίρα (share, portion) was well recognizable, might explain the popularity of that wish among Jews. The great frequency of εὐμοίρει in Beth She'arim[23] could be explained along these lines. If this thesis is correct, then we may regard all εὐμοίρει inscriptions of Beth She'a-rim as testimonies of belief in a life in the world to come, albeit of unspecified nature.

Another frequent formula of pagan origin in Beth She'arim –

---

[20] The works by Cavallin and Fischer (*inter alios*) have clearly demonstrated this point. Nagakubo's dissertation (see n. 1), however shaky its argumentation may sometimes be, also stresses this variety, especially in Beth She'arim.

[21] Robert, *BE* 1956 no. 182.

[22] Cf. Lieberman, *Greek in Jewish Palestine* 72-74, although my suggestion is somewhat different from his.

[23] BS II nos. 2, 3, 4, 5, 6, 7, 9, 13, 26, 27, 33, 47, 52, 56, 57, 69, 124, 129, 130, 171, 173, 187.

although also found in Jewish epitaphs elsewhere – is θάρσει, οὐδεὶς ἀθάνατος.[24] This expression, with its variants (often οὐδεὶς ἀθάνατος is omitted), has been explained in various ways ranging from 'banale, trostlose Wendung' to an expression of 'courage et confiance' with respect to eternal life.[25] It is very difficult to say what in each individual case may have been the associations this expression evoked. At first sight it may seem to be an expression of resignation: no one is immortal, death is common to all people, so try to be courageous in the face of the inevitable. It cannot be ruled out that such sentiments existed among Jews, who definitely did not all believe in immortality of the soul or resurrection of the body.[26] That belief in afterlife was not part and parcel of everybody's Judaism is clearly evidenced by the slightly cynical epitaph of a Roman Jew called Leo (no. 32*), which runs 'Friends, I await you here!' (amici, ego vos hic exspecto) and by two Jerusalem inscriptions one of which calls upon the survivors to enjoy themselves by eating and drinking (εὐφραίνεσθε οἱ ζῶντες, τὸ δὲ λοιπὸν [...] πεῖν ὄμα φαγεῖν),[27] whereas the other simply says, 'No one can go up [from the grave]'.[28] There is, however, some evidence that θάρσει, οὐδεὶς ἀθάνατος was also used by Jews who did believe in a blessed afterlife. In one of the Beth She'arim catacombs we find two inscriptions by one and the same hand, BS II 193 and 194.[29] The first runs θαρσεῖτε, πατέρες ὅσιοι, οὐδεὶς ἀθάνατος, and the second is

---

24 See CIJ nos. 314, 335, 401, 450, 539, 544, 782, 1209; BS II 22, 29, 39, 40, 41, 43, 59, 84, 87, 89, 102, 193. The list is not exhaustive. Instead of θάρσει one also finds εὐψύχει.

25 Delling, Speranda futura 39, takes it to be an expression of gloomy resignation without any hope of afterlife; the more optimistic interpretation is advocated by Simon, Θάρσει 65.

26 Think, for example, of the Sadducees; see J. le Moyne, Les Sadducéens, Paris: Gabalda, 1972, 167-175.

27 Published by Lifshitz in RB 73 (1966) 248-257, where he also refers to the many pagan parallels, e.g. in Peek, GV 716, 721, 905, 1112, 1218, 1301, 1333, 1925, 1978, 1987, 2029, etc. Cf. Lk. 12:19 and 1 Cor. 15:32. It should be added that the frequently occurring nihilistic pagan formula non fui, fui, non sum, non curo (often abbreviated as n.f.f.n.s.n.c.) has no Jewish parallels.

28 F. M. Cross, A Note on a Burial Inscription from Mount Scopus, IEJ 33 (1983) 245-246.

29 Lifshitz, ZDPV 78· (1962) 73-74; Nagakubo, Investigation 222-238.

the already quoted εὐτυχῶς τῇ ὑμῶν ἀναστάσει. This seems to indicate that the use of the θάρσει formula could well go together with a belief in the resurrection. Moreover, θαρρεῖν/θαρσεῖν is already used by Plato in the context of a discussion of afterlife and immortality (*Phaedo* 63e, 78b, 87e, 95c), and in the famous Codex Bezae (D) at Lk. 23:43 (quoted above) Jesus' answer to the repentant criminal significantly is: "*Keep courage* (θάρσει), today you will be with me in Paradise". Also 4 Macc. 17:4 leaves us in no doubt that θάρρει is used there in a context of expectation of a glorious after-life. So there certainly was a use of θαρρεῖν/θαρσεῖν in connection with afterlife with very positive overtones. The exhortation θάρσει, οὐδεὶς ἀθάνατος, and certainly θάρσει alone (which is frequent in Beth She'arim) was probably meant "to encourage the deceased to meet the dangers involved in the passage to the next world coura-geously".[30] The use of θαρρεῖν in several passages in the New Testament demonstrates that it is employed most often in situations of real and dangerous tests which can be passed or afflictions which can be borne.[31] The passage to the next world is beset with dangers, according to ancient conceptions, because inimical powers or de-mons will try to bar the deceased from entry into a new and blessed existence.[32] Not only pagan Greeks and Romans but also Jews and Christians knew the notion of a dangerous heavenly ascent of the dead. Θάρσει wishes the dead the courage they need to be able to bring this journey to a successful conclusion. So there is good reason to connect this phrase with a positive belief in a blessed afterlife, even though that need not be the case in every instance.[33]

---

[30] Lifshitz, *Beth She'arim* II 224.

[31] See the fine study of the word by C. Spicq, *Notes de lexicographie néo-testamentaire* I, Fribourg: Éditions universitaires – Göttingen: Vandenhoeck, 1978, 367-371.

[32] See e.g. F. Cumont, *After Life in Roman Paganism*, New Haven: Yale University Press, 1922, 148-169, and his *Recherches sur le symbolisme funéraire des Romains*, Paris: Geuthner, 1942 (repr. New York: Arno, 1975), 104-176.

[33] Firmicus Maternus, *De errore profanarum religionum* 22, 1, quotes the famous exclamation in the (Osiris?) mysteries, θαρρεῖτε μύσται τοῦ θεοῦ σεσωσμένου, ἔσται γὰρ ἡμῖν ἐκ πόνων σωτηρία. This formula indicates that in mystery religions as well θαρρεῖν was used in connection with 'salvation from pains', probably referring to afterlife; see R. Joly, L'exhortation au

Leontopolis (Tell el-Yehudieh)

From Leontopolis in Egypt we have some testimonies to belief in some unspecified form of afterlife. In 1510 the deceased woman states that her soul has gone to the holy ones (ψυχὴ δ' εἰς ὁσίους ἔπετε); in 1513 the dead says, ἐλέους ἐλπίδα ἀγαθὴν προσδέχο- μαι, 'I await a good hope of mercy', *i.e.*, I have good and hopeful expectations of God's mercy, which clearly demonstrates an opti- mistic look at the final judgement; and in 1536 it is said of the dead woman that her spirit is [destined] for eternal life (*nishmᵉtah lᵉhayye 'olam*). Again, there is no clear picture of the nature of this 'eternal life' or this dwelling of the soul with the holy ones, although the reference seems to be to the immortality of the soul rather than to a bodily post-mortal existence. Ἐλπὶς ἀγαθὴ ἐλέους refers to judge- ment without any hint as to the nature of life after judgement.

Elsewhere in Egypt we find in no. 1534 the Hebrew formula *naphsho biṣror hahayyim*, 'his soul (be) in the bundle of the living', which is in fact a non-literal quotation of 1 Sam. 25:29 (it is also found in this form in no. 661 from Spain). Although in the story of 1 Sam. 25 the words "the soul of my master will be bound in the bundle of the living by the Lord" do not have any eschatological meaning, in post-biblical Judaism this biblical verse was interpreted in an eschatological sense.[34] The 'bundle of the living' is then the transcendent place where the souls of the righteous find their rest with God. In medieval and modern times the words "may his/her soul be bound in the bundle of the living" became the most fre- quently used funerary formula on Jewish tombstones, very often in abbreviation (תנצבה).

Astral immortality

Another form of afterlife (other, that is, than bodily resurrection) is astral immortality, an immensely popular notion in educated pagan

---

courage (ΘΑΡΡΕΙΝ) dans les mystères, *REG* 68 (1955) 164-170.

[34] See O. Eissfeldt, *Der Beutel der Lebendigen*, Berlin: Akademie Verlag, 1960, 28-40; also Berger, *Weisheitsschrift* 179-180. Both refer to the frequent occurrence of the formula in epitaphs from the Crimea (ed. D. Chwolson, 1865) which are, however, of dubious antiquity.

circles in the Hellenistic and Roman world.[35] There is literary evidence that this notion had penetrated into Jewish circles as well.[36] Among the inscriptions it is only no. 788 (from Corycos in Cilicia) which clearly expresses this idea: "Don't be despondent, for nobody is immortal except One, He who ordered this to happen (and) who has placed us in the sphere of the planets (ὃς εἰς σφαῖραν πλανη‐ τῶν κατέστησεν ἡμᾶς)". This indicates that the author of this epitaph believed that, probably right after death, the deceased is granted by God to dwell among the planets or stars and to experience eternal bliss by being a heavenly body. It should be borne in mind that heavenly bodies were regarded as living beings, most often as angels.[37] The deceased thus becomes an angelic or heavenly being that lives the eternal life of a heavenly body. 'Body' should be put between quotation marks here, for this notion certainly does not imply belief in a bodily resurrection.[38]

Judgement

As was to be expected, there are only very few references to the eschatological judgement or to condemnation or hell in our inscriptions. We only have some allusions to the post-mortal fate of tomb-violators in the curse-inscriptions. It is not certain whether the threats with 'the sickle of the curse' should be interpreted in an eschatological sense (see above on nos. 768 and 769), but there are

---

[35] F. Cumont, *Lux Perpetua*, Paris: Geuthner, 1949, 142-188; idem, *After Life* 91-109, esp. 96-106; M. P. Nilsson, *Geschichte der griechischen Religion* II, München: Beck, 2nd ed. 1961, 278-279.

[36] See e.g. Dan. 12:3; 1 Enoch 104:2; 4 Macc. 17:5; 4 Ezra 7:97 (cf. 125); 2 Baruch 51:10.

[37] See my *Sentences of Pseudo-Phocylides* 186-188; Cavallin, *Life After Death* 203-205; W. Bousset – H. Gressmann, *Die Religion des Judentums im späthellenistischen Zeitalter*, Tübingen: Mohr, 1926, 322-323; Hengel, *Judentum und Hellenismus* 358-360.

[38] Fischer, *Eschatologie* 229, thinks it is not impossible to also interpret in this astral sense no. 306 containing only the name ΑΣΤΗΡ, which usually is a rendering of Esther but might here indicate the notion that the deceased has become a star (ἀστήρ). This remains doubtful. Goodenough, *Jewish Symbols* II 9: "the name of the woman, if such it was, lent itself so well to such a pun".

other, more unambiguous epitaphs. The Roman no. 526 ends a threat with *ultor erit Deus Israel in saeculum*, 'the God of Israel will be a revenger until eternity'; and in no. 652 we find, in a similar context, κατὰ τοῦ μελλητικοῦ μηδεὶς ἀνοίξῃ. There is no doubt that τὸ μελλητικόν (= τὸ μέλλον) refers to the coming judgement (cf. the expression 'the coming wrath' in 1 Thess. 1:10), so that the correct translation probably is: 'let no one open (this tomb) in view of the coming (judgement)', the implication being, of course, that trespassing would entail eternal condemnation. The clearest expression of the expectation of a final judgement is found in some epitaphs from Asia Minor in which the tomb-violator is warded off with the warning ἕξει κρίσιν πρὸς τὸν θεόν ('he will undergo judgement before God') or ἕξει πρὸς τὴν κρίσιν ('he will have to face judgement').[39] The latter expression reminds us of the Eumeneian formula – found particularly in Christian texts but also in Jewish and pagan ones – ἔσται αὐτῷ πρὸς τὸν θεόν in the 'sickle of the curse' inscription, no. 769 (see above in Ch. 3). And finally we have from Beth She'arim the already quoted BS II 162, 'anyone who removes this woman, He who promised to revive the dead will Himself judge (κρινεῖ) him'. So warnings against tomb-violation are the only context in which belief in a judgement or post-mortal punishment is brought to expression.[40]

This does not imply that it is only the authors of these epitaphs who believe in a final judgement. Nor can it be said that the writers of the vast majority of epitaphs in which there is no (clear) sign of belief in afterlife were non-believers in this respect. In spite of the fact that belief in the resurrection of the body was a much more central tenet in Christianity from the beginning than in Judaism, in ancient Christian epitaphs, too, this belief finds expression only seldomly.[41] But it is reasonable to think that, although this tenet was

---

[39] Published by Robert, *Hellenica* XI-XII (1960) 381-413 ('Épitaphes juives d'Éphèse et de Nicomédie'), esp. 387 and 392 (= *TAM* IV [1], ed. F. K. Doerner, Vienna: Oest. Akad. der Wiss., 1978, 375, 376).

[40] Whether the threats against tomb-violators in Beth She'arim (BS III 1 and 2) that they will die 'with a bad end' (*beᵉsoph bish*) should be seen as refernces to the final judgement is uncertain.

[41] See I. Kajanto, The Hereafter in Ancient Christian Epigraphy and Poetry, *Arctos* 12 (1978) 27-53.

rarely explicitly mentioned, it was tacitly assumed. Of course we cannot extrapolate this to the situation in the Jewish inscriptions. But it can make us aware of the fact that the *argumentum e silentio* is dangerous here, too. Many more Jews may have believed in some form of afterlife than seems to be apparent from the epitaphs, but in fact we have no way of knowing. But it cannot be stated on the basis of our evidence that belief in the bodily resurrection, as expressed so clearly in the inscription of Regina (476),[42] was an undisputed dogma among Jews in the imperial period. We find a wide variety of attitudes, ranging from nihilism, via the conviction that the immortal soul will dwell among the righteous ones or the stars, to belief in the resurrection of the body.

---

[42] The Regina inscription says that she *meruit sedem venerandi ruris habere* ('she deserved to possess an abode in the hallowed land', line 8). There has been much dispute over whether the *venerandum rus* is Paradise or the Land of Israel. Leon, *Jews* 249, takes it to mean Paradise; so does Frey *ad loc*. But Cavallin, *Life* 168, Fischer, *Eschatologie* 235, and Delling, Speranda futura 42, take it to mean that by her resurrection Regina will have a place in the holy land, referring to [Strack-] Billerbeck, *Kommentar zum NT* III 828-9 and IV 1198. There Billerbeck quotes some later rabbinic testimonies to the effect that the resurrection will take place in the land of Israel. This does not imply that our inscription should be interpreted as sharing this notion, but it has to be conceded that *venerandum rus* is an odd expression for Paradise. The matter must remain open.

IX. Ancient Jewish Epitaphs and the New Testament

Although the majority of Jewish epitaphs dates from the post-NT period, they can nevertheless shed light on some NT problems, and sometimes the NT may shed light on problems in the epitaphs. Many inscriptions from the second through fifth century contain data that are relevant for early Christian studies exactly as the early rabbinic literature (which also dates from the second through fifth century) is relevant for NT studies, however slippery a field the comparison between these two corpora may be. It may be said that in NT scholarship the study of Jewish inscriptions has by and large been neglected. In modern exegetical literature one finds little awareness of the existence, let alone the relevance, of a sizeable corpus of data concerning the life and the ideas of Jews in Palestine and the diaspora in the Hellenistic and Roman periods.[1] In this chapter a very provisional and cursory attempt will be made to show, for some topics, what this relevance might be.

Distribution

To begin with the provenance of the inscriptions, the very wide geographical spread of the epitaphs demonstrates with much greater force than the literary sources that Jews lived all over the ancient world, from Morocco and Spain in the West to Babylonia in the East. We did already know from ancient authors that by the turn of the era the majority of the Jews no longer lived in Roman Palestine,

---

[1] G. H. R. Horsley's five volumes, *New Documents Illustrating Early Christianity* (1981-1989) are a favourable exception, as are also Martin Hengel's works.

just as in our days still more Jews live outside the land of Israel than within it. Several ancient writers, both Jews and pagans, give testimony to the fact that in the first century there was no part of the world left that did not have its share of Jewish population.[2] It is the inscriptions, however, that enable us to check these statements and establish their veracity. And this check reveals that there is little exaggeration in our sources. Unequal though the geographical spread of the inscriptions may be (with its over-representation of material from Rome and Egypt), it turns out to be true that almost every country of the ancient world had Jews among its inhabitants. James, the brother of Jesus, states at the apostles' council in Jerusalem that "Moses has been preached *in every city* from of old and is read in the synagogues on every sabbath" (Acts 15:21). We can say that the inscriptions support the overall correctness of this only slightly exaggerated statement. And the same can be said of the list of countries enumerated by Peter in his famous Pentecostal speech (Acts 2:9-11).[3]

The fact that such a great number of epitaphs have been found at Rome indicates that there must have been a sizeable Jewish community there – the estimates vary from 10.000 to 60.000 for the first century.[4] The threat posed to this community by early Christian preaching must have been considerable, and the ensuing tension is reflected both in the final chapter of the book of Acts and in the Epistle to the Romans itself. The fact that Christianity often made its first converts among diaspora Jews and Godfearers (at least according to Acts) should not make us believe that Christianity gained an easy and quick victory over Judaism. On the contrary, both inscriptions and literary sources clearly indicate that Jewish communities

---

[2] See e.g. Philo, *Legatio ad Gaium* 214; Josephus, *Bellum* II 398, VII 43; *Oracula Sibyllina* III 271; Strabo, *ap.* Josephus, *Antiquitates* XIV 115; Seneca *ap.* Augustine, *De Civitate Dei* VI 11. All these passages are quoted in full in my essay Jews and Christians in Aphrodisias, in my *Essays on the Jewish World* 166.

[3] See C. J. Hemer, *The Book of Acts in the Setting of Hellenistic History*, Tübingen: Mohr, 1989, 222-223. For an extensive survey of diaspora settlements (based for a very great part on epigraphical evidence) see M. Stern, The Jewish Diaspora, in Safrai – Stern (edd.), *The Jewish People in the First Century* I 117-183, and also Schürer, *History* III 1-86.

[4] See our chapter on age at death for more details.

continued to flourish till the end of antiquity. In some areas, especially parts of Asia Minor, Judaism was so strong and influential that the church had little chance to get a foothold or had great problems in not losing its own members to the synagogue.[5] Jewish inscriptions testify to the high and influential positions Jews had reached in the pagan society of Asia Minor. It was only after Constantine, when the church was backed by the state and imperial measures began to curtail the Jews' rights and so to paralyze its propaganda,[6] that Christianity was able to gain the upper hand in its struggle with Judaism over the pagan world.

Greek and Hellenism

We have noted the heavy preponderance of Greek in our inscriptions: some 70% are in this language, circa 12% are in Latin, and circa 18% are in Hebrew and Aramaic. If we leave Palestine out of account, the percentage of Greek inscriptions rises to at least 85%, those in Latin are around 10%, and less than 5% are Semitic (or bilingual). If we take only Palestine, even then the Greek epitaphs are good for some two thirds of the whole. That is to say that in the diaspora knowledge of Hebrew (and Aramaic) was well-nigh lost, and that in Palestine for a great part of the population the daily language was Greek. This is an impressive testimony to the enormous influence Hellenistic culture had exercised upon Jews both in their mother country and in the diaspora. As Martin Hengel has recently demonstrated, this was already the situation at the turn of our era in the heartland of the Jewish people, Judaea.[7] About 40% of the inscriptions from Jerusalem dating to the early Imperial period are in Greek, and the inhabitants were expected to be able to read them. And in a first century CE tomb of a Jewish family in Jericho, called the Goliath family because of their extraordinary stature,

---

[5] See my Jews and Christians in Aphrodisias, *Essays* 166-181.
[6] See for this esp. A. Linder, *The Jews in Roman Imperial Legislation*, Detroit: Wayne State University Press – Jerusalem: The Israel Academy of Sciences and Humanities, 1987.
[7] M. Hengel, *The 'Hellenization' of Judaea in the First Century after Christ*, London: SCM Press, 1990.

more than half of the epitaphs are in Greek.[8] Already in the pre-Christian centuries Jewish Palestinian authors wrote works in Greek.[9] In later centuries, even the rabbis and their families in Beth She'arim phrased many of their epitaphs in Greek. Also the tomb-inscriptions of the vast majority of other pious Jews who wanted to be buried in the same soil as the great Rabbi Judah ha-Nasi, are in Greek.[10] This is not to say that Hebrew and Aramaic ever died out completely as languages for the Jews; that has never been the case. Especially the eastern diaspora always continued to speak in a Semitic language. But in the first five centuries of our era, which is exactly the period in which the rabbinic literature in Hebrew and Aramaic came into existence, a majority of the Jews in Palestine and the western diaspora spoke Greek.

This is important for the history of early Christianity. The translation of the early Jesus tradition from Aramaic into Greek took place early, within one generation after the life of Jesus,[11] and this Greek translation turned out to be of so much greater use that nobody bothered to preserve the Aramaic original. With the Greek version, everyone could be reached, the Jews too. Early Christianity started as a Jewish sect in an Aramaic-speaking milieu. But even before it emancipated itself from its Jewish matrix so as to become an independent religious movement, it dropped Aramaic and adopted Greek as its linguistic vehicle.[12] It was not only Paul who wrote his letters in Greek; others did so too, even perhaps Jesus' brother, James, who remained so much more within the Jewish milieu than his 'feindlicher Bruder', Paul.[13] The fact that all the documents we have from the first seven decades of the history of an originally Jewish movement are in Greek can be fully explained against the

---

[8] See R. Hachlili, The Goliath Family in Jericho: Funerary Inscriptions from a First Century A.D. Jewish Monumental Tomb, *BASOR* 235 (1979) 31-70.

[9] Hengel, *Judentum* 191-195; *Hellenization* 22-23.

[10] B. Lifshitz, L'hellénisation des Juifs de Palestine, *RB* 72 (1965) 520-538.

[11] The sayings source Q was probably composed in the fourties in Greek; for the most recent discussion see J. S. Kloppenborg, *The Formation of Q*, Philadelphia: Fortress, 1987.

[12] G. Mussies, Greek as the Vehicle of Early Christianity, *NTS* 29 (1983) 356-369.

[13] See J. N. Sevenster, *Do You Know Greek? How Much Greek Could the First Jewish Christians Have Known?*, Leiden: Brill, 1968, 15 *et al.*

background just sketched. And even though it can hardly be doubted that Jesus' own teaching was in Aramaic, it is equally beyond doubt that he understood and probably was even able to speak Greek. The synoptic stories about Jesus' meetings with the centurion of Capernaum, with Pilate, and with the Syro-Phoenician woman, presuppose that "he was capable of carrying on a conversation in Greek".[14] It is the inscriptions that show us that it was not only the highly educated upper classes but also the common men who made use of this language for various purposes.[15]

With knowledge of the Greek language gradually and inevitably came knowledge of Greek literature and Greek literary conventions, and also knowledge of Greek ideas, philosophical notions, popular beliefs, etc.[16] Apart from the many literary proofs in Jewish-Hellenistic writings, the epitaphs demonstrate that Jews had adopted all sorts of Hellenistic conventions and ideas. We find there Greek hexametric and iambic poems; we find Greek literary motifs like death as marriage to the god of the netherworld; we find Greek mythological figures such as Hades, Charon, Lethe, and others; we find all kinds of concepts and formulas of pagan origin (although probably filled with a new sense in many [but how many?] cases, e.g. Moira); we find the Greek notion of astral immortality; we find Greek epigraphical conventions like the metrical epitaph or the dialogue of the deceased with the passer-by; etc., etc.[17] And all this not only in the diaspora but also in Palestine, and not only in later centuries but from the Hellenistic period onwards.

This is not to say that Judaism gave up its own identity and diluted its central conceptions so as to be able to accommodate to Hellenistic thought. In 'mainstream' Judaism, Hellenistic culture was adopted

---

[14] Hengel, *Hellenization* 17.

[15] E. M. Meyers – J. F. Strange, *Archaeology, the Rabbis and Early Christianity*, London: SCM, 1981, 90: "It appears that sometime during the first century B.C.E. Aramaic and Greek changed places as Greek spread into the countryside and as knowledge of Aramaic declined among the educated and among urban dwellers".

[16] Hengel, *Judentum* and *Hellenization*, both *passim*.

[17] Examples of all this can easily be found in the previous chapters. Apart from the literary and epigraphical sources, Jewish art in the Roman period is also heavily influenced by Greek examples and motifs. There are pagan mythological motifs even in the funerary art of the Beth She'arim catacombs.

only in so far as it did not undermine the essential religious tenets of the Jewish faith. Nonetheless, the evolution of religious concepts in the post-biblical period was not just a matter of inner-Jewish developments, it was a process in which Hellenistic civilization played a part that was much greater than that of a thin cultural veneer. This is not the place to give a survey of Greek influences on post-biblical Judaism, but I do want to emphasize (with scholars like Hengel) that early Christianity came into existence within a very much hellenized Judaism. Therefore, it may come as no surprise that in the New Testament we find many Hellenistic literary forms, notions and ideas.[18] These most often were not innovations in early Christianity (in the sense that the Christians began to expose themselves to pagan influences right from the start), but they were part of the Jewish heritage.[19] (Needless to say that this point of view also has its relevance for the study of the relations between Hellenism and early Christianity.) The profound cultural changes that took place in Judaism all over the ancient world during the centuries around the turn of the era are of the greatest importance for the investigation of the New Testament and early Christian religion and literature. Again, Jewish epitaphs show us that these changes did not remain limited to members of upper class circles only.

Values

In our study of the *epitheta ornantia* we saw a relatively high number of adjectives beginning with φιλ-, both in pagan and Jewish epitaphs. The New Testament uses 12 compound adjectives with φιλ-, but there is little overlap with the typically Jewish epithets here. Φιλόνομος, φιλέντολος, φιλοσυνάγωγος, φιλόλαος are all

---

[18] K. Berger, Hellenistische Gattungen und Neues Testament, *ANRW* II 23, 2 (1984) 1031-1432. H. O. Guenther, Greek: Home of Primitive Christianity, *Toronto Journal of Theology* 5 (1989) 247-279.

[19] In other publications I have emphasized that my research in the *Corpus Hellenisticum Novi Testamenti* project in Utrecht was not to deny the *Jewish* matrix of the NT but rather to gauge the extent to which this matrix had been transformed by Greek culture. See P. W. van der Horst – G. Mussies, *Studies on the Hellenistic Background of the New Testament*, Utrecht: Universiteitspers, 1990.

lacking in the New Testament. This is a distinctive difference because it indicates that in the New Testament the centrality of the Torah has been replaced by other values and that the synagogue no longer functions as the religious community (λαός) in which the Christians are at home. This becomes even clearer when one looks at the abundance of titles of religious officials in the synagogue community, which through their sheer preponderance over indications of secular professions demonstrate how great the role of the synagogue was in Jewish life in the Roman Empire. This also applied to the church but in spite of all its Jewish heritage (reflected, for example, in a term like 'elders'), the nomenclature completely changed as the religions grew further apart.

The centrality of the Torah and the ideal of study of the Torah is also apparent, as we have seen, in terms like νομομαθής, νομοδι-δάσκαλος, σοφῶν μαθητής, μαθητὴς εὐδίδακτος, *discipulina bona, colens legem, eruditus*. If we interpret these terms correctly, we see again an important difference with early Christianity. Not only was the Torah no longer central for the early Christians, but also and especially the growing emphasis on the importance of study and knowledge in rabbinic Judaism (even to the point of it becoming equivalent to worship)[20] was not taken over in Christianity. The tone was set for early Christians by Jesus' word in Mt. 11:25: "I praise you, Father, Lord of heaven and earth, because you have hidden these things from the wise and the learned and revealed them to little children". It was, however, the emphasis on study as worship that has become such an important factor in shaping the identity of the Jewish people up to the present day and which has enabled it to maintain that identity in spite of all the persecutions, especially by Christians. This element kept them together and gave direction to the life of the communities, and in antiquity it made these communities often look like a group of philosophers, which evoked the admiration of pagan Hellenistic outsiders.[21]

The aforesaid does not imply, however, that the inscriptions present us with a picture of communities with a rabbinic orientation

[20] B. T. Viviano, *Study as Worship*, Leiden: Brill, 1978.
[21] On Jews as philosophers see the quotations from Theophrastus, Megasthenes and Clearchus in Stern, *GLAJJ* nos. 4, 14 and 15; also M. Hengel, Der alte und der neue "Schürer", *JSS* 35 (1990) 58-59.

or under the sway of the rabbis. On the contrary, the fact that almost no rabbis are mentioned in the inscriptions outside of Palestine and that, moreover, the word *rabbi* in an epitaph mostly seems to mean 'important person' rather than 'Rabbi',[22] gives us the decided impression that the diaspora communities developed largely outside rabbinic control till the very end of antiquity. Apart from the very few epitaphs – only five or six out of 1600! – which seem to emphasize the importance of Torah study (which of course was not an exclusively rabbinic activity), nothing whatsoever in our inscriptions suggests any distinctive rabbinic ideas. There are strong reasons to doubt whether Rabbi Judah's Mishnah ever exercised binding authority in the first centuries after its compilation. We should bear in mind that the Mishnah was never translated from Hebrew into any other language in antiquity, unlike the Bible, so that presumably very few outside the academies could read and study it.[23] It would seem that until the end of the Talmudic age there was a greater variety of traditionally pious but non-rabbinic Judaism than many would have us believe. It is important for students of early Christianity to realize that the great variety of Judaisms in the New Testament period, which we have only too slowly become aware of, did not disappear after 70, and not even after 200. Some groups may have disappeared in this period, but that does not mean that all Jews turned 'rabbinic' after 70 or 200. The Hellenistic Synagogal prayers in the *Apostolic Constitutions*, the *Epistle of Anna to Seneca*, the *Testament of Solomon*, the *Sefer Yeṣirah*, the *Sefer ha-Razim*, the anti-rabbinic strands in the *Hekhalot* literature, and perhaps also the recently published Wisdom treatise from the Cairo Genizah, are all of them witnesses to the remarkable variety of colour and shape in post-70 and even post-200 Judaism.[24] The epitaphs are another important witness to this rich pluralism in Judaism of late antiquity.

---

22 See Cohen's 'Epigraphical Rabbis'.

23 See Goodenough, *Jewish Symbols* XII (1965) 51. For opposition to Rabbi Judah's Mishnah even in rabbinic circles see D. Weiss Halivni, The Reception Accorded to Rabbi Judah's Mishnah, in E. P. Sanders e.a. (edd.), *Jewish and Christian Self-Definition* II, London: SCM, 1981, 204-212.

24 For a later period one may point to the Karaite writings. For the controversy over the date of the Genizah Wisdom text see the publications by K. Berger and

Proselytes and Godfearers

Some dozens of epitaphs mention proselytes and Godfearers, both being groups of non-Jews, the first of which have fully converted to the Jewish faith, the second being those pagans who felt more or less attracted to aspects of the Jewish religion and also kept some of the commandments by choice but who did not take the final step to conversion. Both types are known from the New Testament. It has already been remarked that recent denials of the existence of a distinct class of Godfearers have been refuted decisively by the discovery of a new Jewish inscription in which three clearly distinct categories are mentioned: Jews, proselytes, Godfearers.[25] The very great number of Godfearers in this inscription (no less than 54) has made us aware of the fact that the 12 $\theta\epsilon o\sigma\epsilon\beta\epsilon\hat{\iota}\varsigma$ recorded in the epitaphs that are known to date are probably only a negligibly tiny fraction of the total number of these pagan sympathizers. If the Aphrodisias inscription, which now looks exceptional, actually reflected an average situation, then we would have to think in terms of many tens of thousands of pagan Judaizers in the Roman Empire throughout the first centuries of our era. And the literary sources we referred to earlier indeed give us reason to think in such terms. If, in addition, we may trust the reports in the book of Acts that many early Christian converts came from these circles, one realizes that this group of sympathizing Godfearers had an ambiguous value as viewed from the standpoint of Christian missionaries. On the one hand, pagans who were already inclined to reject polytheism and felt attracted to the high ethical standards of Judaism but were repelled by some ritual precepts, notably circumcision and kashrut, were a favourable target group for early Christian preachers. On the other hand, precisely the fact that Judaism was able to win over so many pagans to a position on the fringe of the synagogue, made Christians only too aware of the fact that Judaism was a vital religious force and made itself felt as an attractive alternative for pagan religiosity. The competition with this rival would be very hard; and this created great tensions between church and synagogue. Judaism and Christia-

---

H. P. Rüger mentioned in the bibliography.
[25] Reynolds – Tannenbaum, *Jews and Godfearers at Aphrodisias* (1987); also Hengel, *JSS* 35 (1990) 43.

nity were waging a war over the pagan soul; and Christianity, which in the eyes of the ancients was something of an upstart, had a very hard struggle to oust Judaism, with its much older and therefore more venerable traditions,[26] from the strong position it had built up in the ancient world.

This strong position made itself felt especially with women, as we have already noticed. Our epitaphs give the impression that women felt attracted to Judaism more than men and became not only sympathizers or Godfearers but even proselytes. At least 50% of our epigraphical proselytes and ca. 80% of the Godfearers are women. This is a high percentage in view of the under-representation of women in our material. That women were more readily inclined to convert to Judaism than men because it entailed less incisive consequences for them, is nowhere stated explicitly in ancient sources, but it stands to reason. The New Testament confirms this picture. When the book of Acts describes the conflict between Paul and the Jews in Pisidian Antioch, it is said: "The Jews incited the Godfearing women of high standing and the leading men of the city" (13:50). It is obvious that among the Godfearers of that city women – and women of high standing at that – were in the majority, probably even to such an extent that the author does not even mention male Godfearers. Later, in Philippi, Paul looks for a synagogue on the sabbath and speaks to the women who were gathered there. One of these women, who becomes a Christian, is explicitly said to have been a Godfearer (Acts 16:13-14), with the possible implication that the other women were too. Again, men are not even mentioned here. Still later, in Thessalonica, Paul succeeds in winning over to his message a considerable number of Godfearing women from upper class circles. Out of sheer jealousy, Luke says, the Jews created a great uproar in the city and attacked the house of Paul's host (Acts 17:4-6). This recurring picture in Acts is confirmed by the data in our epitaphs. The New Testament does not mention female proselytes to Judaism, as the inscriptions do, but it is obvious that becoming a Godfearer was often a first step in the direction of full

---

26 On the motif 'older is better' see now P. Pilhofer, *Presbyteron kreitton. Der Altersbeweis der jüdischen und christlichen Apologeten und seine Vorgeschichte*, Tübingen: Mohr, 1990.

conversion, the final step that was taken more easily by women than by men.

Belief in afterlife

The data our epitaphs yield concerning age at death – with an average of 28 years – are of interest for New Testament scholars mainly in that they make us aware of the short life expectancy in the Roman Empire. However intractable these data may be from a statistical point of view, they at least make clear that the average life-span was very much shorter than in our days (in First World countries at least). One wonders whether the fact that probably not even half of those born reached adulthood, would not create an immense longing for a happy afterlife, if only to make up for the loss of so many years in so many lives. There is no way to find an answer to that question, one can only speculate about it.

From literary sources we can deduce with certainty that the period under consideration (300 BCE – 700 CE) was exactly the period in which Judaism slowly but steadily developed various forms of belief in afterlife. Resurrection of the body was only one of the options, but as the most typically Jewish alternative this option gained the upperhand towards the end of our period. In the New Testament period and a considerable time thereafter, however, this doctrinal monopoly had not yet been achieved. Several notions competed with one another, as is testified not only by the written sources but also by our epitaphs, where we find a variety of notions ranging from nihilism to the eternal dwelling of the immortal soul among the heavenly beings or the resurrection of the body. Even though resurrection was part and parcel of the Christian faith from the beginning – in contrast to Judaism – we can find also in the New Testament some uncertainties and discrepancies about the exact nature of life after the resurrection. When in 1 Cor. 15 Paul states that in the resurrection we will have a 'spiritual body' (σῶμα πνευματικόν, v. 44), because "flesh and blood cannot inherit God's kingdom, neither does the perishable inherit imperishability", that is certainly a different conception from that of Luke, who has Jesus say after his resurrection that he wants something to eat and that they should not be troubled: "Look at my hands and my feet. It is me myself! Touch me and see, a spirit (πνεῦμα) does not have flesh and bones, as you see I have" (Lk. 24:39). Paul seems to adhere to a more spiritualizing view of the resurrection 'body' than Luke does.[27] Nevertheless, the variety of points of view concerning this matter in the New Testament is not as great by far as the wide range of notions we meet in our epitaphs.[28]

It is interesting to see that among the various notions of afterlife in the inscriptions there is also attested, albeit only in one epitaph, the belief in astral immortality. When no. 788 states that God "has placed us into the sphere of the planets", that can hardly mean anything else than that the deceased are believed to have become heavenly bodies, a very widespread belief in late antiquity. This notion, which has ancient roots in Greek religious philosophy, seems to have penetrated into some Jewish circles, as is testified by texts like Daniel 12:3: "Those who are wise shall shine like the brightness of the firmament; and those who turn many to righteousness (shall shine) like the stars for ever and ever"; *1 Enoch* 104:2: "Now you shall shine like the lights of heaven and you shall be seen"; 4 Macc. 17:5: "Not so majestic stands the moon in heaven as you stand, lighting the way to piety for your seven starlike sons, honoured by God and firmly set with them in heaven". All three texts make these statements in the context of afterlife (cf. also Wisdom 3:7).[29] Matthew has Jesus say: "Then the righteous will shine like the sun (ὡς ὁ ἥλιος) in the kingdom of their Father" (13:43). Of course, this may just mean that the righteous will share in God's glory which will make them shine or radiate, but the explicit mention of the sun as a point of comparison and the fact that the Greek word ὡς can

---

[27] Cf. C. J. de Vogel, Reflexions on Phil. I 23-24, *NT* 19 (1977) 262-274, who also stresses this point, albeit from a different angle.

[28] For a general orientation I refer the reader to C. F. Evans, *Resurrection and the New Testament*, London: SCM Press, 1970; Ph. Perkins, *Resurrection. New Testament Witness and Contemporary Reflection*, London: Chapman, 1985.

[29] See further e.g. *4 Ezra* 7:97 "it is shown to them how their face is to shine like the sun and how they are to be made like the light of the stars, being incorruptible from then on" (cf. 125); *2 Baruch* 51:10 "they will be like the angels and be equal to the stars". For context and background see Cavallin, *Life after Death* 203-204.

mean 'having the nature of'[30] may perhaps justify the consideration that some echo of a belief in astral immortality is heard here. But we cannot be sure about this, the more so since it is such an isolated case in the New Testament.[31]

There is another saying of Jesus, this time reported by Luke, which brings us perhaps closer to the theme in one of the epitaphs. In the parable of the rich fool, Jesus has the man say to himself, after he has stored all his riches: "Take it easy, eat, drink, enjoy yourself" (ἀναπαύου, φάγε, πίε, εὐφραίνου, Lk. 12:19b), and after having said this the man dies. Significantly enough, this kind of call is found in numerous pagan epitaphs, in which the deceased appeals to the survivors to enjoy life in all respects (*carpe diem*), especially with respect to food, drink, and sex.[32] Now we need not assume that Jesus is polemicizing here against a pagan attitude towards life, for we have evidence that the same sentiments were also entertained in sceptical Jewish circles, which felt they received support from the book of Qoheleth (see e.g. Qoh. 5:17, 8:15, 9:7). In a Jerusalem inscription, which is certainly Jewish, we find the following exhortation by the deceased:[33] "Enjoy yourselves, you who are still alive, and further [...] eat and drink together" (εὐφραίνεσθε, οἱ ζῶντες, τὸ δὲ λοιπὸν [...] πεῖν ὄμα φαγεῖν).[34] This epitaph, to be sure, is the only Jewish one we know with this motif, but it clearly demonstrates that in some Jewish circles (Sadducees?) this view of life was accepted, and it is not for nothing that in the parable Jesus has God react to it by 'you fool' (12:20; cf. also 1 Cor. 15:32!).

---

[30] See D. Daube, On Acts 23: Sadducees and Angels, *JBL* 109 (1990) 494.

[31] Cf. Apoc. 1:20 where the 7 stars are identified with the 7 angels, and the explicit relationship between the resurrected and the stars in 1 Cor.15:39-43. For a balanced discussion see now M. E. Stone, *Fourth Ezra,* Minneapolis: Fortres Press, 1990, 244-245 (*ad.* 7:97).

[32] Lattimore, *Themes* 260-263. The theme occurs also in literature.

[33] Published by B. Lifshitz, Notes d'épigraphie palestinienne, *RB* 73 (1966) 248-257.

[34] Reading and translation are not absolutely certain in some minor details, see Lifshitz *ad loc.* Robert, *BE* 1977 no. 342, draws attention to the fact that in this type of inscriptions εὐφραίνεσθαι always means 'banqueter'.

Persons known from the New Testament

Let us finally ask the question whether there are any epitaphs extant of persons known to us from the New Testament. This question is not easy to answer as we will see. We can leave aside the ossuary inscription of "Jesus, the son of Joseph" because both names are too common for us to be surprised by this collocation.[35] In 1962 Avigad published a number of first century CE ossuary inscriptions from the Kidron Valley (just outside Jerusalem). One of the inscriptions mentions that the bones in the ossuary are those of 'Alexander, the son of Simon'. This is written on the front and on the back in Greek, but on the lid of the ossuary is written in Greek 'of Alexander', and in Hebrew letters the words 'Alexandros QRNYT'.[36] The final word can be read as *qornit*, which is the name of an aromatic plant; then it would be a nickname for Alexander. The editor, however, tentatively suggests another possibility, namely to read these letters as meaning 'the Cyrenian'. There are some linguistic difficulties which mean that this solution is not beyond any doubt, but the fact that other persons in these ossuaries also probably come from Cyrene,[37] strengthens the suggestion. If it could be made more certain, we would have the epitaph of a Jew from Cyrene, named Alexander, with a father called Simon. In the passion narrative of Mark, we read that the Roman soldiers compelled a passer-by, Simon of Cyrene, the father of Alexander, to carry Jesus' cross (15:21). Of course, this may be a case of sheer coincidence, for one may argue that the names Alexander and Simon are too common to establish such a connection with Mark's story. That is certainly true, but on the other hand this is the only instance we have of the combination 'Alexander the son of Simon' and, if the possibility that they were from Cyrene could be made a certainty, there is at least a good chance that we have here the ossuary of the son of the man who

---

[35] See P. Figueras, *Decorated Jewish Ossuaries*, Leiden: Brill, 1983, 13 with n. 89. Curious is also the Roman inscription 459 for *Maria vere benedicta*, which is certainly Jewish but sounds very Christian.
[36] N. Avigad, A Depository of Inscribed Ossuaries in the Kidron Valley, *IEJ* 12 (1962) 9-12.
[37] Sevenster, *Dou You Know Greek?* 146-147.

carried Jesus' cross.[38] But it may be clear that there are here many uncertainties.

Another recently published inscription can be connected to Acts 4:6. There we read that after the arrest of Peter and John in the temple of Jerusalem, there was a meeting of the rulers and elders of the people, and present as well were Annas the high priest, and Caiaphas, and John (Johannes), and Alexander, and all who were of the high-priestly family. An ossuary recently found in the neighbourhood of Jerusalem mentions in Aramaic that it contains the bones of ''Yehohanah, daughter of Yehohanan, son of Theophilus the high priest'.[39] The title 'high priest' here belongs not to Yehohanan but to Theophilus who we know was appointed to this office in 37 CE (Josephus, *Ant.* 18:123-124). His father was Annas (Ḥanan, Ananus in Josephus), who is mentioned several times in the New Testament. Annas, father-in-law of Caiaphas, was involved in the trial of Jesus (John 18: 13, 24) and in the arrest of Peter and John in Acts 4. Four of Theophilus' brothers served as high priests between 16 and 62 CE, one of which was Ananus who had Jesus' brother James killed in 62, which cost him his high-priesthood (Josephus, *Antiquitates* 20:200-201).[40] In Acts 4:6 we also meet a certain Johannes who belonged to the high-priestly family, a man about whom we know nothing, but who may quite well be identical to Yehohanan, the father of the buried woman, whose name appears on her ossuary. All in all, what we have here is the epitaph of the great-granddaughter of Annas, who was also the great-niece of Caiaphas and probably the daughter of the unknown John in Acts 4:6. So this case is much more certain than the one of Alexander, son of Simon, but here we do not actually have the tomb-inscription of a person known from the New Testament. The harvest is not rich, it should be conceded, but the future may bring some more surprises.[41]

---

38 See also Hengel, *Hellenization* 67 n. 39.
39 D. Barag – D. Flusser, The Ossuary of Yehohanah granddaughter of Theophilus the High Priest, *IEJ* 36 (1986) 39-44.
40 See e.g. G. Theissen, *Lokalkolorit und Zeitgeschichte in den Evangelien*, Fribourg: Universitätsverlag – Göttingen: Vandenhoeck & Ruprecht, 1989, 184-185.
41 For a general survey of NT names occurring in Acts which are also found in Jewish inscriptions see Hemer, *The Book of Acts* 221-239.

Although not an inscription of a person mentioned in the New Testament, it is worthwhile to draw attention to the epitaph on one of the ossuaries of the already mentioned Goliath family in Jericho.[42] It runs, "The ossuary of Theodotus, freedman of Queen Agrippina". We know from Josephus and other sources that in the course of the two centuries around the turn of the era many Jews were taken captive by the Romans and sold into slavery. Many of them came into the service of the emperors themselves. If they were manumitted and became freedmen (*liberti[ni]*), which often happened (Philo, *Legatio* 155), they sometimes formed their own groups. Theodotus was freed by Queen Agrippina, who was the wife of the emperor Claudius and the mother of Nero. After being set free, Theodotus returned to his family in Israel. Now in Acts 6:9 we read that some of those who belonged to the so-called synagogue of the freedmen (τινες τῶν ἐκ τῆς συναγωγῆς τῆς λεγομένης τῶν Λιβερτίνων) and to other synagogues went into dispute with Stephen. We may infer from the way Luke formulates the phrase that freedmen were organized in their own synagogue in Jerusalem, which even retained the original Latin term for these ex-slaves, *libertini*.[43] Our Theodotus may have been a member of this or a similar synagogue, but again we are moving in the realm of speculation.

Conclusion

There is much more that could be said about our topic. Especially New Testament lexicography can profit from a close scrutiny of the vocabulary of these Jewish epitaphs. Since Moulton and Milligan,[44] no systematic attempt has been made to collect all the relevant lexicographical evidence from the thousands of inscriptions (and papyri) published in the last 60 years. Even though Frey's Corpus has been used for the compilation of the later editions of Bauer's Lexi-

---

[42] R. Hachlili, *BASOR* 235 (1979) 33 and 46.
[43] Schürer, *History* II 428 n. 8, and G. Schneider, *Die Apostelgeschichte* I, Freiburg: Herder, 1980, 435 n. 19.
[44] J. H. Moulton – G. Milligan, *The Vocabulary of the Greek Testament Illustrated from the Papyri and Other Non-Literary Sources*, London: Hodder and Stoughton, 1930.

con,[45] much work still remains to be done. Fortunately, an international team of scholars has taken up this challenge under the leadership of the Australian scholars Greg Horsley and John Lee.[46] Naturally the Jewish inscriptions will play a not unimportant role in this project. Two illustrative examples may suffice here. One is the inscription from Beth She'arim which asks the Lord to remember the deceased (BS II 184); its relation to and relevance for the use of μνήσθητι in Lk. 23:42-43 has already been dealt with in the previous chapter. We further note that Paul's conviction that "woman is the glory (δόξα) of man" (1 Cor. 11:7) is also expressed by the Roman Jew Sophronius who inscribes his wife's tombstone with the words ἡ δόξα Σωφρονίου Λουκίλλα εὐλογημένη, 'the glory of Sophronius (was) the blessed Lucilla' (135). Many more examples could be adduced. But the author hopes that the material discussed in this chapter, however briefly, has made clear that Jewish epitaphs deserve to be no longer neglected by New Testament scholars.

---

[45] See now esp. W. Bauer – K. & B. Aland, *Wörterbuch zum Neuen Testament*, Berlin – New York: W. de Gruyter, 6th ed. 1988.

[46] See C. J. Hemer, Towards a New Moulton-Milligan, *NT* 24 (1982) 97-123; G. H. R. Horsley, *New Documents* 5 (1989) 1-2.

X. Selected Epitaphs

In this final chapter I will present a small sample of ancient Jewish epitaphs in their original languages with a translation and very brief explanatory notes. The texts will here be printed in the orthography in which they are written on the tombstones (or ossuaries), that is, without any correction in spelling or grammar. Accents, breathings, subscript iotas, word-divisions, and interpunction will, however, be added by me (so ἐνθάδε κεῖται is actually written on the stone as ΕΝΘΑΔΕΚΕΙΤΑΙ, and ἐν εἰρήνῃ ἡ κοίμησις αὐτοῦ is written as ΕΝΕΙΡΗΝΗΗΚΟΙΜΗΣΙΣΑΥΤΟΥ). Existing translations will be used where possible, but often adapted or corrected. In order to enable the reader to discern what is preserved text and what is reconstruction by epigraphists, I will first give a list of the current diacritical signs which are nowadays used in classical epigraphy. It is called the Leiden system and comprises the following signs:

(ααα) = resolution of an abbreviation
{ααα} = cancelled by the editor
[ααα] = lacuna in the inscription
[[ααα]] = deletion in the original
<ααα> = omission in the original
ạạạ = uncertain letters
... = illegible letters

I. CIJ 123 (Rome, imperial period)

θάρσι, Ἰουλία Ἐμιλ-
2   μ' ία ἐτῶν
καλῶς ἔζησας μετὰ
4   τοῦ ἀνδρός σου. εὐ-
χαριστῶ τῇ προνοίᾳ
6   καὶ τῇ ψυχῇ σου.

*Keep courage, Julia Emilia, aged 40 years. You lived a good life
with your husband. I am grateful for your thoughtfulness and your
personality.*

For unclear reasons the numeral μ' (=40) is placed at the beginning
of line 2 instead of at the end. Θάρσι = θάρσει (for the meaning see
Ch. 8). The expression of gratitude for the wife's *pronoia* and *psyche* is unparalleled in the rest of our corpus.

II. CIJ 358 (Rome, imperial period):

     Θεόδοτος τροφεὺς τέκνῳ γλυκυτ[ά]τ[ῳ].
2   Εἴτε σε, Ἰοῦστε, τέκνον, ἐδυνάμην σα-
     ρῷ χρυσέῳ θεῖναι θεψάμενος. Νῦν, δέσ-
4   ποτα, ἐν εἰρήνῃ κόμησιν αὐτοῦ, Ἰοῦστον,
     νήπιον ἀσύκριτον, ἐν δικαίωματί σου.
6   [Ἐ]νθάδε κεῖμε Ἰοῦστος ἐτῶν δ' μηνῶν η', γλυ-
     κὺς τῷ τροφέων.

*Theodotus, the foster father, to his most sweet child.
Would that I, who reared you, Justus, my child, were able to place
you in a golden coffin. Now, Oh Lord, (grant) in your righteous
judgement a sleep in peace to Justus, an incomparable child.*

    *Here I lie, Justus, 4 years (and) 8 months, who was sweet to my
foster father.*

Note that, after the dedication, the text is addressed first to Justus,
then to God, and is followed by words which the deceased child himself is supposed to have spoken. Line 2: Εἴτε stands for εἴθε and
σαρῷ for σορῷ. Line 3: θεψάμενος is an error for θρεψάμενος,
not θαψάμενος; a form of τρέφω is more fitting to a situation with
a τροφεύς and a θρεπτός. Line 4: κόμησιν is one of the many
variant spellings of κοίμησιν. The construction of lines 4-5 is unclear; the vocative δέσποτα indicates that it is a prayer to God, so
probably some such form as an optative or imperative of δίδωμι is
to be suppleted, which has κοίμησιν as its object. (On prayers beginning with (καὶ) νῦν see my article Hellenistic Parallels to Acts
3-4, in P. W. van der Horst – G. Mussies, *Studies on the Hellenistic
Background to the New Testament,* Utrecht: Universiteit, 1990,

150.) For the possible implications of this prayer see the chapter on afterlife. Instead of the accusative Ἰοῦστον one expects a dative. Line 5: ἀσύκριτον = ἀσύγκριτον, *incomparabilis*. Δικαίωμα must here have the sense of 'righteous judgement' or 'justice'. Line 6: κεῖμε = κεῖμαι. Line 7: τῷ τροφέων should be read as τῷ τροφεῖ ὤν.

III. CIJ 418 (Rome, imperial period)

    Ἐνθάδε κεῖντε Φορτου‾
2   νᾶτος καὶ Εὐτρόπις νήπιοι φι-
    λοῦντες ἀλλήλους ὃς ἔζησεν
4   Φορτουνᾶτος ἔτη τρεῖς καὶ μῆν-
    ας τέσσαρες καὶ Εὐτρόπις ὃς ἔ-
6   ζησεν ἔτη τρια καὶ μῆνας ἐπ-
    τά. ἐν εἰρήνῃ ἡ κοίμησις
8   αὐτῶν.
    εἰς μίαν
10   ἀπέθαναν ἡμέραν.

Here lie Fortunatus and Eutropius, children who loved each other, Fortunatus, who lived 3 years and 4 months, and Eutropius, who lived 3 years and 7 months. In peace be their sleep. They died on the same day.

Possibly these two young and little friends were killed in the same accident. Noteworthy features are: the inverted order of the words ὃς ἔζησεν Φορτουνᾶτος in lines 3-4; the fact that line 4 reads ἔτη τρεῖς whereas line 6 has the correct ἔτη τρία; the accusative ending of τέσσαρες in line 5; εἰς ἡμέραν for ἐν ἡμέρᾳ in lines 9-10; and the ending -αν in ἀπέθαναν in line 10.

IV. CIJ 611 (Venosa, fifth to sixth cent. CE):

*   Hic ciscued Faustina,*
2   *filia Faustini pat(ris), annorum*
    quattuordecim mηnsurum
4   *quinque, que fuet unica paren-*
    turum, quei dixerunt trηnus

6   *duo apostuli et duo rebbites, et*
    satis grandem dolurem fecet pa-
8   *rentebus et lagremas cibitati.*
    que fuet pronepus Faustini,
10 *pat(ris), nepus Biti et Acelle,*
    qui fuerunt maiures cibitatis.
12 משכבה שׁל פוסטינה
    נוח נפשׁ שׁלום

The translation of the Latin lines is:
*Here lies Faustina, daughter of Faustinus her father, 14 years (and)
5 months old, who was the only (child) of her parents. Two apostles
and two rabbis spoke a lament over her, and she caused a very great
grief to her parents and tears to the city. She was the great-grand-
child of Faustinus, father, and grandchild of Vitus and Asella, first
citizens of the city.*
The translation of the Hebrew lines (which actually stand between
lines 8 and 9 of the Latin text on either side of a picture of a menorah) is:
Resting place (or: bed) of Faustina; may (her) soul rest, peace.

Line 1: *ciscued = quiescit.* Line 3: *mηnsurum,* as *trηnus* in 5, uses
the Greek η in the middle of a text in Latin script. Line 4: *que fuet =
quae fuit.* Line 4-5: *parenturum* instead of *parentum,* as if from *pa-
rentus.* Line 5: *quei = cui; trηnus =* θρήνους. Line 6: on *apostoli* (=
sheliḥim) and *rebbites* see our remarks in ch. 6. Line 7-8: *dolurem
fecet parentebus = dolorem fecit parentibus.* Line 8: *lagremas =
lacrimas; cibitati = civitati.* Line 9: *que fuet pronepus = quae fuit
pronepos.* Line 10: *pater* is here probably a (late) designation of a
high municipal official (it was often an abbreviation of *pater civitatis*), as is *maiures cibitatis = maiores civitatis* in 11; *nepus Biti et
Acelle = nepos Viti et Asellae.*

V. CIJ 701 (= *GV* 1217; Larissa, Thessaly, second to third cent. CE)

    Μαρία 'Ιούδα
2   Λεοντίσκου
    δὲ γυνή. τῷ
4   λαῷ χαί-

ρειν.

6   [χαί]ροις ἀνθρώπων πεπ[νυ-
μέν]ε ὅστις ὑπάρχει.

*Maria, daughter of Juda and wife of Leontiskos. Farewell to the
people. May you rejoice, wise man, whoever you are.*

This is the only (partly) poetic Jewish epitaph in Greek outside of
Egypt and Palestine where most of them were found (12 in Leontopolis, 2 in Beth She'arim; further only a Latin one in Rome). It is a
typically Larissan epitaph in that it is one of a unique series of
twelve (699-708c) from that city which all contain the greeting
formula τῷ λαῷ χαίρειν, in which *laos* has the meaning of 'local
Jewish community' (see our Ch. 3 and Robert, *Hell.* III 103-4, XI-
XII 260-2, *BE* 1976 no. 333). Frey translates "Maria Juda, wife of
Leontiskos", but Lifshitz has rightly pointed out that "the genitive
which follows the name of a woman usually indicates the name of
her father, the husband being indicated by the formula γυνὴ δὲ τοῦ
δεῖνος" (Proleg. to CIJ 80). The metrical closing line wishes the
passer-by good luck with a phrase which has a distinctly Homeric
flavour.

VI. CIJ 725 (Rheneia, second to first cent. BCE):

Ἐπικαλοῦμαι καὶ ἀξιῶ τὸν θεὸν τὸν
2   ὕψιστον, τὸν κύριον τῶν πνευμάτων
καὶ πάσης σαρκός, ἐπὶ τοὺς δόλῳ φονεύ-
4   σαντας ἢ φαρμακεύσαντας τὴν τα-
λαίπωρον ἄωρον Ἡράκλεαν ἐκχέαν-
6   τας αὐτῆς τὸ ἀναίτιον αἷμα ἀδί-
κως, ἵνα οὕτως γένηται τοῖς φονεύ-
8   σασιν αὐτὴν ἢ φαρμακεύσασιν καὶ
τοῖς τέκνοις αὐτῶν, κύριε ὁ πάντα ἐ-
10   φορῶν καὶ οἱ ἄγγελοι θεοῦ, ᾧ πάσα ψυχὴ ἐν τῇ σήμερον ἡμέρᾳ ταπεινοῦται
12   μεθ' ἱκετείας, ἵνα ἐγδικήσῃς τὸ αἷμα τὸ
ἀναίτιον ζητήσεις καὶ τὴν ταχίστην.

I call upon and pray to God the Most High, the Lord of the spirits and of all flesh, against those who have treacherously murdered or poisoned the poor Heraclea, who died untimely, and who have unjustly shed her innocent blood; may the same happen to them who have murdered or poisoned her and to their children, Lord, you who see everything, and you, angels of God, for Whom every soul humiliates itself on this day with supplications, (hoping) that you revenge her innocent blood and settle your account with them as soon as possible.

This very unusual epitaph with a prayer for vengeance is found on two tombstones from Rheneia, a little island near Delos. The text of the two stones, one in Bucharest and one in Athens, is identical except for the name of the girl. It is written almost without errors, which is exceptional. The best discussion still is the one by A. Deissmann, *Licht vom Osten*, Tübingen: Mohr, 4th ed. 1923, 351-362, who drew attention to the many echoes of LXX vocabulary and phraseology. Ἐπικαλεῖσθαι, ἀξιοῦν, θεὸς ὕψιστος, ἐκχεῖν αἷμα ἀναίτιον, πᾶσα ψυχή, ταπεινοῦσθαι, αἷμα ἐκδικεῖν, etc., are all of them common terms and expressions in the LXX. For κύριος τῶν πνευμάτων καὶ πάσης σαρκός see Num. 16:22 and 27:16; πνεύματα are here angels, as in Hebr. 1:14 (and cf. I Clem. 64). For καὶ τοῖς τέκνοις αὐτῶν see Ex. 20:5 and Num. 14:18. Κύριε ὁ πάντα ἐφορῶν is reminiscent of LXX Job 34:23, Esth. 5:1, 2 Macc. 7:35, 3 Macc. 2:21 (and again I Clem. 64). Most interesting is the mention of 'the day on which every soul humiliates itself with supplications'. It reminds one strongly of Lev. 23:29, πᾶσα ψυχή, ἥτις μὴ ταπεινωθήσεται ἐν αὐτῇ τῇ ἡμέρᾳ ταύτῃ, which is about fasting on the Day of Atonement. So what we most probably have here is a prayer for vengeance on Yom Kippur, which was evidently celebrated by the Jewish community on pre-Christian Delos. On the Jews (and Samaritans) of Delos see now the full documentation in Schürer, *History* III 70-71. (Unfortunately I have not been able to consult M. T. Couilloud, *Les monuments funéraires de Rhénée*, Paris 1974).

VII. CIJ 752 = TAM V 2, 1142 (Thyatira, early second cent. CE)

Φάβιος Ζώσιμος κατασκευάσας σορὸν ἔθετο ἐπὶ τόπου
καθαροῦ, ὄντος πρὸ
2   τῆς πόλεως πρὸς τῷ σαμβαθείῳ ἐν τῷ Χαλδαίου περι-
βόλῳ παρὰ τὴν δημοσίαν ὁδὸν ἑαυτῷ, ἐφ᾽ ᾧ τεθῇ, καὶ τῇ
γλυκυτάτῃ
4   αὐτοῦ γυναικὶ Αὐρηλίᾳ Ποντιανῇ, μηδενὸς ἔχοντος
ἑτέρου
ἐξουσίαν θεῖναί τινα εἰς τὴν σορὸν ταύτην. ὃς δ᾽ ἂν
τολμήσῃ ἢ ποιήσῃ
6   παρὰ ταῦτα, δώσει εἰς μὲν τὴν πόλιν τὴν Θυατειρηνῶν
ἀρ-
γυρίου δηνάρια χείλια πεντακόσια, εἰς δὲ τὸ ἱερώτατον
ταμεῖον δηνάρια
8   δισχείλια πεντακόσια, γεινόμενος ὑπεύθυνος ἔξωθεν τῷ
τῆς τυμβωρυχίας νόμῳ. ταύτης τῆς ἐπιγραφῆς ἐγράφη
ἁπλᾶ δύο
10 ὧν τὸ ἔτερον ἐτέθη εἰς τὸ ἀρχεῖον. ἐγένετο ἐν τῇ
λαμπροτάτῃ
Θυατειρηνῶν πόλει ἀνθυπάτῳ Κατιλλίῳ Σεβήρῳ μηνὸς
Αὐδναίου τρισ-
12 καιδεκάτῃ ὑπὸ Μηνόφιλον Ἰουλιανοῦ δημόσιον.

Fabius Zosimus, who had this sarcophagus made, put it on a holy place located before the city, near the sabbateion *in the Chaldaean quarter, alongside the public road, for himself, in order to be deposited there, and for his very sweet wife Aurelia Pontiane, but no one else has the right to deposit someone into this sarcophagus. But if someone dares to do so or acts contrary to these (rules), he will have to pay 1500 silver denaria to the city of the Thyatirans and to the most holy treasury 2500 silver denaria, and, moreover, he falls under the law of tomb violation. Two copies of this inscription have been written, one of which has been deposited in the archive. This has been done in the most illustrious city of the Thyatirans when Catillius Severus was consul, on the 13th of the month Audnaios, by Menophilus the public notary, the son of Julianus.*

This second century CE epitaph is an instance of the type discussed at the end of Chapter III (under the heading 'Curses'). It is a carefully written inscription of a probably well-to-do and well-educated Jew in Thyatira. Interesting is the term σαμβαθεῖον, which is probably identical to σαββατεῖον in the meaning of 'synagogue' (see Josephus, *Ant.* XVI 164), although the meaning of 'sanctuary of the Chaldaean Sibyl Sambethe' cannot be excluded; see Krauss, *Synagogale Altertümer* 25-27, and *contra* Krauss (*et al.*) P. Hermann in *Tituli Asiae Minoris* V 2, Vienna: Oesterreichische Akademie der Wissenschaften, 1989, 406 (lit!), who argues that the expression '*sambatheion* in the Chaldaean quarter' strongly suggests that the sanctuary of the Chaldaean Sibyl Sambethe is meant here. Be that as it may, "the community to which this 'Sabbath House' belonged cannot, however, have been a fully orthodox Jewish one for, according to the inscription, a burial place was situated in its vicinity" (Schürer, *History* III 19; but see *ibid.* II 440 n.63: 'perhaps a shrine of the Chaldaic Sibyl').

VIII. BS II 127 (Beth She'arim, first half of the third cent. CE)

Κεῖμαι Λεοντείδης νέκυς [Σ]αφο[ῦς υἱὸς 'Ιοῦ]στος
2 ὃς πάσης σοφίης δρεψάμενος κ[αρπὸ]ν
   λεῖψα φάος, δειλ[οὺς γ]ονέας ἀκα[χημέν]ους αἰε[ί],
4 αὐτοκασιγνήτους [τ]ε, οἴμοι, ἐ[ν οἷς Β]εσάρ[οις]
   καί γ' ἐλθ[ὼν ἐ]ἰς "Αδην 'Ιοῦστο[ς ... αὐτ]όθι κεῖμα[ι],
6 σὺν πόλλοισιν ἐοῖς, ἐπὶ ἤθελε Μοῖρα κραταίη.
   Θάρσει, 'Ιοῦστε, οὐδεὶς ἀθάνατος.

I, the son of Leontius, lie dead, Justus, the son of Sappho,
who, having plucked the fruit of all wisdom,
left the light, my poor parents in endless mourning,
and my brothers too, alas, in my Beth She'arim.
And having gone to Hades, I, Justus, lie here
with many of my own kindred, since mighty Fate so willed.
Be of good courage, Justus, no-one is immortal.

This is one of the two poetic inscriptions from Beth She'arim (for the other one see the next item). It is written in alternating dactylic hexameters and pentameters (disticha), as is usual in epigrams. It is a clear proof that Palestinian Jews were not only familiar with the Greek language but also with Greek literature, for the poem is full of Homeric phraseology and diction (although from a metrical point of view the poem is far from faultless). In line 1 Λεοντείδης is already an imitation of Homeric patronymics (cf. 'Ατρείδης for 'son of Atreus'). In line 2 the emphatical πάσης σοφίης seems to indicate that it was not only Jewish wisdom (*i.e.* Torah study) but also Greek learning that Justus had been involved in. In epigrams *sophia* is often used for 'excellence in one of the arts'. "The Jew Justus, a citizen of that town which was for many decades a center of Jewish scholarship, and apparently also the author of the inscription, used this expression in the sense accepted in his Hellenized environment" (Schwabe-Lifshitz *ad loc.,* p. 100; on p. 101 they rightly emphasize that "in this one hexameter [read: pentameter] concepts from two different worlds meet and are combined"). Sirach 6:19-20 also speaks of the 'fruits' of wisdom. Λιπεῖν φάος in line 3 is a Homeric expression (*Od.* XI 93), as is ἀκαχημένους (*Od.* IX 62, 105, 565, etc.; on the faulty prosody here see Schwabe-Lifshitz 102). Αὐτοκασίγνητος for 'brother' in line 4 is very common in Homer. Βέσαρα (line 4) for Beth She'arim occurs also in Josephus. 'To go to Hades' in line 5 in the sense of 'to die' is common both in Homer and in funerary epigraphy. In Jewish writings 'Hades' had lost its religious-mythological meaning (God of the underworld); hence the LXX translators used it to render *she'ol,* and it occurs 10 times in the New Testament. Μοῖρα κραταίη in line 6 (a typically Homeric verse ending) seems to be more difficult to reconcile with Jewish ideas. Moira was the Greek goddess of fate, but apparently Justus sees no problem in using the term, in the tradition of Greek epigrams, to say that it was his destiny to die young. In line 6 ἐπί = ἐπεί. On the θάρσει formula in line 7 see the discussion in the chapter on afterlife.

IX. BS II 183 (Beth She'arim, second half of the third cent. CE)

Καρτερίης τόδε σῆμα λίψανον φέρει φθιτὸν
2   ἄφθιτον ἠὲ λαμπρὰν σῷζον μνίαν γεναίης.
θήκατο δέ μιν ἐνθάδε Ζηνοβία
4   μητέρος ἑῆς τίουσα [ἐφ]ημοσύνας.

τοῦτό σοι, μακαρτάτη, καρπὸς σὸς ἐδίματο
6   ἣν τέκες ἐξ ἀγανῶν εὐσεβίην λαγόνων,
    ῥέζει γὰρ κλυτὰ ἔργα ἐνὶ φθιμένοις αἰεί,
8   ὄφρα δὴ ἄμφω καὶ μετὰ τέρμα βίου
    νέον ἠδ' ἀσκύλευτον αὖθις ἔχοιτε πλοῦτον.

This tomb contains the dwindling remains of Karteria,
preserving forever the illustrious memory of a noble woman.
Zenobia brought her here for burial,
fulfilling thus her mother's request.
For you, most blessed of women, your offspring,
whom you bore from your gentle womb, your pious daughter
– for she always does actions praiseworthy in the eyes of mortals –
built this monument, so that even after the end of life's term
both of you may enjoy again new and indestructible riches.

This epitaph is metrically more deficient than the previous one (there is an intermingling of dactyls and trochees and the length of syllables is often ignored), but the spelling is correct apart from thrice ι instead of ει. Lines 1-4 contain a statement about mother and daughter, lines 5-7 address the mother, lines 8-9 address both mother and daughter. Again there is much Homeric phraseology and diction (ἄφθιτος, ἠέ, τίω, ἑός, ῥέζω, κλυτὰ ἔργα, ὄφρα, etc.; for details see Schwabe-Lifshitz *ad loc.*, pp. 157-167). Zenobia is called 'pious' here because she always performs 'praiseworthy deeds', in this case especially the proper burial of her mother in the way this woman had asked her daughter to do it. The editors take the 'new and indestructible riches' to be the splendid tomb of Karteria, but it seems more natural to see this as a reference to the 'treasure in heaven' that 'neither moth nor rust' can destroy and no thieves can steal (Matt. 6:20), that is, eternal life.

X. CIJ 1300 (Jerusalem, Kidron Valley, early imperial period)

כוכה דנה עביד
לגרמי אבהתנה
ארך אמין תרתין
ולא למפתח עליהון

This tomb was made for the bones of our fathers. Its length is two cubits. And do not open it above them.

The Hebrew word *kokh*, here Aramaic *kokhah*, actually means cavity or cave, but it has developed the special meaning 'burial chamber' (in a rock). The indication of the length is unique. 'Do not open it' is the shortest formula against tomb violation to be found; see the final paragraph in chapter 3 on forms and formulas.

XI. CIJ 1490 (Leontopolis/Tell el-Yehudieh, 117 BCE)

    ὧδ' ὑπὸ τὸ σπιλάδος μέλαθρον, ξένε, κε[ῖται?...]
2   Δημᾶς, γῆρας ἀφεὶς μητρὸς ἐλεινοτά[της]
    καὶ τέκνα νήπι' ἐλεινὰ καὶ αὐστηρὰν πα[ράκοιτιν],
4   πολλῶν ἀνθρώπων βοιθὸς ἐὼν σοφ[ίᾳ?]
    κλαύσατε τὸν προλιπόντα τὸ σεμνότα[τον ...]
6   καὶ πόλιν, ἀνθρώπων δ' ἤθεα καὶ φιλίαν.
    Δ[η]μᾶς ᾧ[ς] (ἐτῶν) λη',
8   (ἔτους) νδ', 'Αθ[ὺ]ρ γ'.
    Καὶ σύ, 'Αλέξανδρε,
10 πασίφιλε καὶ ἀνέγ-
    κλ[η]τε, χρη[στ]έ, χ[αῖρε].

Here under the shelter of this stone, stranger, lies ...
Demas, deserting the old age of his very pitiable mother
and his pitiable little children and his mourning wife.
He helped many men by his skill.
Weep for the man who has left the most honourable ...
and his city, and the abodes and friendship of men.
Demas, about 38 years old, in the 54th year, the third of (the month)
Hathyr. You too, Alexander, friend of all and without reproach,
excellent one, farewell.

The best edition and most extensive discussion of this epitaph is by E. Bernand, *Inscriptions métriques de l'Égypte gréco-romaine* (1969) 89-92, on the basis of whose treatment I have slightly corrected D. M. Lewis' translation in CPJ III 153. It consists of 3 disticha in poetic vocabulary and a prose ending. The restorations at the end of lines 1-5 are far from being certain. In line 1 it is possible to read κεῖμαι instead of κεῖται. Αὐστηρός (3) usually means 'harsh, bitter, severe', but here a sense like 'bitterly grieving' seems required. The fact that βοηθός (4) was pronounced as βοιθός enabled the poet to use it in this pentameter. Several scholars assume that Demas had been a doctor, but 'helping many men by his skill' (?, or: understanding, if one reads συνέσει) may also refer to another profession. The πόλις of line 6 is Onias' temple-city, Leontopolis. Lines 9-11 are an inscription by another hand, added later.

XII. CIJ 1511 (Leontopolis, first cent. CE)

Εἰμεὶ ἐγὼ Ἰησοῦς, ὁ φὺς δὲ Φαμεῖς, παροδεῖτα,
2 (ἐξήκοντα ἐτῶν) ἦλθον δ' εἰς Ἀείδαν.
κλαύσατε δὴ ἄμα πάντας τὸν ἐξαπίνης μεταβάντα
4 εἰς μυχὸν αἰώνων, ἐν σκοτίᾳ διάγειν.
καὶ σὺ δέ, Δωσίθεε, κατάκλαέ με· σοὶ γὰρ ἀνάγκη
6 δάκρισι πικροτάτοις τύμβῳ ἐμῷ προχέειν·
τέκνον ἐμοὶ εἶ ς[ύ], ἐγὼ γὰρ ἀπῆλθον ἄτεκ<ν>ος:
8 κλαύσατε πάντες ὁμοῦ Ἰησὸν δυσμενέα.

I am Jesus, my father was Phameis, passer-by,
I went to Hades when I was sixty years old.
Weep all together for the one who has suddenly gone
to the secret place of eternity to dwell in darkness.
And you, Dositheus, weep for me, for it is your duty
to pour libations of bitterest tears on my tomb.
You are my child, for I have gone away childless.
All weep together for Jesus, the lifeless.

This poetic epitaph from the beginning of the common era has been well edited and discussed by Bernand, *Inscriptions métriques* 92-95. Line 1: Jesus was a very common name among Jews as a look in A. Schalit's *Namenwörterbuch zu Flavius Josephus* (Leiden: Brill, 1968) immediately shows. The father (φύς = φύσας) of Jesus has an Egyptian name (elsewhere spelled as Παμῆς). Line 2: the age of the deceased is indicated not by words but by the figure for 60. Line 3: πάντας stands for πάντες (see line 8), a vulgarism caused by the fact that the endings of the nominative and the accusative plural tended to merge in Koine Greek (as we have seen in the chapter on the languages). In other epitaphs from Leontopolis as well, the wayfarer is often called upon to weep (see the chapter on forms and genres). Line 4 makes clear that the expectation of post-mortal existence here scarcely differs from the Old Testament view of the gloomy *she'ol*. Lines 5-7 probably address Jesus' foster child, whom he, a childless man, regards as his own child. In line 7 the engraver wrote ἄτεκος. Δυσμενής in line 8 usually means 'hostile', which is impossible here. Possibly it means 'without μένος' in the sense of vital force, vitality; hence the translation 'lifeless' (Frey renders 'malheureux').

XIII. CPJ 1530A (Leontopolis, early imperial period?)

Πεντήκο<ν>τα τριῶν ἐτέων κύκλον ἤδ' ἀνύσαντα
2   αὐτὸς ὁ πανδαμάτωρ ἥρπασεν εἰς Ἀίδην.
    ὦ χθὼν ἀμμοφανής, οἷον δέμας ἀμφικαλύπτις
4   Ἀβράμου ψυχῆς τοῦ μακαριστοτάτου.
    οὐκ ἀγέραστος ἔφυ γὰρ ἀνὰ πτόλιν, ἀλλὰ καὶ ἀρχῇ
6   πανδήμῳ ἐθνικῇ ἐστέφετ' ἐν σοφίᾳ.
    δισσῶν γάρ τε τόπων πολιταρχῶν αὐτὸς ἐτειμῶ
8   τὴν διμερῆ δαπάνην ἐξανύσας χάρισιν.
    πάντα δέ σοι, ἐπέοιχ' ὅσα τοι, ψυχή, πρὶν ἔκευθες,
10 καὶ τέκνων ἀγαθῶν αὔξομεν γενεή.
    ἀλλὰ σύ, ὦ παροδεῖτα, ἰδὼν ἀγαθοῦ τάφον ἀνδρὸς
12 ὅν τε κατευφημῶν τοῖα φράσας ἄπιθι·
    "γαῖαν ἔχοις ἐλαφρὰν εἰς τὸν ἅπαντα χρόνον".

When he had already achieved the span of 53 years,
he who tames all himself snatched him off to Hades.
O sandy earth, what a body you hide
of the soul of the most blessed Abramos.
For he was not without honour in the city, but wore the wreath
of magistracy for the whole people in his wisdom.
For you were honoured with the leadership of two places,
generously performing the double duty.
And everything which was fitting to you, soul, before you hid yourself,
we, your family of good children, are increasing.
But you, passer-by, seeing the grave of a good man,

say these fair words to him and depart:
'May the earth be light on you for ever'.

The dates that have been suggested for this epitaph range from the first to the fourth century CE. See the edition and discussion by Bernand, *Inscriptions métriques* 95-100 (with the bibliography at 95-96). Lewis, CPJ III 162, adopts Louis Robert's suggestion that Abramos had been the head of two local Jewish communities. Notable is the absence of any expression of belief in life after death, even in the case of an honoured community leader. In line 1 πεν-τήκοτα is again an indication of the dropping of the *nun* in vulgar pronunciation. Line 2: πανδαμάτωρ is often used as an epithet of time (or the personified Χρόνος). Line 3: ἀμμοφανής is a hapax but well-chosen in view of the bright yellow sand in the Egyptian desert. Line 4: μακάρ and μακαριστότατος are frequently used of the dead. Lines 5-6: ἀρχῇ depends on ἐστέφετο, he was honoured (lit. crowned with a wreath) with a magistracy over the whole community (ἀρχὴ πάνδημος ἐθνική belonging together; ἔθνος is frequently used to designate a Jewish community, cf. ethnarch). Line 7: πολιταρχῶν means that Abraham was the head of the πολίτευμα of the Jews in Leontopolis. Lines 9-10 are very hard to translate; Bernand renders: "Tu as eu tous les honneurs convenables, chère âme, avant d'être enfoui, et, lignée de bons enfants, nous y ajoutons". Lewis' translation, 'everything which was fitting to your spirit', ignores the vocative character of ψυχή, which is often used as a term of affection for the deceased. Line 13: the adding of this verse with the well-known wish *sit tibi terra levis* causes the poem to end with two pentameters, which is very unusual.

XIV. CIJ 68 (Rome, second to third cent. CE)

> *Cresces Sinicerivs*
> 2 *Ivdevs proselitvs*
> *vixit ann XXXV*
> 4 *dormitione acce-*
> *pit. mat dvl flv*
> 6 *svo fec qvd ips mihi*
> *deb facere. VIII Kl*
> 8 *Ian*

Crescens Sinicerius, a Jew (and) proselyte, lived 35 years and fell asleep. His mother did for her sweet son what he himself should have done for me. December 25.

This Latin inscription by a mother for her son who had converted to Judaism, shows many peculiarities in spelling and abbreviation. In corrected form the text is as follows: *Crescens Sinicerius Iudaeus proselytus vixit annis XXXV, dormitionem accepit. Mater dulci filio suo fecit quod ipse mihi debuit facere. VIII Kalendas Ianuarias.* For the motif of protest against the fact that parents have to bury their child instead of the other way round, see Lattimore, *Themes* 187-191.

XV. CIJ 643a (Aquileia, Italy, sixth cent. CE?)

	Hic requiescit
2	*Petrus qui Papa-*
	rio fil(ius) Olympii Iu-
4	*daei solusque*
	ex gente sua
6	*ad XRI(sti) meruit*
	gratiam perveni-
8	*re et in [hanc] s(an)c(t)am*
	aulam digne sepul-
10	*tus est sub d(ie) pr(i)d(ie)*
	id(us) iul(ias) ind(ictione) quarta.

Here reposes Petrus, who (is called also) Papario, son of Olympius the Jew, and who alone of his family has deserved to attain the grace of Christ and was becomingly buried in this holy aula on the 14th day of July in the 4th indiction.

This epitaph is unique in that it is the only one of a Jew converted to Christianity. As Lifshitz rightly remarks (Prolegomenon to CIJ I 50), "The convert is proud that he alone of his family has embraced the Christian religion". The Latin *gens* could also be interpreted as 'nation', but that would seem to be less fitting here. For the *indictio* system see E. J. Bickerman, *Chronology of the Ancient World*, London: Thames & Hudson, 1980 (rev. ed.), 78-79.

XVI. SEG VIII 13 (Nazareth?, first cent. CE?)

Διάταγμα Καίσαρος·
2 Ἀρέσκει μοι τάφους τύνβους
τε, οἵτινες εἰς θρησκείαν προγόνων
4 ἐποίησαν ἢ τέκνων ἢ οἰκείων,
τούτους μένειν ἀμετακεινήτους
6 τὸν αἰῶνα. ἐὰν δέ τις ἐπιδίξῃ τι-
νὰ ἢ καταλελυκότα ἢ ἄλλῳ τινὶ
8 τρόπῳ τοὺς κεκηδευμένους
ἐξερριφφότα ἢ εἰς ἑτέρους
10 τόπους δώλῳ πονηρῷ μετατεθεικότα ἐπ' ἀδικίᾳ τῇ τῶν
12 κεκηδευμένων ἢ κατόχους ἢ λί-
θους μετατεθεικότα, κατὰ τοῦ
14 τοιούτου κριτήριον ἐγὼ κελεύω
γενέσθαι καθάπερ περὶ θεῶν
16 ἐς τὰς τῶν ἀνθρώπων θρησκ-
κίας. πολὺ γὰρ μᾶλλον δεήσει
18 τοὺς κεκηδευμένους τειμᾶν.
καθόλου μηδενὶ ἐξέστω μετα-
20 κεινῆσαι· εἰ δὲ μή, τοῦτον ἐγὼ κεφαλῆς κατάκριτον ὀνόματι
22 τυμβωρυχίας θέλω γενέσθαι.

*Ordinance of Caesar: It is my pleasure that graves and tombs –
whoever has made them as a pious service for ancestors or children
or members of their house – (5) that these remain unmolested in
perpetuity. But if any person lay information that another either has
destroyed them, or has in any other way cast out the bodies which
have been buried there, or (10) with malicious deception has trans-
ferred them to other places, to the dishonour of those buried there,
or has removed the headstones or other stones, in such a case I
command that a trial (15) be instituted, protecting the pious services
of mortals, just as if they were concerned with the gods. For beyond
all else it shall be obligatory to honour those who have been buried.
Let no one remove them for any reason. (20) If anyone does so,
however, it is my will that he shall suffer capital punishment on the
charge of tomb robbery.*

This is not a Jewish tomb inscription. Nevertheless I have included it here since it is of interest for the present study. The inscription, now in the Bibliothèque Nationale in Paris, was most probably found in Nazareth. It contains an imperial edict or rescript concerning tomb-violation. The date of the inscription is a much debated matter, sug-gestions ranging from the first century BCE to the second century CE. Franz Cumont, the first editor of the inscription (Un rescrit impérial sur la violation de sépulture, *Revue historique* 163 [1930] 241-266), suggested that, owing to the altercations between Jews and Christians over what had happened to the body of Jesus, and in order to prevent the occurrence of future disturbances arising from simi-lar circumstances, Pilate inquired of Tiberius what should be done; the inscription would then be an extract of the emperor's response, engraved on a slab of marble and set up at Nazareth where Jesus had lived and which had been hostile to him. This must be regarded as absolutely unproven. "The most that can be said with assurance is that the ordinance was promulgated after a particularly serious violation of sepulture. (...) If in fact the ordinance was published in Palestine some time prior to the death of Jesus, then (...) at the time of the resurrection there was in force a severe law against tampering with buried bodies, the consequences of infringing which the panic-stricken disciples are very unlikely to have braved" (B. M. Metzger, The Nazareth Inscription Once Again, in his *New Testament Stu-dies: Philological, Versional, and Patristic*, Leiden: Brill, 1980, 90-91). In any case, this inscription makes clear again that the sanctity of tombs was a matter of great concern, even on the imperial level, in the early Roman Empire. The translation presented above is by Metzger (p. 77 of the above-mentioned article, which has a very useful bibliography on pp. 91-92). From his philological notes I select only the following:

Lines 3-4: the syntax is odd, one expects ἐποιήθησαν. Line 10: δώλῳ (= δόλῳ) πονηρῷ represents the *dolo malo* of the Latin original. Lines 20-22: κεφαλῆς κατάκριτον and ὀνόματι τυμβωρυχίας are again Latinisms for *poena capitis* and *nomine sepulchri violati*.

SELECT BIBLIOGRAPHY

F. M. ABER, Epitaphs: testimonies to Jewish living, *Judaism* 6 (1957) 311-318

M. ALEXIOU – P. DRONKE, The Lament of Jephtha's Daughter: Themes, Traditions, Originality, *Studi Medievali* (third series) 12 (1971) 819-863

L. J. ARCHER, *Her Price is Beyond Rubies. The Jewish Woman in Graeco-Roman Palestine*, Sheffield: Sheffield Academic Press, 1990

N. AVIGAD, A Depository of Inscribed Ossuaries in the Kidron Valley, *IEJ* 12 (1962) 1-12

— Aramaic Inscriptions in the Tomb of Jason, *IEJ* 17 (1967) 101-111

— *Beth She'arim III: Catacombs 12-23*, Jerusalem: Massada,1976

B. BAGATTI – J.T. MILIK, *Gli scavi del "Dominus Flevit" (Monte Oliveto-Gerusalemme)* I: La necropoli del periodo romano, Jerusalem: Franciscan Publishing House, 1958

D. BARAG – D. FLUSSER, The Ossuary of Yehoḥanah Granddaughter of the High Priest Theophilus, *IEJ* 36 (1986) 39-44

S. W. BARON, *A Social and Religious History of the Jews* I, Philadelphia: Jewish Publication Society, 1952

F. BECKER, *Die heidnische Weiheformel D.M. auf altchristlichen Grabsteinen,* 1881 (non vidi)

P. BENOIT, L'inscription grecque du tombeau de Jason, *IEJ* 17 (1967) 112-113

F. BÉRARD – D. FEISSEL e.a., *Guide de l'épigraphiste. Bibliographie choisie des épigraphies antiques et médiévales*, Paris: Presses de l'Ecole Normale Supérieure, 1989 (2nd ed.)

K. BERGER, *Die Weisheitsschrift aus der Kairoer Geniza*, Tübingen: Francke, 1989

E. BERNAND, *Inscriptions métriques de l'Egypte gréco-romaine*, Paris: Les Belles Lettres, 1969

H. W. BEYER – H. LIETZMANN, *Die jüdische Katakombe der Villa Torlonia in Rom,* Berlin: W. de Grüyter, 1930

B. BLUMENKRANZ, Quelques notations démographiques sur les Juifs de Rome des premiers siècles, *Studia Patristica* IV 2 (ed. F. L. Cross), Berlin: Akademie Verlag, 1961, 341-7

— Premiers témoignages épigraphiques sur les Juifs en France, in S. Lieberman – A. Hayman (edd.), *Salo Wittmayer Baron Jubilee Volume* I, Jerusalem: American Academy for Jewish Research, 1974, 229-235

Y. le BOHEC, Inscriptions juives et judaïsantes de l'Afrique Romaine, *Antiquités Africaines* 17 (1981) 165-207

— Juifs et judaïsants dans l'Afrique romaine, *ibid.* 209-229

W. BOUSSET – H. GRESSMANN, *Die Religion des Judentums im späthellenistischen Zeitalter*, Tübingen: Mohr, 1926 (3rd ed.)

B. BOYAVAL, Remarques sur les indications d'âges dans l'épigraphie funéraire grecque d'Égypte, *ZPE* 21 (1976) 217-243

— Tableau général des indications d'âge de l'Égypte gréco-romaine, *Chronique d'Égypte* 52 (1977) 345-351

C. BRIXHE, *Essai sur le grec anatolien du début de notre ère*, Nancy: Presses universitaires de Nancy, 1984

B. J. BROOTEN, *Women Leaders in the Ancient Synagogue,* Chico: Scholars Press, 1982

F. E. BROWN, Violation of Sepulture in Palestine, *AJP* 52 (1931) 1-29

A. R. BURN, Hic breve vivitur. A Study of the Expectation of Life in the Roman Empire, *Past & Present* 4 (1953) 1-31

— Review of Nordberg, *Biometrical Notes* (1963), *JRS* 55 (1965) 253-7

W. M. CALDER, The Eumeneian Formula, in W. M. Calder – J. Keil (edd.), *Anatolian Studies Presented to W. H. Buckler*, Manchester: Manchester University Press, 1939, 15-26

A. CALDERINI, *Epigrafia*, Torino: Società Editrice Internazionale, 1974

H. C. C. CAVALLIN, *Life after Death. Paul's Argument for the Resurrection of the Dead in 1 Cor. 15. Part I: An Enquiry into the Jewish Background*, Lund: Gleerup, 1974

— Leben nach dem Tode im Spätjudentum und im frühen Christentum I: Spätjudentum, *ANRW* II 19, 1 (1979) 240-345

B. CHILTON, The Epitaph of Himerus from the Jewish Catacomb of the Via Appia, *JQR* 79 (1988/89) 93-100

J. E. CHURCH, *Beiträge zur Sprache der lateinischen Grabinschriften*, diss. München 1901 (non vidi)

D. CHWOLSON, *Achtzehn hebräische Grabschriften aus der Krim*, St. Petersburg: Akademie der Wissenschaften, 1865

M. CLAUSS, Probleme der Lebensalterstatistiken aufgrund römischer Grabinschriften, *Chiron* 3 (1973) 395-417

— Ausgewählte Bibliographie zur lateinischen Epigraphik der römischen Kaiserzeit (1.-3. Jh.), *ANRW* II 1 (1974) 796-855

S. J. D. COHEN, Epigraphical Rabbis, *JQR* 72 (1981/82) 1-17

B. F. COOK, *Greek Inscriptions*, London: British Museum, 1987

M.T. COUILLOUD, *Les monuments funéraires de Rhénée*, Paris 1974 (non vidi)

F. M. CROSS, A Note on a Burial Inscription from Mount Scopus, *IEJ* 33 (1983) 245-6

F. CUMONT, *Afterlife in Roman Paganism,* New York: Dover, 1922

— *Le symbolisme funéraire des Romains*, Paris: Geuthner, 1942

— *Lex Perpetua*, Paris: Geuthner, 1949

G. DAGRON – D. FEISSEL, *Inscriptions de Cilicie*, Paris: Boccard, 1987

G. DELLING, Speranda Futura, in his *Studien zum Neuen Testament und zum hellenistischen Judentum*, Göttingen: Vandenhoeck & Ruprecht, 1970, 39-44
— *Die Bewältigung der Diasporasituation durch das hellenistische Judentum*, Berlin: Evangelische Verlagsanstalt, 1987

K. DIETERICH, *Untersuchungen zur Geschichte der griechischen Sprache von der hellenistischen Zeit bis zum 10. Jhdt. n. Chr.*, Leipzig: Teubner, 1898 (repr. Hildesheim: Olms, 1970)

E. DINKLER, Schalom – Eirene – Pax: Jüdische Sepulkralinschriften und ihr Verhältnis zum frühen Christentum, *Riv. Arch. Crist.* 50 (1974) 121-144

O. EISSFELDT, Der Beutel der Lebendigen (= Berichte über die Verhandlungen der sächsischen Akademie der Wissenschaften zu Leipzig, Phil.-hist. Klasse 105,6), Berlin: Akademie Verlag, 1960

U. M. FASOLA, Le due catacombe ebraiche di Villa Torlonia, *Riv. Arch. Crist.* 52 (1976) 7-62

D. FEISSEL, Notes d'épigraphie chrétienne (V): Μυστήριον dans les épitaphes juives et chrétiennes, *BCH* 105 (1981) 483-488
— Notes d'épigraphie chrétienne (VII), *BCH* 108 (1984) 575-9
— La Bible dans les inscriptions grecques, in C. Mondésert (ed.), *Le monde grec ancien et la Bible,* Paris: Beauchesne, 1984, 223-231
— *Receuil des inscriptions chrétiennes de Macédoine du IIIe au VIe siècle* (BCH Suppl. 8), Paris: Boccard, 1983

L. H. FELDMAN, Proselytes and "Sympathizers" in the Light of the New Inscriptions from Aphrodisias, *REJ* 148 (1989) 265-305

J. FERRON, Inscriptions juives de Carthage, *Cahiers de Byrsa* 1 (1950) 175-206
— Épigraphie juive. Un hypogée juive, *Cahiers de Byrsa* 6 (1956) 99-117

A. FERRUA, Addenda et corrigenda al CIJ, *Epigraphica* 3 (1941) 30-46
— Iscrizioni paleocristiane in una raccolta privata, *Riv. Arch. Crist.* 59 (1983) 321-333

P. FIGUERAS, *Decorated Jewish Ossuaries*, Leiden: Brill, 1983

U. FISCHER, *Eschatologie und Jenseitserwartung im hellenistischen Diasporajudentum,* Berlin: W. de Gruyter, 1978

J. A. FITZMYER – D. J. HARRINGTON, *A Manual of Palestinian Aramaic Texts*, Rome: Pontifical Biblical Institute Press, 1978

J. B. FREY, *Corpus Inscriptionum Judaicarum*, 2 vols., Rome: Pontificio Istituto di Archeologia Cristiana, 1936-1952; reprint of vol. I with a Prolegomenon by B. Lifshitz, New York: Ktav, 1975
— La signification des termes ΜΟΝΑΝΔΡΟΣ et Univira, *Recherches de science religieuse* 20 (1930) 48-60
— La vie de l'au-dela dans les conceptions juives au temps de J.-C., *Biblica* 13 (1932) 129-168

B. FRIER, Roman Life Expectancy. The Pannonian Evidence, *Phoenix* 37 (1983) 328-344

G. FUKS, Where Have All the Freedmen Gone? On an Anomaly in the Jewish

Grave-Inscriptions from Rome, *JJS* 36 (1985) 25-32

K. GALLING, Die jüdischen Katakomben in Rom als ein Beitrag zur jüdischen Konfessionskunde, *Theologische Studien und Kritiken* 103 (1931) 352-360

E. GERNER, Tymborychia, *Zeitschrift der Savigny-Stiftung für Rechtsgeschichte (Rom. Abt.)* 61 (1941) 230-275

F. T. GIGNAC, *A Grammar of the Greek Papyri of the Roman and Byzantine Periods*, 2 vols., Milano: Cisalpino-Goliardica, 1975-1981

E. R. GOODENOUGH, *Jewish Symbols in the Greco-Roman Period,* 13 vols., New York: Pantheon, 1953-1968

A. A. GORDON, *Illustrated Introduction to Latin Epigraphy*, Berkeley – Los Angeles: University of California Press, 1983

C. H. GRANDGENT, *An Introduction to Vulgar Latin*, New York: Hafner, 1962

E. GRIESSMAIR, *Das Motiv der Mors Immatura in den griechischen metrischen Grabinschriften,* Innsbruck: Universitätsverlag, 1966

B. A. van GRONINGEN, *Greek Palaeography*, Leiden: Sijthoff, 1967

R. HACHLILI, The Goliath Family in Jericho: Funerary Inscriptions from a First-Century A.D. Jewish Monumental Tomb, *BASOR* 235 (1979) 31-65

P. A. HANSEN, *Carmina epigraphica graeca*, 2 vols., Berlin: W. de Gruyter, 1983-1989 (more volumes to follow)

A. G. HARKNESS, Age at Marriage and Death in the Roman Empire, *TAPA* 27 (1896) 35-72

M. HENGEL, *Judentum und Hellenismus*, Tübingen: Mohr, 1969, 2nd ed. 1973 (E.T. London: SCM, 1974)

— *The 'Hellenization' of Judaea in the First Century after Christ,* London: SCM, 1990

— Der alte und der neue 'Schürer', *JSS* 35 (1990) 19-72

H. HOMMEL, Juden und Christen im kaiserzeitlichen Milet, in his *Sebasmata* II, Tübingen: Mohr, 1984, 200-230

G. H. R. HORSLEY, *New Documents Illustrating Early Christianity*, 5 vols., North Ryde, N.S.W.:Macquarie Ancient History Documentary Research Centre, 1981-1989

P. W. van der HORST, *The Sentences of Pseudo-Phocylides*, Leiden: Brill, 1978

— *De onbekende god. Essays over de joodse en hellenistische achtergrond van het vroege christendom*, Utrecht: Rijksuniversiteit, 1988

— *Essays on the Jewish World of Early Christianity*, Fribourg: Universitätsverlag – Göttingen: Vandenhoeck & Ruprecht, 1990

P. W. van der HORST – G. MUSSIES, *Studies on the Hellenistic Background of the New Testament*, Utrecht: Rijksuniversiteit, 1990

T. ILAN, Notes on the Distribution of Jewish Women's Names in Palestine in the Second Temple and Mishnaic Periods, *JJS* 40 (1989) 186-200

J. JUSTER, *Les Juifs dans l'empire romain,* 2 vols., Paris: Geuthner, 1914

G. KAIBEL, *Epigrammata graeca ex lapidibus conlecta,* Berlin: Riemer, 1878

I. KAJANTO, *A Study of the Greek Epitaphs of Rome*, Helsinki: Academia

Scientiarum Fennica, 1963
— *On the Problem of the Average Duration of Life in the Roman Empire*, Helsinki: Academia Scientiarum Fennica, 1968
— The Hereafter in Ancient Christian Epigraphy and Poetry, *Arctos* 12 (1978) 27-53

L. H. KANT, Jewish Inscriptions in Greek and Latin, *ANRW* II 20,2 (1987) 671-713

A. KASHER, *The Jews of Hellenistic and Roman Egypt*, Tübingen: Mohr, 1985

C. M. KAUFMANN, *Handbuch der altchristlichen Epigraphik*, Freiburg: Herder, 1917

G. KITTEL, Das kleinasiatische Judentum in der hellenistisch-römischen Zeit, *TLZ* 69 (1944) 9-20

G. KLAFFENBACH, *Griechische Epigraphik*, Göttingen: Vandenhoeck & Ruprecht, 2nd ed. 1966

S. KLEIN, *Jüdisch-Palästinisches Corpus Inscriptionum (Ossuar-, Grab- und Synagogeninschriften)*, Pressburg: Loewit, 1920 (non vidi)

M. KLEYWEGT, *Ancient Youth. The Ambiguity of Youth and the Absence of Adolescence in Greco-Roman Society*, Amsterdam: Gieben, 1991

L. KOEP – E. STOMMEL – J. KOLLWITZ, Bestattung, *RAC* 2 (1954) 194-219

A. KONIKOFF, *Sarcophagi from the Jewish Catacombs of Ancient Rome. A catalogue raisonne*, Stuttgart: Franz Steiner, 1990

W. KORNFELD, Jüdisch-aramäische Grabinschriften aus Edfu, *Öster-reichische Akademie der Wissenschaften Anzeiger* 110 (1973) 123-137

H. KOSMALA, *Hebräer – Essener – Christen,* Leiden: Brill, 1959

B. KÖTTING, Univira in Inschriften, in his *Ecclesia Peregrinans* I, Münster: Aschendorff, 1989, 345-355

A. T. KRAABEL, Jews in Imperial Rome, *JJS* 30 (1979) 41-58

R. S. KRAEMER, Hellenistic Jewish Women. The Epigraphical Evidence, *SBL Seminar Papers 1986*, 183-200
— A New Inscription from Malta and the Question of Women Elders in the Diaspora Jewish Communities, *HTR* 78 (1986) 431-438
— Non-Literary Evidence for Jewish Women in Rome and Egypt, *Helios* 13 (1986) 85-101
— On the Meaning of the Term 'Jew' in Greco-Roman Inscriptions, *HTR* 81 (1989) 35-53

S. KRAUSS, *Synagogale Altertümer*, Hildesheim: Olms, 1966 (= Berlin 1922)
— Die jüdischen Apostel, *JQR* 17 (1905) 370-383

P. KRETSCHMER, Die Inschriften der jüdischen Katakombe am Monteverde, *Glotta* 12 (1923) 192-194

J. KUBINSKA, *Les monuments funéraires dans les inscriptions grecques de l'Asie Mineure,* Warsaw: Centre d'archéologie méditerranée, 1968

F. KUDLIEN, Jüdische Ärzte im römischen Reich, *Medizinhistorisches Journal* 20 (1985) 36-57

D. C. KURTZ – J. BOARDMAN, *Greek Burial Customs,* London: Thames &

Hudson, 1971

P. LAMPE, *Die stadtrömischen Christen in den ersten beiden Jahrhunderten*, Tübingen: Mohr, 1989 (2nd ed.)

R. LATTIMORE, *Themes in Greek and Latin Epitaphs*, Urbana: University of Illinois Press, 1942 (repr. 1962)

H. J. LEON, *The Jews of Ancient Rome*, Philadelphia: Jewish Publication Society, 1960

— The Jews of Venusia, *JQR* 44 (1953-54) 267-284

— The Language of the Greek Inscriptions from the Jewish Catacombs at Rome, *TPAPA* 58 (1927) 210-233

L. I. LEVINE, *The Rabbinic Class of Roman Palestine in Late Antiquity*, Jerusalem – New York: Yad Izhak Ben-Zvi – The Jewish Theological Seminary of America, 1989

S. LIEBERMAN, *Greek in Jewish Palestine*, New York: Jewish Theological Seminary, 1942, 2nd ed.1965

— *Hellenism in Jewish Palestine*, New York: Jewish Theological Seminary, 1950

B. LIER, Topica Carminum Sepulcralium Latinorum, *Philologus* 62 (1903) 445-477, 563-603; 63 (1904) 54-65

H. LIETZMANN, Jüdisch-griechische Inschriften aus Tell el Yehudieh, *ZNW* 22 (1923) 280- 286

B. LIFSHITZ, *Donateurs et fondateurs dans les synagogues juives*, Paris: Gabalda, 1967

— Fonctions et titres honorifiques dans les communautés juives, *RB* 67 (1960) 58-64

— Inscriptions grecques de Césarée en Palestine, *RB* 68 (1961) 115-126

— La vie de l'au-delà dans les conceptions juives, *RB* 68 (1961) 401-411

— Inscriptions de Césarée en Palestine, *RB* 72 (1965) 97-107

— L'hellénisation des Juifs en Palestine, *RB* 72 (1965) 520-538

— Notes d'épigraphie palestinienne, *RB* 73 (1966) 248-257

— Beiträge zur palästinischen Epigraphik, *ZDPV* 78 (1962) 64-88

— Beiträge zur griechisch-jüdischen Epigraphik, *ZDPV* 82 (1966) 57-63

— Varia epigraphica, *Epigraphica* 26 (1974) 78-100

— Du nouveau sur l'hellénisation des Juifs de Palestine, *Euphrosyne* n.s. 3 (1970) 113-133

— Varia epigraphica, *Euphrosyne* n.s. 6 (1973-74) 23-48

— Jérusalem sous la domination romaine, *ANRW* II 8 (1977) 444-489

— Les Juifs de Venosa, *Rivista di Filologia e di Istruzione Classica* 90 (1962) 367-371

G. LÜDERITZ, *Corpus jüdischer Zeugnisse aus der Cyrenaika*, Wiesbaden: Reichert, 1983

O. MARUCCHI, *Christian Epigraphy. An Elementary Treatise with a Collection of Ancient Christian Inscriptions Mainly of Roman Origin*, Chicago: Ares, 1974 (= Rome 1910)

G. MAYER, *Die jüdische Frau in der hellenistisch-römischen Antike,* Stuttgart: Kohlhammer, 1987

B. MAZAR, *Beth She'arim I: Catacombs 1-4,* Jerusalem: Massada Press, 1973

B. M. METZGER, The Nazareth Inscription Once Again, in his *New Testament Studies,* Leiden: Brill, 1980, 75-92

E. M. MEYERS – J. F. STRANGE, *Archaeology, the Rabbis and Early Christianity,* London: SCM Press, 1981

E. M. MEYERS – A. Th. KRAABEL, Archaeology, Iconography, and Non-Literary Written Remains, in R. A. Kraft – G. W. E. Nickelsburg (edd.), *Early Judaism and its Modern Interpreters,* Atlanta: Scholars Press – Philadelphia: Fortress Press, 1986, 175-210

E. MIRANDA, Due iscrizioni greco-giudaiche della Campania, *Riv. Arch. Crist.* 55 (1979) 337-341

A. MOMIGLIANO, Un documento della spiritualità dei Giudei Leontopolitani, *Aegyptus* 12 (1932) 171-172

P. MONCEAUX, Enquête sur l'épigraphie chrétienne d'Afrique, II: Inscriptions juives, *Revue archéologique* n.s. 3 (1904) 354-373

L. MORETTI, Iscrizioni greco-giudaiche di Roma, *Riv. Arch. Crist.* 50 (1974) 213-9

— Statistica demografica ed epigrafia: durata media della vita in Roma imperiale, *Epigraphica* 21 (1959) 60-78

J. H. MOULTON – G. MILLIGAN, *The Vocabulary of the Greek Testament Illustrated from the Papyri and Other Non-Literary Sources,* London: Hodder & Stoughton, 1930

N. MÜLLER – N. A. BEES, *Die Inschriften der jüdischen Katakombe am Monteverde zu Rom,* Leipzig: Harassowitz, 1919

G. MUSSIES, *The Morphology of Koine Greek as Used in the Apocalypse of John,* Leiden: Brill, 1971

— Greek in Palestine and the Diaspora, in S. Safrai – M. Stern (edd.), *The Jewish People in the First Century* (CRINT I 2), Assen: Van Gorcum, 1976, 1040-1064

— Greek as the Vehicle of Early Christianity, *NTS* 29 (1983) 356-369

S. NAGAKUBO, *Investigation into Jewish Concepts of Afterlife in the Greek Beth She'arim Inscriptions,* diss. Duke University, Durham NC, 1974 (unpubl.)

G. NAHON, *Inscriptions hébraïques et juives de France médiévale,* Paris: Les Belles Lettres, 1986

J. NAVEH, The Ossuary Inscriptions from Giv'at ha-Mivtar, *IEJ* 20 (1970) 33-37

— Varia Epigraphica Judaica, *Israel Oriental Studies* 9 (1979) 17-31

— Another Jewish Aramaic Tombstone from Zoar, *HUCA* 56 (1985) 103-116

A. D. NOCK, Tomb violations and Pontifical Law, in his *Essays on Religion and the Ancient World,* 2 vols., Oxford: OUP, 1972, II 527-533

— Sarcophagi and Symbolism, *ibid.* 606-641

H. NORDBERG, *Biometrical Notes. The information on ancient Christian inscriptions from Rome concerning the duration of life and the dates of birth and death*, Helsinki: Academia Scientiarum Fennica, 1963

J. OEHLER, Epigraphische Beiträge zur Geschichte des Judentums, *MGWJ* 53 (1909) 292-302; 443-452; 525-538

M. OGLE, The Sleep of Death, *Memoirs of the American Academy in Rome* 11 (1933) 81-117

A. PARROT, *Malédictions et violations de tombes,* Paris: Geuthner, 1939

W. PEEK, *Griechische Versinschriften* I, Berlin: Akademie Verlag, 1955
— *Griechische Grabgedichte,* Berlin: Akademie Verlag, 1960

R. PENNA, Les Juifs à Rome au temps de l'apotre Paul, *NTS* 28 (1982) 321-347

J. PIRCHER, *Das Lob der Frau im vorchristlichen Grabepigramm der Griechen,* Innsbruck: Universitätsverlag, 1979

G. PFOHL, *Bibliographie der griechischen Versinschriften*, Berlin 1964
— *Elemente der griechischen Epigraphik*, Darmstadt: Wissenschaftliche Buchgesellschaft, 1968
— *Das Studium der griechischen Epigraphik*, Darmstadt: Wissenschaftliche Buchgesellschaft, 1977
— Grabinschrift (gr.), *RAC* XII (1983) 467-514

Ch. PIETRI, Grabinschrift (lat.), *RAC* XII (1983) 514-590

D. PIKHAUS, *Levensbeschouwing en milieu in de Latijnse metrische inscripties,* Brussel: Vlaamsche Academie van Wetenschappen, 1978

E. PUECH, Note d'épigraphie latine palestinienne, *RB* 89 (1982) 210-221
— Inscriptions funéraires palestiniennes, *RB* 90 (1983) 481-533

W. M. RAMSAY, *The Cities and Bishoprics of Phrygia*, 2 vols., Oxford: Clarendon Press, 1895-1897

J. REYNOLDS – R. TANNENBAUM, *Jews and Godfearers at Aphrodisias*, Cambridge: Cambridge Philological Society, 1987

L. et J. ROBERT, *Bulletin Épigraphique*, 10 vols. + 5 index vols., Paris: Les Belles Lettres, 1972-1987

L. ROBERT, *Hellenica*, 13 vols., Paris: Maisonneuve, 1940-1965
— *Opera Minora Selecta*, 5 vols., Amsterdam: Hakkert, 1969-1989
— *Études anatoliennes*, Paris: Boccard, 1937
— *Nouvelles inscriptions de Sardes*, Paris: Librairie d'Amérique, 1964
— Malédictions funéraires grecques, *CRAI* 1978, 241-289
— *Die Epigraphik der klassischen Welt* , Bonn: Habelt, 1970

E. S. ROSENTHAL, The Giv'at ha-Mivtar Inscription, *IEJ* 23 (1973) 72-81

H. P. RÜGER, *Die Weisheitsschrift aus der Kairoer Geniza,* Tübingen: Mohr, 1991

S. SAFRAI – M. STERN (edd.), *The Jewish People in the First Century*, (CRINT I), 2 vols., Assen – Philadelphia: Van Gorcum – Fortress, 1974-1976

G. SANDERS, L'idée du salut dans les inscriptions latines chrétiennes, in U.

Bianchi – M. J. Vermaseren (edd.), *La soteriologia dei culti orientali nell' impero romano*, Leiden: Brill, 1982, 352-400

J. E. SANDYS – S. G. CAMPBELL, *Latin Epigraphy*, Groningen: Bouma's Boekhuis, 1969

A. SCHEIBER, *Jewish Inscriptions in Hungary From the Third Century to 1686*, Budapest: Akadémiai Kiadó – Leiden: Brill, 1983

E. SCHÜRER, *The History of the Jewish People in the Age of Jesus Christ*, 3 vols. in 4, rev. ed. by G. Vermes, F. Millar and M. Goodman, Edinburgh: Clark, 1973-1987

M. SCHWABE – B. LIFSHITZ, *Beth She'arim II: The Greek Inscriptions*, Jerusalem: Massada, 1974

J. N. SEVENSTER, *Do You Know Greek? How Much Greek Could the First Jewish Christians Have Known?*, Leiden: Brill, 1968

A. R. R. SHEPPARD, Jews, Christians and Heretics in Acmonia and Eumenia, *Anatolian Studies* 29 (1979) 169-180

M. SIMON, Θάρσει, οὐδεὶς ἀθάνατος, in his *Le christianisme antique et son contexte religieux* I, Tübingen: Mohr, 1981, 63-81

J. Z. SMITH, Fences and Neighbors, in W.S. Green (ed.), *Approaches to Ancient Judaism* II, Chico: Scholars Press, 1980, 1-25

M. SMITH, The Image of God: Notes on the Hellenization of Judaism, *BJRL* 40 (1958) 473-512

H. SOLIN, Juden und Syrer im römischen Reich, in G. Neumann – J. Untermann (edd.), *Die Sprachen im römischen Reich der Kaiserzeit*, Bonn: Habelt, 1980, 301-330

— Juden und Syrer im westlichen Teil der römischen Welt, *ANRW* II 29, 2 (1983) 587-789

I. di STEFANO MANZELLO, L. Maccius Archon, centurio alti ordinis. Nota critica su *CIL* VI, 39084 = *CII* I, 470, *ZPE* 77 (1989) 103-112

M. STERN, *Greek and Latin Authors on Jews and Judaism*, 3 vols., Jerusalem: The Israel Academy of Sciences and Humanities, 1974-1984

E. STOMMEL, Domus Aeterna, *RAC* IV (1959) 109-128

J. H. M. STRUBBE, Vervloekingen tegen grafschenners, *Lampas* 16 (1983) 248-274

— "Cursed be he that moves my bones", in C. A. Faraone – D. Obbink (edd.), *Magika Hiera. Ancient Greek Magic and Religion*, Oxford: Oxford University Press, 1991, 33-59

R. W. SUDER, *Hebrew Inscriptions: A Classified Bibliography*, Selinsgrove: Susquehanna University Press, 1984

S. SZYSZMAN, Les inscriptions funéraires découvertes par A. Firkowicz, *Journal Asiatique* 263 (1975) 231-264

V. TCHERIKOVER – A. FUKS, *Corpus Papyrorum Judaicarum*, 3 vols., Cambridge: Harvard University Press, 1957-1964

P. THOMSEN, *Die lateinischen und griechischen Inschriften der Stadt Jerusalem*, Leipzig: Hinrich, 1922

— Die lateinischen und griechischen Inschriften der Stadt Jerusalem, *ZDPV* 64 (1941) 203-256

M. N. TOD, Laudatory Epithets in Greek Epitaphs, *Annual of the British School at Athens* 46 (1951) 182-190

K. TREU, Die Bedeutung des Griechischen für die Juden im römischen Reich, *Kairos* 15 (1973) 123-144

L. B. URDAHL, Jews in Attica, *Symbolae Osloenses* 43 (1968) 39-56

V. VÄÄNÄNEN, *Introduction au Latin vulgaire*, Paris: Klincksieck, 1963

A. M. VÉRILHAC, Παῖδες ἄωροι. *Poésie funéraire*, 2 vols., Athens: Athens' Academy Press, 1978-1982

H. S. VERSNEL, Beyond Cursing: The Appeal to Justice in Judicial Prayers, in C. A. Faraone – D. Obbink (edd.), *Magika Hiera. Ancient Greek Magic and Religion*, Oxford: Oxford University Press, 1991, 60-106

M. WAELKENS, *Die kleinasiatischen Türsteine. Typologische und epigraphische Untersuchungen der kleinasiatischen Grabreliefs mit Scheintür,* Mainz: Philip von Zabern, 1986

G. WAGNER – R. G. COQUIN, Stèles grecques et coptes d'Egypte, *BIFAO* 70 (1971) 161-162 (non vidi)

S. WIDE, Ahôroi biaiothanatoi, *ARW* 12 (1909) 224-233

A. G. WOODHEAD, *The Study of Greek Inscriptions*, Cambridge: CUP, 1982 (2nd ed.)

Indices

Index of Passages

Inscriptions

CIJ

5	71
7	91
9	91
18	91
21	72, 109, 110
24	91
28	64
32*	121
36	91
37	72
45	102
53	91
55	117
67	91
68	46, 72, 157-158
72	116
78	117
79	64, 99, 114
81	103
85	89, 90
86	38
88	89, 93
89	114
93	93
95	91
99	91, 92
100	95
102	29, 91
105	104
106	47, 91
109	99
110	117
118	117
119	64, 91
120	89
121	91
122	91
123	52, 144-145
125	89, 91
132	109
135	143
136	104
142	91
145	91
146	91, 92
147	91
148	31, 47, 91
149	91
152	29
158	103
166	107
168	102
172	93
177	91
180	91, 92
190	108
193	95, 117
198	117
201	37, 95
202	71, 72, 109

203	67
210	99, 117
211	117
212	117
215	33, 108
216	90
221	91
222	72
224	33
225	91
228	117
229	33
236	27
239	33
242	103, 104
248	33
250	117
256	72
264	33
265	92
266	89
268	104
279	91
281	117
282	92
283	32
284	33, 89, 91-92
285	71, 109
286	27
289	89
296	69
298	117
301	91
306	124
315	96, 108
316	89
317	90
318	28, 91
319	32, 93-94
320	102
324	90
325	89
333	95, 99
336	92
337	90, 94
340	117
346	96
347	96
349	32
351	91
353	91
354	70
355	96
358	52, 116, 145-146
361	28
363	29
364	117
365	95, 116
368	91
370	37, 70
375	96
378	91
379	70
381	102
383	92
390	116
392	103
397	32, 89
398	89
402	89
405	91
408	91
416	89
418	114, 146
425	91
433	91
456	91
457	89
460	33, 114
462	72, 109
464	43
465	90
466	46
470	90
476	49, 51, 112, 126
480	27
482	114
483	89

Bible

Other Ancient Writings

1 Enoch 104:2	138
4 Ezra 7:97	124, 138
2 Baruch 51:10	124, 138
Josephus, *Bellum* II 398	128
VII 43	128
Antiquitates XX 200	141
Oracula Sibyllina III 271	128
Philo, *Legatio* 214	128
Pseudo-Philo, *LAB* 40:6	48
Pseudo-Phocylides 112	42
Mishna:	
Sanhedrin 10:1	120
Shabbath 1:3	93
Sheqalim 2:5	44
Sotah 7:7-8	92-93
Sukkoth 4:6	93
Ta'anith 1:14	93
Yoma 7:1	92
Talmud Bavli:	
Eruvin 53a	44

Pesahim 49b	92

Pagan

Dio Cassius 37, 17, 1	70
Sophocles, *Antigone*	47
Euripides, *Iphigeneia Aul.*	47
—, *Alcestis* 463-4	54
Anthologia Palatina VII	47, 50, 54
Plato, *Phaedo* 63e, 78b, 87e, 95c	122

Christian

Cod. Theod. XVI 8,4.6. 13-4	94, 105, 110
Firmicus Maternus, *De errore* 22:1	122
John Chrysostom, *Adv. Iud.* 2:4-6; 4:3	110

Index of Names and Subjects

addressing the deceased 52-54
addressing the passer-by 49-52
afterlife 115-126, 137-140
agamos 47
age-rounding 76-77, 82-83
Agrippesioi 86
ahoroi 45-46
Alexander from Cyrene 140
anagnostes 97
Anastasius 117
Aphrodisias 21, 71
Aquila 37-38
ara (altar) 42-43
Aramaic 36-37, 130
archegissa 106
archigerousiarches 91
archisynagogos 92-93, 105-106
archon 89-90
astral immortality 123-124, 138-
139
ateknos 47
Augustesioi 86
average age at death 73-84

benememorius 38, 65
Beth She'arim 118-122, 151-153
Biblical quotations in epitaphs 37-39
bibliographical aids 13-15
biribbi 97
Bolumnesioi 86
bomos 42-43
bundle of the living 38-39, 123

childbirth (as cause of death) 104
Christianity 127-143
CIJ, supplements to, 13-15
conversion to Christianity 158